PRAISE FOR
SUPPLY CHAIN S1...
AND FINANCIAL METRICS

"This book is a milestone in the evolution of supply chain planning literature. It presents a comprehensive methodology for connecting supply chain improvements to business performance, a topic that has not often been addressed. I would recommend this book as a must-read to all supply chain practitioners."
Harpal Singh, CEO, Arkieva

"Bram has been instrumental at Barco in identifying and defining our challenges in supply chain, working capital management and order fulfilment and in delivering a model that helped our organization to manage these challenges in a more thoughtful way. It drove our people to have a more comprehensive look at our business and in considering the different dimensions and possible impact in these domains."
Carl Vandenbussche, VP Investor Relations, Barco

"A very timely book. As the fundamentals of supply chain are being redefined by the digital revolution, it is absolutely needed for supply chain executives to become much more proficient with the financial metrics of supply chains to assess the benefits and costs of those technologies. Metrics beyond cost, like cash, are going to define the future evolution of digital supply chains and change current practices dramatically.
Prof Dr Carlos Cordon, LEGO Professor of Strategy and Supply Chain Management, IMD

"Bram is a leader in helping companies maximize value in supply chain management. This book will be helpful in changing the dialogue of supply chain leaders to balance metrics and align on supply chain strategy."
Lora Cecere, Supply Chain Visionary and Founder, Supply Chain Insights

"This is a great book that makes a perfect bridge between strategy, supply chain management and finance. Too many books dig deeper and deeper within their discipline. This book is an exception and convincingly shows how strategic choices have a huge impact on the most important supply chain parameters and metrics. A true recommendation."
Prof Dr Kurt Verweire, Professor, Strategy, Vlerick Business School

"This book is a great contribution in the evolution of business and supply chain excellence to a more holistic approach to create sustainable business performance and results. It provides a clear picture and extensive guidance for leaders to connect all the dots of a chosen business strategy with a supply chain strategy, and links this to the right business performance measurement. Bram DeSmet has created a masterpiece which can

be used for any business transformation and I am convinced that winning companies will implement the methods described in the book as part of their business excellence journey towards sustainable success."
Frank Vorrath, VP Global Supply Chain, Johnson Controls

"Bram DeSmet has created a must-read resource for anybody looking to improve financial metrics by working on supply chain strategy or even the connection between the two. In his unique style, he builds from simple concepts and takes the reader to a viewpoint that is easy to follow, while promising to deliver great impact for those who understand and implement. The connection he provides to implementable technology makes it complete and a resource for all kinds of readers, from those interested in theory, just the implementation, or a combination thereof. A must-read for supply chain professionals."
Sujit Singh, COO, Arkieva

"With this decisive book, Bram DeSmet has cracked the nut of translating business strategy into practical supply chain metrics."
Martijn Lofvers, CEO and Chief Trendwatcher at Supply Chain Media

"Bram DeSmet has in this book brought together very authentic and deep insights in managing supply chain strategies and their impact on financial performance; both on the P&L as well as on free cash and working capital. The dependencies in the triangle become crystal-clear. The book is a joy to read and very insightful for practical use. A treasure to have and a pleasure to read."
Ton Geurts, CPO / SVP Supply Chain Excellence, Bekaert

"Supply chain management is very often only looked at from a single axis: keeping the inventory as low as possible. In some cases you will find a more mature management approach looking at two axes: minimize inventory and maximize customer satisfaction. Seldom does supply chain management focus on the impact on the bottom line of their decisions. This book provides a great outline on how to manage all at the same time."
Johan Heyman, VP Operations, Barco

"Bram's book very comprehensively addresses and explains the permanent supply chain challenges of balancing the dimensions of cash, cost, and service. Highly recommended."
Patrick Dittli, Global Director, Supply Chain Management, Metro

"This book provides a practical guide towards formulating and implementing supply chain strategy. Highly recommended for all supply chain professionals!"
Prof Dr Jack van der Veen, Evofenedex Chair Supply Chain Management, Nyenrode Business Universiteit

"Excellent companies have more than good products and marketing, above all they have a perfect supply chain. By using the supply chain triangle of Bram DeSmet, organizations can fulfil their promises to their customers. The supply chain triangle takes care of the right balance between service to customers, the costs customer are willing to pay and the cash the organization must generate to be able to exist and to innovate."
Michel Van Buren, Managing Director, BLMC & Solventure Netherlands

Supply Chain Strategy and Financial Metrics

The Supply Chain Triangle
of service, cost and cash

Bram DeSmet

KoganPage

Publisher's note

Every possible effort has been made to ensure that the information contained in this book is accurate at the time of going to press, and the publishers and author cannot accept responsibility for any errors or omissions, however caused. No responsibility for loss or damage occasioned to any person acting, or refraining from action, as a result of the material in this publication can be accepted by the editor, the publishers or the author.

First published in Great Britain and the United States in 2018 by Kogan Page Limited

2nd Floor, 45 Gee Street	c/o Martin P Hill Consulting	4737/23 Ansari Road
London	122 W 27th Street	Daryaganj
EC1V 3RS	New York, NY 10001	New Delhi 110002
United Kingdom	USA	India

© Bram DeSmet 2017

The right of Bram DeSmet to be identified as the author of this work has been asserted by him in accordance with the Copyright, Designs and Patents Act 1988.

ISBN   978 0 7494 8257 2
E-ISBN   978 0 7494 8258 9

British Library Cataloguing-in-Publication Data

A CIP record for this book is available from the British Library.

Typeset by Integra Software Services, Pondicherry
Print production managed by Jellyfish
Printed and bound in Great Britain by CPI Group (UK) Ltd, Croydon CR0 4YY

To my beloved parents,
for their dedication to my brothers and me

CONTENTS

LIST OF FIGURES

LIST OF TABLES

ABOUT THE AUTHOR

Dr Bram Desmet is adjunct professor at the Vlerick Business School, where he is part of the competence centre of supply chain and operations, and a visiting professor for the Beijing MBA programme at Peking University where he teaches statistics and business analytics. Bram is also the CEO of Solventure, a company that specializes in implementing sales and operations planning using Arkieva software. Before that Bram was a partner in strategy, supply chain and operations at MÖBIUS Research and Consulting.

Bram's research interests are in the domain of strategy, supply chain and advanced analytics. He combines academic research with practical applications. He obtained his PhD in the topic of multi-echelon inventory optimization and applied it at companies such as Agfa-Gevaert and Daikin Europe. At Solventure he is developing a new forecasting solution based on the use of leading macro-economic indicators. Customers there include companies, such as Bekaert, that are linked to automotive and/or construction and their economic cycles.

With this book Bram hopes to contribute to the field of supply chain strategy by combining the fields of strategy, supply chain and finance. Bram appreciates your thoughts and feedback. He can easily be reached via his contact page on LinkedIn.

FOREWORD

Frank Vorrath, Johnson Controls

Several global megatrends are driving disruptions, challenges and opportunities for companies. Changing demographics encompassing a move towards urbanization with a surging middle class concentrated in urban areas and aging populations; energy availability and resources; sustainability and regulations; digitalization – these all create challenge and opportunities for companies to grow. We live in a new world, an engagement, an ecosystem-driven economy where everything around us is changing exponentially. In the future a company won't only compete against other companies. Every company is and will be part of an ecosystem, and success will depend on how they can create a strong and sustainable ecosystem that is able to compete and win in the marketplace.

Sustainable business growth, liquidity and profitability are top priorities for organizations, their employees and shareholders. Customer expectations have changed and customers now want to buy products or services in different and faster ways. Reliability, responsiveness and agility are more important than ever before, and focusing just on cost will not deliver the desired outcome in respect of sustainable business growth, liquidity and profitability. Many organizations are stuck in their old understanding, mindset and behaviour.

For many years strategic supply chain management has not been understood well enough, and supply chain professionals are battling to earn their seat at the C-Suite table. We have entered a 'perfect storm' in the life cycle of supply chain management. A fundamental shift in mindset and behaviour is required to transform organizations to be ready to compete and win in this new world of an engagement and ecosystem-driven economy.

Supply Chain Strategy and Financial Metrics by Dr Bram Desmet will help to overcome this challenge, and provides a practical framework how to connect a business strategy and supply chain strategy with the marketplace. The reader will understand through Dr Desmet's framework that any business strategy can be a deliberate choice. The framework first analyses customer buying behaviours in a marketplace, and thereafter connects them with the right business and supply chain strategy, performance measurement and management.

Dr Desmet explains why companies struggle in balancing the triangle of service, cost and cash in their old traditional thinking, mindset and behaviour. Different strategies lead to different trade-offs. The book refers to the well-known Treacy and Wiersema framework of three defined archetypes: operational excellence, customer intimacy and product leadership. A practical solution set is provided for benchmarking and target setting, which are important elements of any chosen business or supply chain strategy.

This book provides valuable information and great insight into strategic supply chain management, and covers all necessary components from setting the right business strategy connected to the right supply chain strategy to financial metrics and performance management.

Dr Desmet provides a foundation for the business C-Suite and any supply chain professional to use market analysis, business strategy and strategic supply chain management connected with new solutions to keep up with ever-changing threats and disruptions. In this new age of global interconnectivity and smart connected ecosystems, it is necessary to provide business executives, supply chain practitioners, both professionals and students, with state-of-the art knowledge on the frontiers of supply chain management.

Is strategic supply chain management part of your business, or is strategic supply chain management your business? We have been waiting to answer this question for a very long time.

I hope you will enjoy reading and learning as much as I did.

Frank Vorrath
Vice President Global Supply Chain, Johnson Controls

FOREWORD

Johan Heyman, Barco

Barco has been working on reducing and controlling inventories in recent years. In the first years, this goes relatively easily. You can reduce inventory without affecting service or cost. As you continue, the trade-off with service and cost becomes more prominent, as captured in the concept of the Supply Chain Triangle, which is central to this book.

At Barco we have actively used the triangle to trigger discussions about that balance. Balancing that triangle also triggers the discussion about aligning targets and incentives across departments. It obliges people to think in multiple dimensions instead of just one dimension, and it requires them to work to a group of shared KPIs instead of only focusing on turnover, cost or inventory.

Barco has been through a major transformation, as described in Chapter 2 of this book. From being a true product leader, we have extended into mid-range products. This redefines the balance in the triangle. As the gross margin on those products on average is lower, we need to take complexity out of the product and the supply chain, and lower the cost and the inventory. Again the triangle has helped us to trigger this type of debate. In our DNA Barco are product leaders. Serving a mid-market segment has been a stretch to our organization. Combining the high-end and the mid-range has forced us to introduce concepts such as modular design, which take some pressure out of the triangle. It allows us to expand the offering while lowering the cost and the inventory.

Supply chain plays a pivotal role in this whole transformation process. Modern organizations are matrix organizations; in our case, this means regional sales organizations combined with product divisions, and a functional back-end organization. A matrix organization requires strong people at the intersection points: they are the oil that makes the matrix work. At Barco these are the supply chain managers.

At Barco our supply chain has expanded from purely operational into a more tactical and strategic role. The Supply Chain Triangle is a helpful tool to challenge the organization and ensure balanced decision making. We have made big steps through processes like sales and operations planning

(S&OP) in balancing service, cost and cash. But there is room for improvement. For instance, the role of supply chain in new product introductions should be stronger, as well as in product life cycle management, or more broadly product portfolio management.

The Supply Chain Triangle can be the compass of the supply chain manager. I warmly recommend it as a useful tool to bring more value to your organization, as I believe it has done for Barco.

Johan Heyman
Senior VP – Global Operations, Barco

PREFACE

After 15 years in the field of supply chain, and almost 10 years after finishing my PhD, I felt it was time to summarize what I had learned, and make a contribution to the development of supply chain thinking, or at least give it a try.

Given my PhD in multi-echelon inventory optimization, and the many projects I did on that topic, I started out with the idea on writing an inventory book; not one giving formulas for safety stock and the EOQ, but more strategic and more conceptual.

Gradually, strategy took over, as through my teaching and consulting assignments I saw how companies lacked an understanding of some basic inventory principles, which boil down to strategic choices. If over the last five years your sales have remained flat, but your number of SKUs has increased by 50%, chances are that your inventory went up. Instead of understanding this 'after the fact', strategy-driven companies realize it upfront and will calculate whether this makes sense, and what can be done to avoid the inventory increase by postponement or modular design.

In 2015, Lora Cecere published her book *Supply Chain Metrics that Matter*. She introduced two-dimensional benchmarking using so-called 'orbit charts' to visualize which companies can improve on both EBIT and inventory turns at the same time, and which ones have fallen behind. I was immediately a fan, and by experimenting with the orbit charts I discovered that different strategies in fact led to different targets for key financial metrics. Based on what I have called 'bang-for-the-buck' lines, I was able to define which strategy was leading to which targets. The underlying reasoning is that investors are indifferent about the strategy as long as you deliver the same EBIT/capital employed – the same bang-for-the-buck.

As I shared my newly developed, more strategic, thoughts with audiences at supply chain conferences worldwide, and as I interviewed senior supply chain professionals in the context of my book, the reactions were enthusiastic. Some of the concepts such as the Supply Chain Triangle are intuitive. Linking them to finance, and linking financial target setting to strategy, was new and ground-breaking. These comments gave me the courage to continue my work and finish the book.

As well as the hardcore supply chain stuff like inventory optimization, I have been lucky to teach strategy to companies. It gave me a detailed understanding of the model of Treacy and Wiersema (1995), which I have gradually had to refine using the model of Crawford and Mathews (2007) to bring more clarity around strategy implementation.

Gradually the pieces of the puzzle started fitting together. The result is this book, which is meant to contribute to the field of supply chain strategy, actually mixing the fields of strategy, supply chain and finance. I hope you will enjoy reading as much as I have enjoyed writing. Not easy at times, but always fulfilling, and triggering me to keep thinking, talking and writing about the subject.

ACKNOWLEDGEMENTS

I want to thank Martijn Lofvers, owner of Supply Chain Media and editor of *Supply Chain Magazine*, for his contribution to Chapter 8 and for connecting me to some of the case studies that made it into this book.

Let me thank Frank Vorrath from Johnson Controls, for the many calls where he gave constructive feedback, and for writing a foreword where he shares his view as a senior supply chain practitioner.

I also want to thank Dirk Holbach from Henkel, Ton Geurts from Bekaert and Tony Heldreth from Owens Corning, for sharing their views on the relevance of the developed concepts and allowing me to include these in the book.

I also want to thank Dr Jack Van Der Veen, Alisson Thomas and Michel Van Buren from the Supply Chain Executive Leadership Platform at Nyenrode. Their enthusiasm on my presentation at SCELP has pushed me forward in getting the concepts further worked out and on paper.

Let me thank André Céron, Martine Pauwels, Erik Pappaert and Jurgen Belsack from Colruyt group in Belgium. For five years I have been teaching strategy, forecasting, inventory and planning in their supply chain academy. This academy has fuelled the development of my thinking.

Let me thank my colleagues at the Vlerick Business School, in particular Dr Ann Vereeck and Dr Kurt Verweire for their advice and encouragements in the early stages of planning the book.

Let me thank all my colleagues at Solventure, for doing without me as their CEO on the multiple days I was unavailable while writing this book. Let me also thank Dr Hendrik Vanmaele for introducing me to the field of supply chain as a complete novice 15 years ago.

Finally let me thank my wife Leen and my kids Matties, Julie and Emiel. I've been writing at home, but equally been absent. Dads should play with their kids instead of writing books. Husbands should help with practical stuff instead of being conceptual.

I hope that all those that have contributed share some of my pride in being able to present this final result. It is our shared result. It has passed through my brain, but it is based on the triggers, the questions, the thoughts, the examples and the support of each one of you.

Thank you all so much.

Introduction

The overall goal of the book, as is expressed by the title, is to link supply chain, strategy and finance through financial metrics. We start gently in Chapter 1, by introducing the Supply Chain Triangle of Service, Cost and Cash. The Supply Chain Triangle captures the balancing act faced by companies. As an example, delivering extra services for your customers can easily increase cost and cash. To understand whether this makes sense, we link the triangle to financial metrics. If service is a driver for sales, combining the service and the cost corner of the triangle defines the margin, as for instance measured by EBIT (earnings before interest and taxes). If we look at the EBIT generated over the cash employed, or more broadly the capital employed (working capital plus fixed assets), we come to the return on capital employed, or ROCE. ROCE is a common financial metric measuring the 'return' (the bang) on the 'capital employed' (the buck), or in spoken language, the 'bang for the buck'. Optimizing ROCE requires optimization across the three corners of the triangle.

Using examples, we will illustrate that many companies still have a functional focus, where sales is primarily concerned with service, operations is primarily focused on cost and finance is concerned with the capital employed. The imperative for alignment lies in the ROCE. The alignment itself is the core task of the supply chain function.

Chapter 2 introduces the strategy model of Treacy and Wiersema (1995), who argue that market leaders pursue one of three strategies:

1 operational excellence, which focuses on keeping costs down to deliver the lowest possible price;

2 product leadership, which focuses on delivering the newest and the highest specification product;

3 customer intimacy, which focuses on delivering the best total solution for specific customer problems.

We show how the three strategies lead to different trade-offs in the Supply Chain Triangle. To be able to guarantee the lowest cost and the lowest price, the operational excellence leader will need to focus on a more basic set of services. A product leader will have a higher capital employed than the operational excellence player, because of the higher complexity of the products and the manufacturing assets. As an investor, from the ROCE principle, I'm OK with the product leader requiring a higher capital employed, as long as his EBIT is higher. Likewise, I'm OK with the operational excellence player working at a lower EBIT, as long as he has a lower capital employed.

Using case studies of Barco and Casio, we illustrate how changes in the strategy are indeed reflected in changes in the EBIT and the capital employed, and how different strategies are in fact just different ways to deliver a comparable ROCE.

Next we compare the EBIT, the capital employed, and the ROCE of multiple food retailers, and find that a hard discounter such as Edeka, working at a much lower EBIT but with much higher asset turns, has a comparable ROCE to a product leader like Whole Foods Market, which has a much higher EBIT, but requires a higher capital employed to deliver its product leadership strategy. Based on these cases, we conclude that different strategies do indeed lead to different targets on service, cost and capital employed, but all with the goal of delivering a comparable ROCE or 'bang-for-the-buck'.

In Chapters 3, 4 and 5, we derive those 'strategy dependent' targets for service, cost and capital employed through financial benchmarking. We combine the service and the cost corner of the triangle into margin, so that we have two dimensions left: margin, and capital employed. In Chapter 3 we analyse different metrics for margin: gross margin, EBITDA (earnings before interest, taxes, depreciation and amortization), EBIT and net profit; and different metrics for capital employed: inventory turns, cash conversion cycle and fixed asset turns.

We conclude that gross margin is a helpful measure for the chosen strategy. Product leaders command a higher premium from their customers, which shows in their gross margin. From the EBITDA, EBIT and net profit metrics, we choose to continue with EBIT, as EBITDA depends on accounting rules for depreciation, and net profit depends on tax optimization. EBIT is closest to the operational margin driven by the supply chain.

For capital employed we conclude we really need all three metrics. Inventory turns is a good measure for the complexity and the health of a business. The cash conversion cycle (CCC) incorporates receivables and payables, which has been a major point of attention for many companies over the last 10 years. Fixed asset turns show how well a company leverages its assets.

We start Chapter 3 by discussing how companies commonly benchmark in only one dimension, for example by looking at the inventory turns of all their competitors and then picking the best performance as the target. This is dangerous and meaningless. For example, we know that a product leader will have a higher inventory than the operational excellence player, but will compensate for that by generating a higher EBIT. If we want to take the strategy into account when benchmarking and setting targets, we need to benchmark pairs of KPIs, for example EBIT and inventory turns. This can be done using so-called 'orbit charts'.

In Chapter 4 we continue our benchmarking journey by adding 'bang-for-the-buck' or 'indifference' lines. We know that as investors we are OK with a product leader requiring more inventory or capital employed, as long as their EBIT is higher. As long as companies generate the same EBIT/inventory, as a proxy for EBIT/capital employed, we are indifferent. We know that companies with a higher EBIT and a higher inventory are likely to be product leaders, whereas companies with a lower EBIT and a lower inventory (or higher turns) are likely to be operational excellence players.

In Chapter 5 we compare three companies on EBIT versus inventory turns, EBIT versus CCC and EBIT versus fixed asset turns. In each of the comparisons we look at which company has the best performance, and we take that as the benchmark. In fact, we take the 'bang-for-the-buck' or 'indifference' curve of that company as the benchmark, meaning that a product leader or operational excellence player will have different targets along that curve, but both leading to the same target ROCE performance.

We then expand the benchmark from three to six companies to get a more complete picture of where the product leadership, operational excellence players and customer intimacy companies are. We use the data of one of the benchmark companies up to 2014, and try to use the technique to set targets for 2015. We show how different strategies lead to different targets, and then afterwards evaluate the actual 2015 performance, and align it with the actual chosen strategy.

The strategic benchmark is hardest for the EBIT versus fixed asset turns. From the six companies only one seems to be close to the target turns. Whereas this could cast doubt on whether the approach is correct, the ROCE comparison for the six companies confirms it – of the six companies, only one is delivering a ROCE of 15%. Using 15% ROCE as a standard or target does indeed imply that most of the companies in the benchmark have a major challenge in improving their asset utilization.

Chapters 3–5 are the most technical, and so the most 'dry'. We have added plenty of exercises so the reader can apply the developed benchmarking methods to his or her company and compare it with competitors. All of this is relatively easy if you have average Excel skills.

While the case studies of Barco, Casio and a group of food retail companies in Chapter 2 show that different strategies lead to different targets, Chapters 3, 4 and 5 develop a benchmark and target setting technique, which allows accounting for the chosen strategy. Chapters 6 and 7 further deepen the set of service, cost and capital employed KPIs, and develop it into a strategy-driven 'KPI dashboard'.

Chapter 6 starts by introducing the strategy model of Crawford and Mathews (2007). Where Treacy and Wiersema consider three strategic options, Crawford and Mathews consider five value drivers: price, access, service, product and experience, and argue that excellence requires making a choice – you can't be the best at everything. You have to choose one driver on which you want to dominate, one driver on which you want to differentiate, and you will have to play at par or even below par on the others. If you don't make a choice, your competitors will, and as a result they will leave you behind in their chosen diversion.

We split the access driver into 'physical access' and 'psychological access', and the product dimension into 'product quality/depth' and 'product breadth'. This allows us to include the three Treacy and Wiersema strategic options as three 'archetypes' in the extended Crawford and Mathews model – which is helpful, given the number of conclusions we based on the Treacy and Wiersema model.

The helpful thing about Crawford and Mathews is that it allows us to deepen the service corner of the Supply Chain Triangle. In fact, in the extended model, service is one of the seven value drivers of the extended model, so for that reason we now talk about the 'value' corner instead of the 'service' corner. Using the checklist of seven value drivers – price, physical access, psychological access, service, product breadth, product quality/depth and experience – we have a more complete set of potential value drivers.

We now also know that companies have to make choices amongst these seven. By knowing their choices, we know their strategy, and once we know their strategy we can better estimate the impact on the cost and capital employed corner of the triangle. So introducing the model of Crawford and Mathews really deepens our understanding.

In Chapter 7 we further deepen the cost and the capital employed corner of the Supply Chain Triangle. Unlike in the SCOR model we stick to commonly used KPIs for cost and capital employed – so we avoid talking about 'cost of supply chain management', but we will talk about the cost of goods sold, about direct and indirect labour and material and any finance terms operational managers already have in their day-to-day reporting.

We conclude Chapter 7 by building a KPI dashboard around the Supply Chain Triangle. Because of the need for balance we always need to report KPIs on value, cost and capital employed together. It is very common, though, for companies to report about OTIF (On-Time-In-Full) service level without reporting on inventories and cost. This is problematic, because only an improvement in the three dimensions at the same time guarantees an improvement in ROCE.

We build up our KPI dashboard in three layers. Layer 1 captures key metrics on the three corners of the Supply Chain Triangle: value metrics (for instance OTIF), cost metrics (for instance cost of goods sold) and capital employed metrics (for instance inventory turns). Layer 2 links them to top-line metrics (for instance growth or net sales), bottom-line metrics (for instance EBIT) and return metrics (for instance ROCE). In a third layer we add process metrics, which function as 'causal' or 'diagnostic' metrics. As an example, an improvement in forecast accuracy will lead to a simultaneous improvement in OTIF, cost and inventory, which makes it an important operational metric to track.

Where Chapters 3, 4 and 5 will help you in setting balanced targets accross the three corners of the triangle, Chapters 6 and 7 will help you in setting up a dashboard to evaluate your progress. In both the target setting and the follow-up it is important to ensure balance across the triangle and avoid bias on one type of metric only. If all metrics improve, life is easy. If some metrics improve to the expense of others, you should assess the impact on ROCE and whether the directon is aligned with the targets set by your chosen strategy.

Once we have built the logic of the KPI dashboard, we show an example of how it can be constructed as an iPad app. We also explain once more how different strategies are different routes to generate a comparable ROCE. An operational excellence leader will have a lower EBIT, but will work with a lower capital employed, whereas a product leader will have a higher gross margin and a higher EBIT, but work with a higher capital employed.

We also discuss the difference between 'primary' and 'secondary' KPIs and how they depend on the strategy. As a product leader the time-to-market and the percentage of turnover from new products are primary KPIs linked to the product leadership. Temporarily failing on those KPIs is more threatening than failing on cost KPIs. Likewise for an operational excellence leader, price points below the market average is a critical KPI. Not having the lowest price in the market, even temporarily, threatens image and reputation, whereas for the operational excellence leader customers will be less demanding on product innovation.

In our concluding Chapter 8, we try to show how this developed thinking differs from the dominant thinking in the 1990s. We start with Martin

Christopher's book *Logistics and Supply Chain Management*, first published in 1992, to summarize strategic thinking and the resulting supply chain thinking at that time.

In summary, the strategy thinking of the 1990s was quite 'closed', in that product differentiation was seen as increasingly difficult, and cost leadership was thought to be the territory of the market leader as volume creates a cost advantage. With two routes closed, the only option left for companies to escape commoditization was to differentiate on service. The result was an increase in variety and volatility, further eroding the cost position and intensifying companies' flight into the service dimension. In this context, the concept of the 'responsive' supply chain, which combined the best of 'lean' and 'agile', promised to improve on service and cost simultaneously.

'Improve on service and cost simultaneously'? Did that get your attention? Well, yes – it got the attention of senior management in the 1990s as well. While all of the above has been essential in the development of supply chain thinking and its adoption, we believe we have reached the limits of what supply chain can do without making choices. We believe it is no longer about making improvements in service and cost: today, for the market leaders, it is about making a strategic choice between service and cost. To come to our concept of the strategy-driven supply chain, we first have to 'open up' the strategic thinking again.

Yes, volume creates a cost advantage – but product leadership is not the privilege of the company with the biggest market share. Think about what hard discounters such as Aldi and Lidl have done over the last 30 years in Europe, and what low-cost airlines like Southwest and Ryanair have achieved in the airline industry. None of them were the biggest when they started.

Likewise for product advantage: yes, competing on product is a dangerous game, as the examples of Kodak and Nokia show – but it's not impossible. Think about how Apple rebounded after Steve Jobs came back as its head in 1996. How did it regain the position of market leader? It did so by delivering innovative and eye-catching products.

We stand with the Crawford and Mathews argument that there are multiple ways to excel in your market, but it requires making a choice. You can't be all things to all people. As we make choices in our value proposition, that has an impact on our supply chain. We don't believe supply chains can be captured in three or four or even six supply chain types such as lean, agile, or responsive. There are as many supply chains as there are strategies. The supply chain has become strategy-driven.

We close the chapter by describing how to implement that strategy-driven supply chain. It starts by making tough choices about your value proposition. It starts by making tough choices about your value proposition. Next you need to 'operationalize' your value proposition through an 'operating model'.

We review two examples of operating models: the one from Treacy and Wiersema (1995), and one from Kaplan and Norton (2004), noting that both lack the supply chain as a crucial element to assess the impact of the value proposition on cost and capital employed. Both focus on process and intangibles such as culture, which are important, but which lack the 'hard stuff' you need to measure a 'hard KPI' like ROCE.

By extending those models with the supply chain we complete our implementation roadmap as follows:

1 Define your value proposition.

2 Define your operating model (including the supply chain).

3 Define the corresponding ROCE level, and return to step 1 if required.

Once your strategy has been defined in this way, you still need to implement it. We share ideas from Kaplan and Norton's *The Execution Premium* on how to organize a successful strategy implementation. In summary, Chapters 3–5 are the more technical and quantitative core of the book, where we make the key argument that different strategies lead to different targets and are in fact different ways to generate a comparable ROCE. Chapters 1, 2, 6 and 7 provide the conceptual models around that, based on the Supply Chain Triangle, finance basics and the strategy models of Treacy and Wiersema and of Crawford and Mathews. Chapter 8 discusses how thinking in the fields of strategy and supply chain has changed since the 1990s – how from a limited set of options, there is a multitude of strategies and supply chains available today. Supply chains have in fact become strategy-driven.

We hope the book will contribute to putting the supply chain at the heart of the strategy discussion, instead of seeing it as a result. We don't believe in translating a business strategy into a supply chain strategy. There simply isn't a business strategy without a supply chain. The value proposition and the operating model, of which the supply chain is an integral part, are like the ying and the yang of your business strategy. Without both you cannot evaluate the shareholder value. There's no business strategy without knowing how you will create value for the shareholder!

The Supply Chain Triangle of service, cost and cash

In this chapter we will introduce the Supply Chain Triangle of Service, Cost and Cash. The Supply Chain Triangle captures the struggle we see in many companies to balance service, cost and cash. We believe that this balancing act is the essence of supply chain management.

In the second part of this chapter we link the Supply Chain Triangle to financial metrics. We will argue that balancing the triangle is about maximizing shareholder value, as measured by the return on capital employed (ROCE). This means that supply chain and finance have the same goal, and have a common interest in aligning the three corners of the Supply Chain Triangle.

What is supply chain management?

There is a great deal of confusion about what exactly 'supply chain management' means. A commonly used definition is that it is the management of the flow of goods and the inverse flow of information and cash, as shown in Figure 1.1. As consumers buy more from the store, the information on increased sales will travel upstream in the supply chain and trigger increased production. The extra production will flow downstream to the shops. Cash is being exchanged for the goods.

This 'process' type of definition is at the heart of the SCOR model. SCOR, or the Supply Chain Operations Reference model, is a process reference model developed and endorsed by the Supply Chain Council. SCOR v10 defined the following key processes: Plan, Source, Make, Deliver and Return. As shown in Figure 1.2, it focuses on the so-called 'extended' supply

Figure 1.1   Managing the flow of goods and the inverse flow of information and cash

chain, where we manage the flow of goods, information and cash from the customer's customer to the supplier's supplier.

SCOR has also developed a set of complementary key performance indicators (KPIs) as the basis for cross-industry benchmarks.

As well as the above 'process' type of definition, many companies have defined supply chain as a function in the organization. The literature abounds with books where supply chain is claimed as an extension of purchasing, or as the new name for logistics. This has added to the confusion about what supply chain management is. In many companies the supply chain manager is responsible for tactical planning across production sites (typically called sales and operations planning, or S&OP), for managing inventory of finished product, and for logistics.

In some companies it also encompasses customer service, in others purchasing, and in yet others operational planning within the production sites. If you include production, 'VP of Supply Chain' would be the new name for the Chief Operating Officer.

A third type of definition, alongside the process and functional definitions, is more strategic. Martin Christopher, emeritus professor of marketing and logistics at Cranfield School of Management, said in 1998 that 'one of the most significant paradigm shifts of modern business management is that individual businesses no longer compete as solely autonomous entities, but rather with supply chains'. It is his belief that given the emerging global competitive environment, the ultimate success of a single business will depend on management's ability to integrate the company's intricate network of business relationships. It's no longer companies competing against companies, it is supply chains competing against supply chains.

Peter Drucker, the late management guru, combined the process view and the strategic view, stating that 'successful supply chain management requires cross-functional integration of key business processes within the

Figure 1.2 Key processes of the SCOR model in the extended supply chain

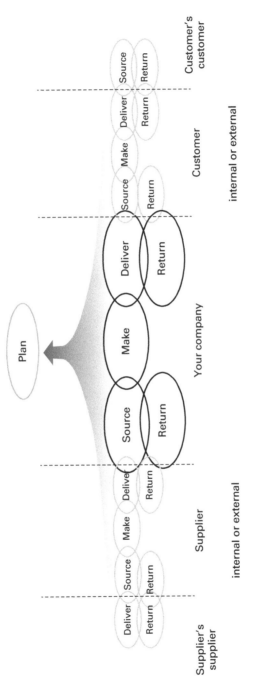

firm and across the network of firms that comprise the supply chain' (1998). The Supply Chain Management Institute has tried to capture that idea in a long list of 'end-to-end' processes, all claimed to be part of supply chain management: customer relationship management, demand management, order fulfilment, manufacturing flow management, supplier relationship management, product development and commercialization, and finally returns management (Lambert, 2008). While it is true that managing end-to-end processes is key to improving the management of the supply chain, it is probably too far a stretch to claim each of these processes as part of a supply chain function.

Reviewing the above confirms the confusion about what supply chain management means. Throughout this book we will give our answer. Central to our answer is the concept introduced in the next section: the 'Supply Chain Triangle'.

The Supply Chain Triangle

Figure 1.3 shows what we will call the Supply Chain Triangle of Service, Cost and Cash. The triangle captures the idea that as organizations, we deliver different types of 'service' to our customers, which comes at a certain 'cost', and requires a certain amount of 'inventory', or more generically 'cash'. Step by step, we will come to the argument that the essence of supply chain management is about balancing this triangle.

Let us first explore each of the corners in more detail.

Figure 1.3   The Supply Chain Triangle of Service, Cost and Cash

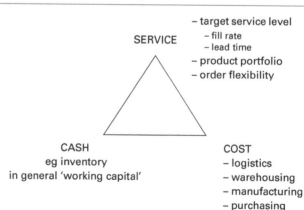

Service

The service corner captures the services that we, as a supply chain, are delivering to our customers. A dominant service metric in the supply chain is the 'service level'. It measures in what percentage of cases we deliver according to the agreed target. There are a myriad of definitions in use. Many companies talk about OTIF, or On-Time-In-Full. Which simply means, we deliver goods 'on time' and 'in full'. That seems straightforward, but it is not.

Do we measure 'on time' against the date of shipment, or against the date of delivery? Are we actually able to confirm the date of delivery? Do we measure against the requested delivery date, or against the confirmed delivery date? How do we promise dates to customers? Do we have standard lead times depending on the customers and the products? Do we promise dates based on the availability of product and/or production?

Do we say 'in full' if the order is delivered in full, with all of its order lines? It is more common for companies to measure the percentage of order lines or the percentage of volume delivered on time and in full. These are called order line or volume fill rates.

Service goes way beyond service level, which is so dominant in supply chain that we often ignore the rest. To give two examples, service extends to the product portfolio and the order flexibility offered. Customers will value a broader product portfolio as an improved service – it allows them to choose the product that is the best fit for purpose. A wider choice allows them to work with fewer suppliers, and this lowers their transaction costs. Order flexibility has to do with how flexible I am with regards to issues such as the timing of ordering, the order quantity, any minimum order amount, any changes to orders already placed, and so on. Customers will value order flexibility as it allows them to be more responsive and avoid unnecessary inventory caused by restrictions on ordering.

Cost

To deliver service, we have costs. Figure 1.3 lists the typical costs associated with the Source, Make and Deliver processes from SCOR. We purchase components or raw materials, we manufacture products in-house or externally, we have the cost of the warehousing for the finished product and we have the logistics cost of shipping our finished product to our customers.

Cash

Where service and cost are easy to grasp, cash is more difficult and requires basic accounting knowledge. We use cash as a synonym for working capital. For working capital we will use the simplified definition in which it equals the inventory plus the accounts receivable, minus the accounts payable. We include a section on accounting basics at the end of this chapter – for now we will assume that basic knowledge as we dig into more detail below.

Inventory is probably the most difficult of the working capital components. There are multiple reasons why companies need to hold inventory. Getting a grip on inventory requires a grip on the different underlying drivers. Figure 1.4 summarizes five key reasons for which we hold inventory. We discuss each of them in more detail.

Cycle stock results from the need to produce or order in batches. The 'lean' philosophy works towards a one-piece flow. However, as long as we are confronted with significant change-over or ordering costs, the well-known EOQ principle (Axsäter, 2015) teaches us that it is more economical to produce in batches. If we produce once a month, the average cycle stock will be two weeks. If we produce once a week, the average cycle stock will be half a week. EOQ teaches us that batch sizes go up as the change-over

Figure 1.4   Five main reasons for which we hold inventory

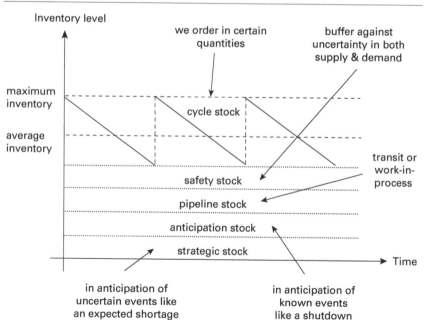

or order costs go up and as the product cost goes down. They are primary drivers of the amount of cycle stock.

Safety stock is a buffer against uncertainty. In an ideal situation, your customer will just wait for you to order your raw materials, make the product, and ship the finished product to the specified location. The ideal situation is, unfortunately, the exception. In a Make-To-Stock environment, the customer expects you to have the finished product available in stock. In a Make-To-Order environment, the customers expects you to keep inventory of raw materials and components and he is willing to wait for manufacturing and distribution to happen. If we take the Make-To-Order example, it implies you will have to order your raw materials and components in the absence of the actual customer orders. That demand uncertainty is covered in a safety stock.

Safety stocks also cover supply uncertainty. Suppliers may be late or deliver less than expected. There may be a quality issue making part or all of the supply unavailable to production. These are examples of supply uncertainty covered by the safety stock.

Anticipation stock is typically the result of your supply planning process. You may build up stock to anticipate a seasonal peak, a tender or a shutdown. These types of planning decisions lead to so-called anticipation stock.

Pipeline stock is the result of lead times. If we ship things per truck, train or boat, it creates 'in transit' inventory. In the process of production we have so-called 'work in progress' or 'WIP', which is all the inventory sitting on the production floor.

Strategic stock is carried to manage potential risks, such as a potential price increase or a shortage in a key raw material. As opposed to (say) a plant shutdown, these events are uncertain. That defines the difference between anticipation and strategic stock. You can consider strategic stock more as hedging and as part of the risk management in your supply chain.

In addition to the above, there are other reasons that companies carry inventory. An example may be a minimum order quantity imposed by a supplier, or the amount of inventory needed in a shop for display purposes. Ordering or displaying five pieces may represent five months of stock if you use or sell only one per month. As a company it is important that you list your key inventory drivers. Adapt the classification to something that works for you.

Inventory balances with cash. If we were able to sell off £20,000 of inventory and get a cash payment, we'd have £20,000 more cash in our bank account. In practice we have payment terms, to both customers and suppliers. The 'accounts receivable' define the amount we still need to receive from our customers. 'Receivables' depend on the payment terms and the speed of collection. If customers need to pay within 30 days, but on average pay only after 45 days, we will have 45 days of sales for which we are waiting to receive the cash. If we can reduce that average from 45 days to 40 days, that creates an extra five days of cash in our bank account.

The 'accounts payable' define the amount we still need to pay to our suppliers. That again depends on the payment terms and our speed of actually paying. If we need to pay after 30 days, but on average we pay after 45 days, it is worth 45 days of goods for which we have not yet spent the cash. If the supplier increases the pressure, our average may shift to 40 days. This requires an extra five days of goods for which we need to provide the cash.

Working capital is the cash we need to keep operations running. It is the cash required to finance the inventory and receivables from our customers, minus the cash we have still kept from our suppliers in the form of payables. An increase in inventory or receivables increases the cash required. An increase in payables towards our suppliers decreases the cash required.

Companies struggle with balance in the triangle

In the previous section we introduced the three corners of the Supply Chain Triangle. In this section we will show that companies struggle with balance in the triangle. Figure 1.5 shows a couple of examples.

Let's start at the top left corner. In a bid to reduce cost, purchasing has, in many companies, started sourcing in the Far East. It will help in lowering cost, but what is often overlooked is that because of the longer lead times, it will increase the average inventory. So we decrease cost, but at the expense of extra inventory. Likewise, production will strive for longer production runs, as longer production runs lead to greater efficiency, and greater efficiency leads to a lower production cost per unit. Longer runs will lower the cost, but again at the expense of extra inventory.

A second example is shown at the top right corner. When faced with peaks in demand, for example through seasonality, an important design question is whether to accommodate the peak by pre-building inventory (the so-called 'level' strategy) or whether to build peak capacity so you can more closely follow the demand as it happens (the so-called 'chase' strategy). Building peak capacity will improve responsiveness to the customer, but it increases the overall investment, so it will increase the overall cost.

Figure 1.5   Companies struggle with balance in the triangle

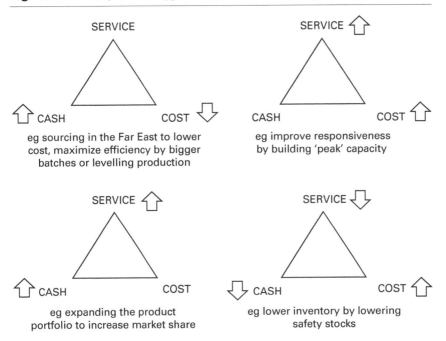

eg sourcing in the Far East to lower cost, maximize efficiency by bigger batches or levelling production

eg improve responsiveness by building 'peak' capacity

eg expanding the product portfolio to increase market share

eg lower inventory by lowering safety stocks

Levelling the peak by pre-building inventory lowers the overall investment and allows production to run more smoothly. This will lower the overall cost, but at the expense of extra inventory.

Though this seems intuitive, in practice it is hard to quantify the value of responsiveness. This offers leeway for operations to always go for the cost-optimal solution of pre-building inventory. The challenge with this approach is that you often can't accurately predict what a customer is going to buy three months from now. As a result you risk having the wrong product, creating both an excess inventory (of the wrong product) and service issues at the same time.

A third example is shown on the bottom left. In your company, marketing and sales may push for an expansion of the product portfolio to increase market share. A wider portfolio will add value for the customer and help to increase market share, but carrying more products will require more inventory. It may also negatively impact cost, as more products may mean more change-overs or longer picking tours in your warehouse.

The fourth example is shown on the bottom right of Figure 1.5. The above examples all push inventory up. In my experience companies have become more concerned with inventory since the financial crisis. As a result, over the last 10 years, many companies have launched multiple working capital reduction projects in a bid to free up cash. Many of them start the year with ambitious programmes attacking the inventory from multiple angles, only to find out around summer that none of the initiatives are really on track and delivering the anticipated benefits. Working capital reduction projects are high-visibility projects, so failing is not an option.

As a result, to save their face and possibly their bonuses, supply chain managers resort to the 'handbrake', which in inventory management means lowering safety stocks. Lowering safety stocks will lower the inventory, but it will also negatively impact the service, and, as service issues arise, trigger all kinds of operational firefighting costs.

So in summary, the first key finding of Figure 1.5 is that the three corners of the triangle are connected. Decisions in one corner almost automatically impact the other corners. A second key finding is that companies struggle with balancing the triangle. We often take decisions with only one of the corners in mind, without assessing the impact on the full triangle. In the next section we explain why this is the case.

Traditional organizations cause tension in the triangle

Figure 1.6 shows a typical and traditional organization chart for a manufacturing company.

We have a management committee existing of a CEO, a CFO, and four VPs responsible for purchasing, for production, for supply chain, and for marketing and sales. Bigger corporations may have matrix variants, but the dominant power typically resides in the functional organization.

Figure 1.6   A traditional organization and the corresponding KPIs

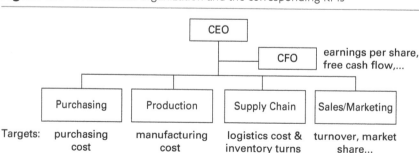

Assume you're the VP of marketing and sales. You step into the car in the morning – what is the first thing you think of? In general, marketing and sales people are driven by top-line metrics such as revenue and market share. What if you're the VP of production? Chances are you'll think of efficiency, as efficiency drives costs. Procurement? Most probably, your first thoughts are about your spend and how to get the spend down. So in general, operations will be cost-driven.

In many companies supply chain will have a double function. On the one hand we are managing an operational process like outbound logistics, on which we are cost-driven. In more and more companies, I see that supply chain has the responsibility for managing global inventories. As we have learned above, managing inventory is about balancing it against service and cost.

The CFO will be driven by financial metrics such as Earnings Per Share (EPS – the net income per share) and free cash flow (FCF – the cash flow from operations minus capital expenditure). We refer to the section on accounting basics at the end of this chapter for more details.

Figure 1.7 maps this traditional organization to the Supply Chain Triangle. It shows that, in general, marketing and sales are pulling the top side of the triangle, whereas operations is pulling the cost side of the triangle.

Before the financial crisis, that was probably about it. There was a tension between sales and operations, with the inventory as a buffer in-between, making often huge swings as a result. Since the financial crisis, the CFO has

Figure 1.7 A traditional organization mapped to the Supply Chain Triangle

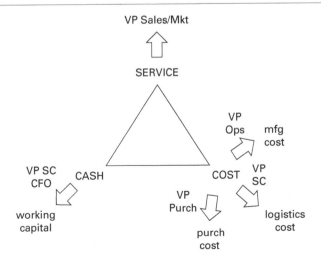

become more concerned with working capital, making inventory a part of the equation, instead of just the result.

Where accounts payable and accounts receivable are relatively straightforward, inventory is more complex. As a result, the CFO will look for a companion when trying to get the inventory under control. The likely candidate is supply chain, as the other functions typically have a conflict of interest. This is the moment when as a VP of Supply Chain you can be given the target to reduce inventories by 30%. You need to be careful in accepting the challenge. Reducing inventories is really about creating balance in the triangle, and balancing the triangle is not something you can do alone!

Increased tension in the triangle as growth stalls

When a company is growing and has healthy profits, there is little incentive for better alignment in the triangle. Yes, maybe working capital has increased and our inventory turns went down, but who will really complain if the company has grown by 20% and has realized a 10% EBIT? Some will probably even argue that the functional KPIs and incentives actually led to the good result. If I'm in sales, I will push back on any changes to the service side so as to keep my room for manoeuvre. If I'm in operations, the extra volumes have helped me to create more efficiency. I'm happy for now, and will push back on any projects that risk making my life more complex.

The trouble starts when growth stalls and profitability drops back. There may be different underlying reasons. The market in general may be slowing down. The market may be disrupted by low-cost players or newer technologies to which I'm late. In any case, the trouble starts when a company or business unit is underperforming compared to the budget that has been put forward. Figure 1.8 shows a possible reaction.

In a typical response, sales will increase the pressure on the service side. They will desperately try to get in any order. They are willing to make any promise that helps, including shorter lead times, expedited shipments, changes in the payment terms, and safety stock at the customer's site.

To sustain profits, operations will start a relentless focus on cost. To lower costs, production prefers big runs and limited changeovers. To lower the purchasing cost, purchasing takes more commitment to the suppliers, typically increasing the inventory risk.

A business in trouble needs cash to turn around the situation. The cash may need to go into the development of new products, the exploration of

Figure 1.8   Increased tension in the triangle as growth stalls

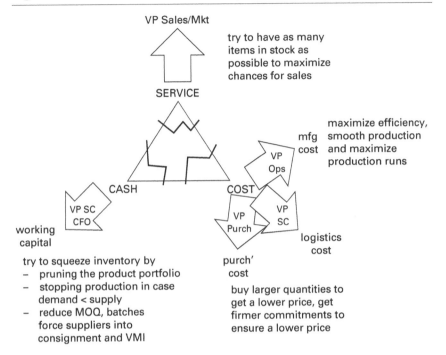

VP Sales/Mkt

SERVICE

try to have as many items in stock as possible to maximize chances for sales

maximize efficiency, smooth production and maximize production runs

mfg cost

VP Ops

CASH

COST

VP SC
CFO

VP Purch

VP SC

working capital

logistics cost

try to squeeze inventory by
- pruning the product portfolio
- stopping production in case demand < supply
- reduce MOQ, batches force suppliers into consignment and VMI

purch' cost

buy larger quantities to get a lower price, get firmer commitments to ensure a lower price

new markets, a rebranding, or a take-over. To generate the cash, we assign the unlucky VP of Supply Chain with the challenge of aggressively reducing inventories, the famous 30%.

Supply chain has its back against the wall. Simplifying the product portfolio will go against sales. Stopping production to control inventories will go against manufacturing. Supplier contracts have just been renegotiated, with a focus on cost instead of cash. We may find ourselves locked into an impossible situation.

The only way to get out of this deadlock is to make joint choices, instead of having each of the departments pulling harder on their side of the triangle. The choice may be to temporarily sacrifice profit and work at higher inventories to 'sweat it out' and sustain market share through a difficult period. If the market is really disrupted by low-cost players or by newer technologies, it may be crucial to generate cash for new investments. As a result we may aggressively cut inventories at the cost of the top-line, to free up the cash to reinvent the company.

So in summary, when times are good, there is little incentive to create alignment. When times are bad, alignment is key, as we can no longer improve on all corners at the same time. It is another illustration of how companies struggle with the triangle, and how that even creates a dangerous catch-22.

Expanding the triangle from cash to capital employed

So far we have focused on the balancing of service, (operational) cost and cash. There are two possible extensions shown in Figure 1.9. The first is accounting for non-operational costs such as R&D and selling, general and administrative expenses (SG&A). These will be important in later chapters as we link the triangle to different strategies. A second is expanding from cash to capital employed, which is the financial term for the sum of the working capital and the fixed assets.

We already gave an example in Figure 1.5. When companies decide to install capacity to cover the peak demand (chase strategy) instead of levelling the demand and pre-building inventory (level strategy), they are in essence creating more service by increasing the fixed assets, as opposed to creating more inventory. Another example could be a company investing in new machines that allow them to provide a broader product range. Not only may we carry more inventory, we may need new investments to create a broader product portfolio. Both are illustrated in Figure 1.10.

Fixed assets are depreciated. If we invest in a production plant or warehouse for £10 million, and we depreciate it over 20 years, then the annual depreciation will be £500,000. As a result, fixed assets always translate into the cost side of the triangle, as is shown in Figure 1.11. We refer to our section on accounting basics at the end of this chapter for more details.

Figure 1.9 Expanding the triangle from cash to capital employed

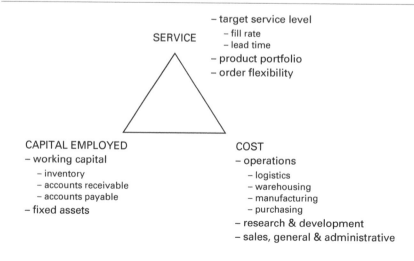

Figure 1.10   Balancing service and capital employed

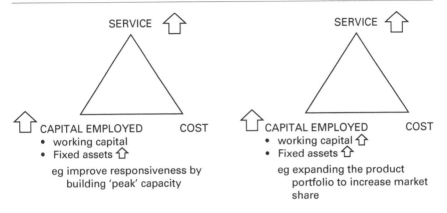

Figure 1.11   Fixed assets translate into the cost corner through depreciation

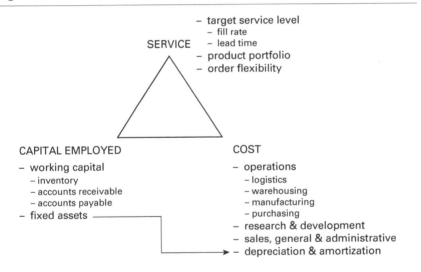

If companies invest in automation, they typically do so to replace the cost of manual labour with a lower cost per unit after the automation. Figure 1.12 visualizes that the cost will only be lower if the annual depreciation is less than the annual saving on labour costs. To take our example of the £10 million investment which is depreciated over 20 years, let's assume the investment is in automation. If the yearly saving in labour cost is £750,000, where the annual depreciation is £500,000, the investment makes sense. It will lower our cost at the expense of a higher capital employed.

Figure 1.12 Lowering manual labour costs by investing in automation

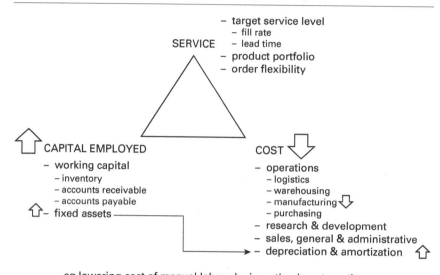

eg lowering cost of manual labour by investing in automation

Figure 1.13 Inventory translates into the cost corner through write-offs

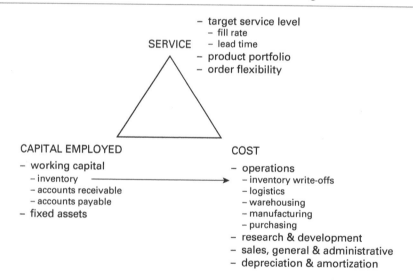

Inventory also translates into the cost corner. Firstly, more inventory requires a bigger warehouse and will increase the warehousing costs. More inventory may also lead to more write-offs. Write-offs are typically charged to the cost of goods sold. For that reason we have shown it in Figure 1.13 under the 'operations' costs.

Aligning the triangle is about optimizing ROCE

Though people from different backgrounds – supply chain, finance, sales, marketing – recognize the tension in the triangle, the dominant thinking is that the tension is 'unavoidable' and that 'this is how companies work'. I do get questions such as 'won't there always be conflicting objectives between sales, operations and finance?' and 'isn't the conflict a source of creative energy?', 'isn't that exactly what keeps companies going?'. Though rightful questions, I believe the answer is no, and the answer lies in taking an investor's perspective.

Figure 1.14 shows that service is a driver for revenue. As we mentioned before, marketing and sales are primarily service driven as they are, in many companies, primarily top-line driven. Most companies have growth objectives. In the absence of breakthrough innovations, it will be tempting to stimulate growth by increasing the services offered to the market.

Though growth is good, it is most often not a goal in itself. As an investor, I would like to see a profit, at least in the long term. Figure 1.15 shows

Figure 1.14 Service is a driver for revenue

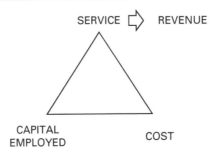

Figure 1.15 Service and cost combine into a profit metric like EBIT

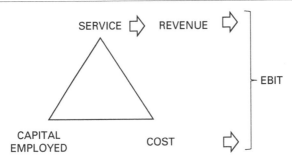

how we can combine the service and the cost side of the triangle into a profit metric like EBIT, the Earnings Before Interest and Taxes.

But as an investor, I am concerned with more than EBIT. If I have two companies generating £100 million of EBIT, but the first requires £2 billion of capital and the second only £1 billion, then I'd rather invest in the second.

As an investor I am really concerned with the EBIT generated over the capital employed – the ROCE. It's OK if your EBIT is a bit lower, as long as you need less capital – or, vice versa, it's OK if you need more capital as long as your EBIT is higher. As an investor I will judge you by the 'bang-for-the-buck', the EBIT you generated over capital employed. That is illustrated in Figure 1.16.

Let's revisit some of the examples from Figure 1.5 with the ROCE principle in mind. Expanding the product portfolio will increase the inventory; it may also require extra investment to be able to produce the extra new products. So what should we do? Is it worthwhile pursuing it? We believe the dominant thinking in companies today is:

1 growth;

2 profit;

3 capital employed.

Some companies are so focused on growth that any initiative supporting growth will automatically get approved. We believe that, in general, companies have become more concerned with profit, so many companies will assess the impact on profit, and if this is promising they will go with the expansion of the product portfolio. In only limited cases do we see companies asking about the impact on their working capital, and what will it do

Figure 1.16   EBIT over capital employed gives a return metric like ROCE

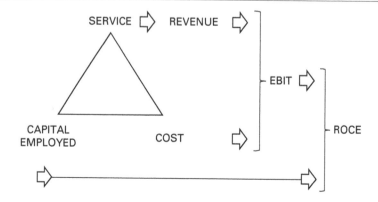

to their ROCE. Companies typically do reflect on the fixed assets, as these may simply be a necessity to buy or install to get to their planned extension.

In the quest for growth, companies over the years add complexity to the service corner. They offer more products, they offer them faster, they get more flexible in honouring customer specific requests. Again, adding service will create value for the customer and support the top-line and your market share. As a result, when supply chain managers try to reduce inventory by pruning the product portfolio, it is typical to get pushback from marketing and/or sales saying: 'You can't cut this product, it's critical to customers A and B. I know it's not profitable but we will lose these customers if we no longer have it.'

So how do we solve this? We start by recognizing that yes, if we stop certain products, it will negatively impact the top-line. If we were able to stop certain products without impact, the top-line would be in a really backward situation! The question we need to ask is, what it will do to our ROCE? In general, as products get to the end of their life, volumes decrease, and because of low-cost competition profits are eroding even faster. At the same time, delivering good service will proportionally require more inventory, or inventory turns will be going down. This negatively impacts 'bang-for-the-buck'. I get less profit for more investment. That's not something I want!

If I look at my product portfolio, it will be clear that some products and customers are positively contributing to my ROCE, where others are lowering it. In supply chain terms we often hear about 'good complexity' versus 'bad complexity'. Bad complexity lowers our ROCE, and should be taken out. But not all complexity is bad. As supply chain people, we'd often like to simplify the service side as to minimize the cost. This is a step too far.

In the next chapter we will show that different strategies lead to different levels of complexity, and each of them can be equally successful. What will however remain is that regardless of the strategy, some complexity will add to the ROCE and some will not. Stripping out bad complexity is best practice. But not every company will strip to the same level. That level depends on your strategy.

Accounting basics: inventory, working capital, and cash generation

In this section we will dig into some accounting basics, which are required for a good understanding of the main text in the book. To better understand the link between inventory, working capital and cash generation, we will introduce and explain the three key financial statements of any publicly listed company: the profit and loss statement, the balance sheet, and the statement of cash flows.

The profit and loss statement (P&L)

Figure 1.17 shows a simplified P&L for an example company.

Let's discuss the different lines. Sales revenue minus the cost of goods sold (COGS) define the gross profit. The COGS are the costs that can be directly attributed to the sale, eg the purchasing cost of the raw materials and the components that go into the finished goods.

Costs that cannot be directly attributed to the sale, such as sales or marketing costs, are grouped into a category called the selling, general and administrative costs, or SG&A.

EBITDA is the earnings before we subtract interest, taxes, depreciation and amortization. If a company invests in a new production facility or a new warehouse, the cost of that investment is spread over its lifetime. This means we can make a £10 million investment this year, and spread the cost over 20 years, ie £500,000 per year. This is called 'depreciation'. If a company invests time or money in the creation of new products or services (R&D), the cost of that investment can also be spread over the lifetime of the product. The yearly cost is called 'amortization'. Notice that 'depreciation' or 'amortization' are not cash-outs as of year 2. The only cash-out is in year 1, when we make the investment.

If the value of our inventory is decreasing, eg because of price evolutions for a key raw material or shelf-life issues, the value reduction is typically charged to the cost of goods sold.

The P&L traces all the revenues and all costs during a period – typically a quarter, a semester or a year. Subtracting all the costs from the revenues that relate to a given period gives the net income or the net profit. the earnings per share (EPS) show the net income per share in the given period.

The balance sheet

The balance sheet shows all that a company owns at a specific moment in time (typically at the end of a year). What a company owns are called the 'assets'. They are shown in Figure 1.18.

Figure 1.17 P&L of an example company

Profit and Loss (2013)		
Sales revenue	£ 75,600	
Cost of goods sold (COGS)	£ −52,920	
Gross profit	£ 22,680	30%
Selling general and administrative (SG&A) Expenses	£ −15,120	
Earnings Before Interest, Taxes, Depreciation & Amortization (EBITDA)	£ 7,560	10%
Depreciation	£ −3,024	
Amortization	£ −	
Earnings Before Interest, Taxes (EBIT)	£ 4,536	6%
Taxes and interest	£ −2,646	
Net income / net profit	£ 1,890	3%
Earnings per share (eg 1,000 shares)	£ 1,89	

Cost that can be directly attributed to the sale, eg purchasing cost

Cost that can NOT be directly attributed to the sale, eg marketing costs

'Investments' in eg warehouses are depreciated, for instance over 20 years. This implies we account for 1/20th of the total cost each year. A depreciation is not a 'cash-out'. The actual cash has been spent when the warehouse was built!

Inventory write-offs are typically in amortization

Figure 1.18 The 'asset' side of an example balance sheet

Balance Sheet (31/12/2012)			Liabilities and owners' equity		
Assets					
Current Assets			*Owners' equity*		
Cash	£	6,600	Paid-in capital	£	15,000
Accounts receivable	£	6,200	Retained earnings	£	800
Inventories	£	5,000			
Total current assets	£	17,800	Total owners' equity	£	15,800
Fixed assets			*Liabilities*		
Property plant equipment	£	20,000	*Current liabilities*		
			Accounts payable	£	8,000
			Short-term bank loans	£	4,000
			Long-term liabilities		
			Long-term bank loans	£	10,000
Total fixed assets	£	20,000	Total liabilities	£	22,000
Total assets	£	37,800		£	37,800

Current assets can be converted into money in the short term. 'Current' refers to 'short-term'

Fixed assets are more difficult to convert into cash. They are 'long-term' assets.

Accounts receivable = turnover that has been invoiced to the customer, but has not yet been paid. eg partners that pay at 30 days or 60 days, consumers that buy on credit of 30 days...

Current assets can be converted into cash in the short term, typically less than a year. Important components of current assets are the cash we have in the bank and the accounts receivable, which is the money we still need to receive from our customers. Inventory is also part of current assets.

Fixed assets cannot easily be converted into cash – for example, plant, properties and equipment in which we have invested in the past.

The balance sheet also shows the financing of these assets. This is again shown in Figure 1.19.

When starting a company, the owners will invest a certain amount of money. This is called the paid-in capital. When the company makes a profit, part of the profit can be returned to the shareholders via a dividend. The shareholders can decide to leave part of the profit in the company as retained earnings. So part of the financing of the assets comes from so-called 'owners' equity' (paid-in capital plus retained earnings).

The second part of the financing is liabilities. Current liabilities are due in the short term. The accounts payable, which is the money still to be paid to suppliers, are part of the current liabilities, as is any type of short-term debt. Investments in fixed assets (plant, warehouses and so on) are typically financed by long-term loans. These are part of the long-term liabilities.

Exercise: Understanding the P&L and the balance sheet

Take the latest financial reports from your company and those of two key competitors. From the P&Ls compare revenue, cost of goods, SG&A, EBITDA, depreciation and amortization, EBIT, net income, and earnings per share.

What do you learn about your profitability compared to your two key competitors?

From the balance sheets, compare the following metrics:

- current ratio – current assets/current liabilities;
- debt ratio – total debt/total assets.

The current ratio is what we call a liquidity measure. It explains how easily the short-term liabilities can be covered by short-term assets like receivables and cash. A ratio below one indicates a lack of liquidity. The debt ratio indicates how much of the total assets is financed by debt rather than equity. Lower debt financing, or a so-called 'lower leverage', makes it easier to get extra debt financing.

Figure 1.19 The 'liabilities and owners' equity' side of an example balance sheet

Balance Sheet (31/12/2012)			Liabilities and owners' equity			
Assets			**Owners' equity**			
Current assets			Paid-in capital	£	15,000	The owners' equity consists of the cash investments made in the company by the shareholders + any earnings that have not been paid as a dividend
Cash	£	6,600	Retained earnings	£	800	
Accounts receivable	£	6,200				
Inventories	£	5,000	*Total owners' equity*	£	15,800	
Total current assets	£	17,800	**Liabilities**			
Fixed Assets			*Current liabilities*			Current liabilities are payable in the short term
Property plant equipment	£	20,000	Accounts payable	£	8,000	
			Short-term bank loans	£	4,000	
			Long-term liabilities			Long-term liabilities are payable in the long term
			Long-term bank loans	£	10,000	
Total fixed assets	£	20,000	*Total liabilities*	£	22,000	
Total Assets	£	37,800		£	37,800	

Accounts payable = costs that have been made and accounted for in the profit-and-loss … but that still need to be paid, eg we pay our suppliers only after 30 days or 60 days

The statement of cash flows

The statement of cash flows explains the difference in the cash position at the end of the previous period and the end of the current period. As explained when discussing the P&L, depreciation of an investment is not a cash-out as of year 2. As a result, when starting from the net profit, we need to add the depreciation (and the amortization) if we want to know actual cash generation (or consumption). If our accounts receivable have decreased, eg from £6,200 at the end of the previous period to £5,000 at the end of the current period, we have been able to 'collect' £1,200 of cash from our customers. As a result, a decrease in the accounts receivable generates cash. An increase in the accounts receivable will consume cash. Likewise, a reduction in inventory and an increase in the accounts payable will generate cash.

Figure 1.20 shows the statement of cash flows for our example company.

The net income is £1,890. We have a depreciation of £3,024. Assuming the investment has been made in earlier years, this is not a cash-out, so we can add it to the net income. Apparently over this period, our accounts receivable have increased, our inventory has increased, and our accounts payable have decreased. As a result the cash we generated – £1,890 plus £3,024 – has been consumed by the increase in the receivables and inventory, and a reduction in the payables.

In fact the cash generated is not sufficient. There is a deficit of -£1,586. This deficit will lower the cash we have available at the bank. If we don't have enough cash in the bank account, we'll need to extend our loans or ask shareholders to increase the capital to finance this deficit.

There is a saying that companies don't go bankrupt from making a loss. They go bankrupt from a lack of cash. The statement of cash flows is instrumental in understanding which are the cash generating factors and which are the cash consuming factors over a given accounting period.

Figure 1.20 shows the so-called 'cash flow from operations'. We can also generate or consume cash from investing activities and from financing activities. The above mentioned investment in a new production facility or warehouse will typically be explained in the cash flow from investments. This is a second and separate part of the overall statement of cash flows. If we make an investment of £10 million in year 1, it will show the £10 million here. If we depreciate over 20 years, we only show £500,000 in the P&L. That £500,000 is not an extra cash-out, so it should be added to the net income in the operations part of the statement of cash flows.

The free cash flow (FCF) equals cash flow from operations minus capital expenditures. A capital expenditure is any investment in non-financial

Figure 1.20 An example statement of cash flows

Statement of cash flows (2013)

Net income	£ 1,890
+ depreciation expense	£ 3,024
+ decrease in accounts receivable	£ -3,000
+ decrease in Inventory	£ -2,500
+ increase in accounts payable	£ -1,000
Cash flow from operations	£ -1,586

The net income or net profit is not equal to the cash we have generated!.

eg as already explained, a depreciation is not a 'cash-out'. The cash has been spent when the investment was initially done. As such, to calculate the actual cash generation, we add the depreciation expense to the net income.

If I decrease my inventory (eg from 5,000£ at the end of 2012 to 4,000£ at the end of 2013) ... then I generate cash.

Likewise, if I decrease my AR (money to receive from customers), or increase my AP (money still to pay to suppliers) ... I also generate cash.

assets, like a new product facility or warehouse. It is called the 'free' cash flow as it represents the cash that is available to further expand production, develop new products, make acquisitions, pay dividends and reduce debt.

If we make a big investment, all or part of the investment may be financed by a new loan or a capital increase by the shareholders. This financing is typically shown in 'cash flow from financing'. That is the third and last part of the overall statement of cash flows.

Figure 1.21 shows that the statement of cash flows can also be derived from comparing the balance sheet at the end of the previous and the current period. The depreciation shows as a reduction of the fixed assets. To come back to our example, each year we account for £500,000 in the P&L. In the balance sheet we reduce the value of the corresponding asset by £500,000 each year. The comparison also shows the increase in the receivables and the inventory, the decrease in the payables. The cash deficit of –£1,586 shows as a reduction of the cash balance from £6,600 to £5,014.

Exercise: Understanding the statement of cash flows

Take the latest two financial reports from your company and those of two key competitors. Try to derive the statement of cash flows by comparing balance sheets from the last two years, as shown in Figure 1.21. Compare your result with the statement of cash flows in the financial reports. Try to understand any differences.

Take a step back and review the following questions: which activities have generated cash? Which have been consuming cash? Was there a net cash generation or consumption? Review for your company and the two key competitors.

Working capital

Working capital is defined as current assets minus the current liabilities. Figure 1.22 shows the working capital for our example company is £5,800.

Throughout the year, working capital can go up and down as the underlying components go up and down. The working capital represents the capital we need in order to have smooth operations. You can consider it the oil in our operational engine.

Figure 1.21 Deriving the statement of cash flows from the balance sheet

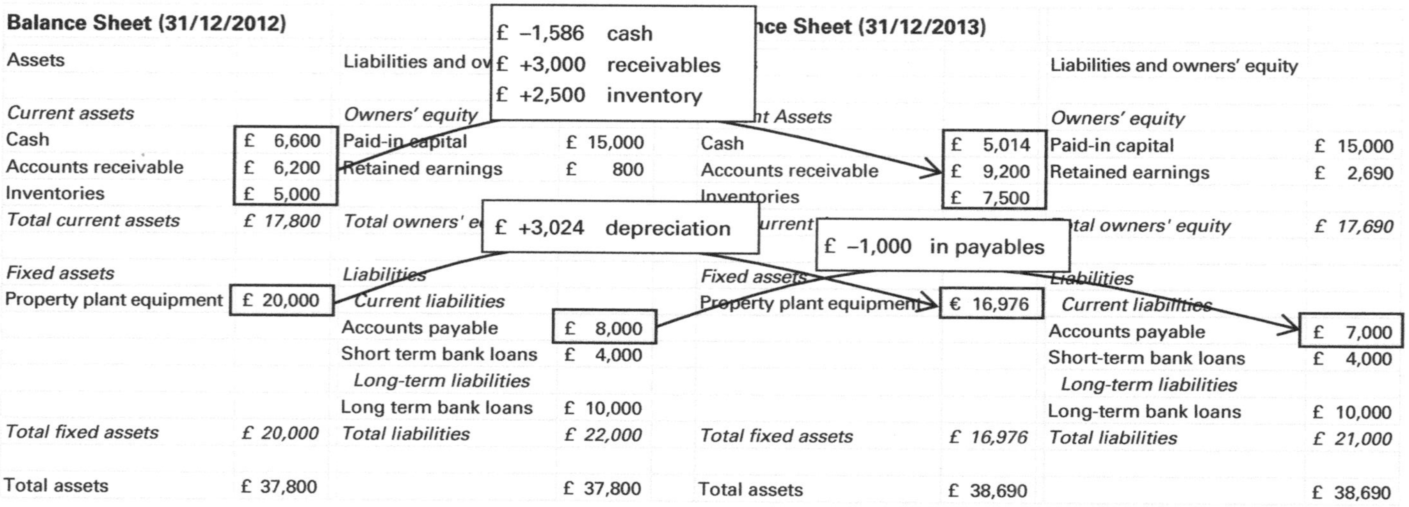

Balance Sheet (31/12/2012)

Assets		Liabilities and owners' equity	
Current assets		*Owners' equity*	
Cash	£ 6,600	Paid-in capital	
Accounts receivable	£ 6,200	Retained earnings	
Inventories	£ 5,000		
Total current assets	£ 17,800		
Fixed assets		*Liabilities*	
Property plant equipment	£ 20,000	*Current liabilities*	
		Accounts payable	£ 8,000
		Short term bank loans	£ 4,000
		Long-term liabilities	
		Long term bank loans	£ 10,000
Total fixed assets	£ 20,000	Total liabilities	£ 22,000
Total assets	£ 37,800		£ 37,800

Balance Sheet (31/12/2013)

Assets		Liabilities and owners' equity	
Current Assets		*Owners' equity*	
Cash	£ 15,000	Paid-in capital	£ 5,014
Accounts receivable	£ 800	Retained earnings	£ 9,200
Inventories			£ 7,500
		Total owners' equity	£ 17,690
Fixed assets		*Liabilities*	
Property plant equipment	€ 16,976	*Current liabilities*	
		Accounts payable	£ 7,000
		Short-term bank loans	£ 4,000
		Long-term liabilities	
		Long-term bank loans	£ 10,000
Total fixed assets	£ 16,976	Total liabilities	£ 21,000
Total assets	£ 38,690		£ 38,690

Annotations:
- £ −1,586 cash
- £ +3,000 receivables
- £ +2,500 inventory
- £ +3,024 depreciation
- £ −1,000 in payables

Figure 1.22 Deriving the working capital

Balance Sheet (31/12/2012)

Assets			Liabilities and owners' equity		
Current assets			*Owners' equity*		
Cash	£	6,600	Paid-in capital	£ 15,000	
Accounts receivable	£	6,200	Retained earnings	£ 800	
Inventories	£	5,000			
Total current assets	£	17,800	*Total owners' equity*	£ 15,800	
Fixed assets			*Liabilities*		
Property plant equipment	£ 20,000		*Current liabilities*		
			Accounts payable	£ 8,000	
			Short-term bank loans	£ 4,000	
			Long-term liabilities		
			Long-term bank loans	£ 10,000	
Total fixed assets	£ 20,000		*Total liabilities*	£ 22,000	
Total assets	£ 37,800			£ 37,800	

£17,800 – £12,000 = £5,800

Figure 1.22 also shows that our working capital is in fact financed by owners' equity and the long-term liabilities. These do not come for free. We typically have a rent on the long-term liabilities. If we pay 5% to the bank, our shareholders will typically expect a higher return, such as 15%. Without going into details, there is a financial metric called the weighted average cost of capital (WACC). This weighs the different types of debt and their corresponding return. For manufacturing and retail companies it typically varies between 8% and 12%.

Figure 1.23 shows that the working capital in our company has increased over the last period, from £5,800 to £10,714. Our current liabilities decreased by £1,000, and current assets increased by £3,914.

Working capital and supply chain

Figure 1.24 shows the primary components of working capital which the supply chain can affect:

- inventory: lowering inventories generates cash;
- accounts receivable: reducing payment terms to clients or improving collection speed generates cash;
- accounts payable: increasing payment terms to suppliers also generates cash

Days of inventory on hand (DIOH), inventory turns, days of sales outstanding (DSO) and days of payables outstanding (DPO) are financial metrics that are commonly used to measure and follow up these key components of

Figure 1.23 An example working capital increase

Balance Sheet (31/12/2012)

Assets			Liabilities and owners' equity		
Current assets			*Owners' equity*		
Cash	£	6,600	Paid-in capital	£	15,000
Accounts receivable	£	6,200	Retained earnings	£	800
Inventories	£	5,000			
Total current assets	£	17,800	Total owners' equity	£	15,800
Fixed assets			*Liabilities*		
Property plant equipment	£	20,000	*Current liabilities*		
			Accounts payable	£	8,000
			Short-term bank loans	£	4,000
			Long-term liabilities		
			Long-term bank loans	£	10,000
Total fixed assets	£	20,000	Total liabilities	£	22,000
Total assets	£	37,800	Total assets	£	37,800

£17,800 – £12,000 = £5,800

Balance Sheet (31/12/2013)

Assets			Liabilities and owners' equity		
Current assets			*Owners' equity*		
Cash	£	5,014	Paid-in capital	£	15,000
Accounts receivable	£	9,200	Retained earnings	£	2,690
Inventories	£	7,500			
Total current assets	£	21,714	Total owners' equity	£	17,690
Fixed assets			*Liabilities*		
Property plant equipment	£	16,976	*Current liabilities*		
			Accounts payable	£	7,000
			Short-term bank loans	£	4,000
			Long-term liabilities		
			Long-term bank loans	£	10,000
Total fixed assets	£	16,976	Total liabilities	£	21,000
Total assets	£	38,690	Total assets	£	38,690

£21,714 – £11,000 = £10,714

+ £4,914

Figure 1.24 Supply chain impacts on working capital

Balance Sheet (31/12/2012)

Assets		Liabilities and owners' equity	
Current assets		*Owners' equity*	
Cash	£ 6,600	Paid-in capital	£ 15,000
Accounts receivable	£ 6,200	Retained earnings	£ 800
Inventories	£ 5,000		
Total current assets	£ 17,800	Total owners' equity	£ 15,800
		Liabilities	
Fixed assets		*Current liabilities*	
Property plant equipment	£ 20,000	Accounts payable	£ 8,000
		Short-term bank loans	£ 4,000
		Long-term liabilities	
		Long-term bank loans	£ 10,000
Total fixed assets	£ 20,000	Total liabilities	£ 22,000
Total assets	£ 37,800		£ 37,800

Sales, Logistics, Manufacturing and Procurement primarily have impact on:

– inventory
– accounts receivable (defined by payment terms for customers and speed of collection)
– accounts payable (defined by payment terms for customers and respecting due dates)

Figure 1.25   DIOH, inventory turns, DSO and DPO

$$DSO = \frac{9,200£}{75,600£/yr} \cdot 365 \ days/yr = 44 \ days$$

$$DPO = \frac{7,000£}{52,920£/yr} \cdot 365 \ days/yr = 48 \ days$$

$$DIOH = \frac{7,500£}{52,920£/yr} \cdot 365 \ days/yr = 52 \ days$$

$$Inventory \ turns = \frac{52,920£/yr}{7,500£} = 7/yr$$

Figure 1.26   The cash conversion cycle

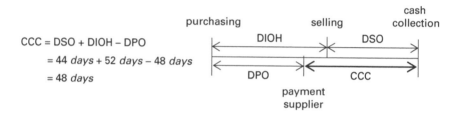

CCC = DSO + DIOH − DPO
= 44 days + 52 days − 48 days
= 48 days

the working capital. They are defined and applied to our example company in Figure 1.25.

Another commonly used metric is the so-called cash conversion cycle (CCC). Figure 1.26 shows its definition and how it applies to our example company.

The CCC indicates the number of days between disbursing cash to suppliers and collecting cash from customers. It is a direct measurement of the key components of working capital. Reducing the CCC lowers the working capital and generates cash. Increasing the CCC increases the working capital and consumes cash.

Exercise: Understanding working capital and the CCC

From the latest two financial reports from your company and two key competitors, derive the working capital for the last two years as shown in Figure 1.22. Calculate and compare the CCC using Figure 1.25 and Figure 1.26. Who has been generating cash from working capital? Who has consumed cash? Do we understand why and how? Which is a sign of weakness – or strength?

Conclusion

In this chapter we have introduced the Supply Chain Triangle of Service, Cost and Cash. We have shown how a traditional functional organization leads to tension in the triangle, as sales people are more service and top-line driven, operations is more cost-driven, and finance is concerned with keeping control of inventory as an important element of working capital, or – in short – cash.

We have expanded the cash corner into a capital employed corner, by adding fixed assets. We can reduce cost by investing in new machines. This is an example of a trade-off between cost and the fixed assets component of the capital employed.

Finally we have shown there is a good reason to reach balance in the triangle. Balancing the triangle leads to an optimization of the ROCE. ROCE measures the EBIT we generate over the capital employed – the so-called 'bang for the buck'. Companies that have a higher ROCE are more attractive to investors. As such, balancing the triangle is a common objective for both supply chain and finance.

At the end of the chapter we have provided an outline of accounting basics. A good understanding of these basics is required for a good understanding of the concepts described in this book.

In the next chapter we will introduce the Treacy and Wiersema strategy model, which describes the three archetypical strategies of operational excellence, product leadership and customer intimacy, and analyse how these different strategies impact the balance in our Supply Chain Triangle.

References

Axsäter, S (2015) *Inventory Control*, Springer, New York

Christopher, M (1998) *Relationships and Alliances: Embracing the era of network competition*, Gower Press, Hampshire

Drucker, P F (1998) Management's new paradigms, *Forbes Magazine*, **10** (2), pp 98–99

Lambert, D M (2008) *Supply Chain Management: Processes, partnerships, performance*, Supply Chain Management Institute

Strategy in the Supply Chain Triangle

In this chapter we will introduce Treacy and Wiersema's strategy model and show how different strategies lead to different trade-offs in the triangle. This is important for two reasons. Firstly, it means that different strategies result in different targets for supply chain metrics such as cost and working capital. Secondly, it means that different strategies lead to different supply chains.

We will show how the different strategies are different routes to delivering value for the shareholder, using return on capital employed (ROCE) as the measure for this. We will conclude the chapter with three case studies. Two cases show the triangle at work at manufacturing companies; a producer of high-tech projection equipment and a producer of electronic watches. The third case study illustrates the triangle at work across multiple companies in food retail.

Let's start by introducing Treacy and Wiersema's strategy model.

Treacy and Wiersema's three strategic options

Treacy and Wiersema (1995) argue that in any sector, a company can be a market leader by excelling at one of three strategies. Either the company is a product leader, is a leader by operational excellence, or leads in customer intimacy. We will give our interpretation of these three archetypes, and then analyse the impact on the Supply Chain Triangle.

Operational excellence

An opex (operational excellence) leader prevails through low-cost and hassle-free, no-nonsense, easy service. They are focused on being the cheapest as well as being easy to deal with. Commonly used examples are the low-cost airlines such as Southwest or Ryanair, who have disrupted the airline sector through a relentless focus on low-cost and hassle-free service.

Operational excellence as a strategy is not to be mistaken for 'lean'[1] or 'operational excellence' as a management philosophy to improve operations, and as originally described in Womack, Jones and Roos (1990). Applying the principles of lean manufacturing will help in reducing throughput times, reducing work-in-progress (WIP) and improving quality measures like the first-pass-yield.[2] An opex will translate these improvements into a lower price for the customer, where a product leader will try to translate that into a shorter time to market. The strategy defines the ultimate goal.

An opex leader has a relentless focus on lowering cost. "In addition to lean, a second important principle or management philosophy is simplicity." into "In addition to lean, a second important principle for an opex leader is simplicity."

An opex leader has a relentless focus on lowering cost. In addition to lean, a second important principle or management philosophy is simplicity. Even without a lot of explanation, we instinctively 'feel' that simplicity drives efficiency, and that efficiency lowers cost, which in turn leads to a lower price. Crawford and Mathews (2007) give the example of Dollar General as a price player. They mention simplicity as a critical success factor for Dollar General.

Simplicity translates into every aspect of the business. One example is limited price points. To keep things simple for the customers, and for the company, Dollar General features only 14 price points, reducing check-out, accounting and inventory time. and allowing suppliers to preprint item prices on the packaging. Dollar General also limits itself to 4,500 SKUs, compared with about 35,000 offered by Wal-Mart.

A comparable example in Europe is Colruyt. Colruyt is a retail group headquartered in Belgium, of which the biggest chain is called Colruyt Lowest Prices. Their slogan is 'simply retail' – simplicity being a core principle to guarantee the 'lowest prices' in their name.

So where does that leave the service delivered by an opex leader? An opex leader doesn't give bad service; on the contrary, it focuses on delivering excellent service, but it is excellence in the basics. Low-cost airlines like Ryanair or Southwest are known to have stripped the flying experience to the basics. There are no meals or free drinks, and they fly to smaller airports. Boarding is via mobile staircases instead of via jetways. They will cut back on numerous service parameters, except for key issues such as on-time departure and arrival.

In their book *Blue Ocean Strategy* (2005), Chan Kim and Mauborgne argue that in many industries competitors have focused on outperforming each other to the point of irrelevance. They consider it a rat race, reaching a level where customers become indifferent to any extras. Cutting down on less important dimensions, or overperformance, is the way to create a 'blue ocean', they suggest – instead of competing in the 'red ocean' where all the big sharks are fighting for the same fish.

Opex leaders will be extra critical in evaluating the 'added value' generated by individual service aspects. They will ensure excellence in those service parameters to which customers are very sensitive, such as on-time departure and landing. Free meals, snacks and jetways will never substitute for leaving and arriving on schedule. Opex players understand that very well. That's why they focus on low cost, but equally on providing a hassle-free service. The essence is in the focus they create.

Product leadership

A product leader prevails by having the newest and highest-spec product, again and again. It is focused on generating a stream of innovative products or services that sell at a significant premium to early adopters and niche markets. The investments in R&D and sales are significant. In fact, with each new product, the product leader is betting its business, as high volumes are required to cover the heavy R&D and sales costs.

A tempting example is Apple. It is clear that Apple has been very successful in launching a series of new products over the last 15 years. It is a dangerous example, though. Certainly, Apple has been successful in launching an impressive series of products – think about the iPod, the iPhone, the iPad, the iMac and many more.

However, Apple wasn't necessarily the first on the market, nor did it have the 'best' product in terms of having the highest specification. Apple has primarily excelled in product design and in marketing. It didn't invent mp3 as a technology, nor the mp3 player. It merely excelled in making it eye-catching and user-friendly, and in making it the hippest product around. This has been extremely rewarding. With a market capitalization of over $600 billion, it has far exceeded any reasonable expectations. However, it's not what I see as a typical product leader.

On one of my trips to China I met the CEO of Sea & Sun Technology Gmbh. The company has a worldwide reputation in the development of innovative products and solutions in the field of water measurement. If you are looking for the most precise equipment, for measurements at an unexplored depth, Sea & Sun Technology will be your partner. The biggest asset of the company is its know-how in water measurement. Know-how is typically an accumulation of decades of experience. It has typically survived many technological evolutions.

It is typical for a product leader to be in niche markets. For Sea & Sun Technology, these are oceanography, limnology, offshore and hydrology.

In general, only niche markets really benefit from the higher specification. Mass markets are not willing to pay the associated premium. They will go with a more average specification, possibly with a previous version of the technology, coming at a lower cost.

Not getting to the big volumes may be the biggest frustration of the product leader, but you can't have it all. As a niche player you will have smaller volumes, but bigger margins. If you're after the bigger volumes, you will typically do so via an operational excellence or customer intimacy model.

In general I prefer smaller companies like Sea & Sun Technology as examples of product leaders over bigger companies like Apple. They are more pure in illustrating that companies can be globally successful by simply having the best product. There are no side effects from their sheer size, which may influence their performance or what they can do in the market.

Customer intimacy

Customer intimacy leaders prevail by having the best knowledge of their key customers, and by providing the best total solution to their challenges. They relieve their key customers from the job of selecting the appropriate products and combining them into a solution. They will proactively define the appropriate answers even before customers have fully realized the question was so relevant.

Coming to a 'total solution' is challenging. It is common for customer intimacy players to work with partners, offering complementary products or services, to come to that total solution. Typical examples come from the maintenance domain; this could be maintenance of your machines or of your buildings. Instead of selling spare parts or MRO materials,[3] a customer intimacy proposition might be to provide maintenance services including preventive maintenance, or to guarantee uptime, as in the end the customer just wants their machines to be up and running.

As well as selling robots, ABB Robotics delivers the following services: inspection and diagnostics, preventive maintenance, refurbishment and reconditioning, condition monitoring and diagnostics, and life cycle assessment. A company like Bosch focuses on software solutions for so-called 'predictive maintenance'. Like preventive maintenance, the idea is to intervene at the 'right' time. They don't wait until a breakdown occurs; at the same time, they avoid stopping the machine unless it's necessary. The idea of 'predictive' maintenance uses (big) data from the equipment to predict the right time.

These are examples where solutions are delivered. They may combine software services with maintenance services and spare parts services into an 'uptime solution'.

An often quoted company with a customer intimacy position is IBM. Certainly IBM has had an important focus on innovation throughout its existence. In 2012 it topped the annual list of US patents for the 20th consecutive year. However, its newest products might not be what IBM is most known or recognized for. In the end it was Microsoft who pioneered a Windows-based operating system for personal computers in the 80s. It was Digital Equipment Corporation (DEC) who pioneered the so-called mini-computers in the 70s. It was Google who took real advantage of making the internet accessible.

The biggest success of IBM has probably always been to provide a full range of IT solutions to customers and to be the trusted partner of the CIO. They were the best at understanding the information technology needs of bigger corporations, and providing tailored solutions. That made and still makes bigger corporations spend large sums of money on IBM products and services.

Compared to a product leader, a customer-intimate company will have a lower R&D cost, but a higher sales cost. It invests more time in building the 'best total solution'. It has more sales people, who spend more time talking to their key customers, to ensure that the solution is well understood and fine-tuned, and finally sold and implemented.

Customer-intimate companies draw value from this positioning. If their customers assembled the solution themselves, by shopping at low-cost players for each of the underlying products and services, they might end up with a lower cost solution, but they would need to put in the effort, which also has a cost, and they would probably have more issues when implementing the solution compared to the customer intimacy player who has done this many times before. This is the reason customers are willing to pay a little bit more to the customer intimacy players, compared to the operational excellence players. It is a premium customers are willing to pay for a one-stop shop solution builder with expertise in solving your problems.

Strategy is about making choices

The good thing about Treacy and Wiersema's model is that it shows that companies have to make choices. We would all like to have the lowest price in the market, with the newest and most customer-intimate offerings.

Treacy and Wiersema help us understand that is impossible. If you don't make a choice, be aware that your competitors will. By focusing on one of the dimensions, they will outperform you. Soon you find yourself being outperformed on each of the dimensions by different competitors. That will leave you stuck in the middle, unappealing to customers, to employees and to investors. We hate to make choices, but we simply have to.

In the next section we will map the three strategies to the three corners of our Supply Chain Triangle. Doing so will reveal that different strategies lead to different trade-offs, and that different trade-offs lead to different supply chains.

Mapping Treacy and Wiersema to the Supply Chain Triangle

Figure 2.1 has extended the Supply Chain Triangle in a third dimension. Instead of three corners, we now have three axes where we can score lower or higher for service, cost and capital employed. For capital employed we will for now focus on inventory. Inventory will prove to be a good metric for the 'complexity' of a business, and we will come to the argument that different strategies imply different levels of complexity. We assume a higher service, a lower cost, and higher inventory turns (meaning less inventory) to be the desired direction, so these are pointing outwards.

Let's start with the service angle. From the previous section it is clear that the opex leader has the most basic service. They deliver excellent service, but

Figure 2.1   The Supply Chain Triangle in three dimensions

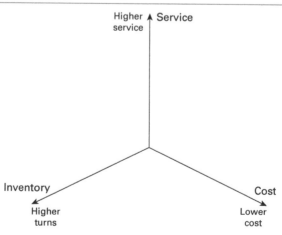

within a strict set of parameters. The more difficult question is how to position the customer intimacy player versus the product leader.

Another difficult question is how to measure service. In the previous chapter we talked about service level and the product portfolio. For product leaders we should probably add product quality or product performance to the service dimension. All of this is intellectually appealing, but difficult to measure and especially difficult to benchmark across companies.

When performing the financial benchmarks we will show later in this chapter, we came to appreciate gross margin as a measure for service. The gross margin compares the selling price to the cost of the goods. The higher the premium that the customer is willing to pay, the higher the service. It tackles two problems at once: we've made the service measurable, and it is easy to benchmark gross margin across companies.

Figure 2.2 shows the updated Supply Chain Triangle.

Given the cost of goods is now included in the service measurement, we will exclude it from the cost axis. That will allow us to focus the cost axis on anything that is added on top of the cost of goods sold. This involves costs like R&D and selling, general and administrative (SG&A) costs. That will be helpful, as we know from the previous section, R&D costs are important for the product leader, and selling costs are important for the customer-intimate company.

Figure 2.3 shows how we position the three strategies on the resulting service axis.

Figure 2.2   The Supply Chain Triangle in three dimensions with gross margin as the service metric

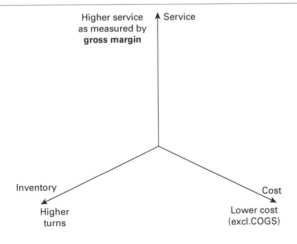

Figure 2.3 Mapping Treacy and Wiersema to the service axis

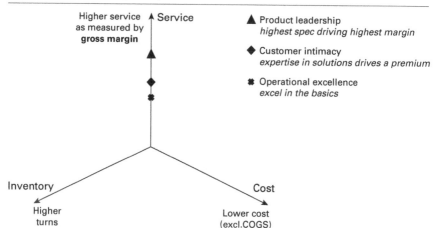

Opex players rank the lowest. They excel in the basics. Their gross margin will be the lowest. If you look at the cost of goods, their mark-up is minimal as they want to ensure the lowest price offer on the market.

The customer intimacy player ranks next. As we've argued in the previous section, customer-intimate companies drive a premium compared to the opex players. The premium comes from the convenience (for customers) of having the one-stop shop, plus the expertise (on which customers can draw) of developing a total solution that is fit for purpose.

The biggest gross margin will be generated by the product leaders. The superiority of their products means that they have little to no competition. That gives them a strong position to negotiate. As they focus on niches where the higher specifications of their products make an important difference, customers are willing to pay a high premium to get the best and the latest product. Niche business is extremely profitable. The challenge for product leaders is to create scale.

Figure 2.4 maps the three strategies to the cost side of the triangle.

Again, the opex leaders are the easiest. They will have the lowest cost, as every fibre of their organization is focused on delivering the lowest cost to be able to offer the lowest price in the market. The difficulty is again in differentiating the product leaders from the customer intimacy players.

In the previous section we discussed that customer intimacy players have a significantly higher sales cost compared to the opex leaders. Developing the best total solution requires time and expertise, and comes at a significant sales cost. As mentioned on the service axis, the good news is that customer intimacy players are able to derive a premium from this.

Figure 2.4   Mapping Treacy and Wiersema to the cost axis

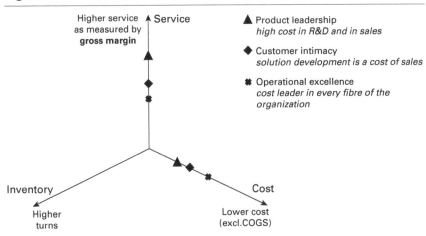

So what about the product leaders? Product leaders typically have less complex product portfolios compared to the customer intimacy players. Their complexity is in the products themselves, instead of the number of products. Explaining complex products and their advantages to niches still requires a significant sales cost. Moreover, product leaders have significant R&D expenses, and for that reason we have put the product leaders at the highest overall cost. The good news is that the product leaders have headroom for this, as they can drive the highest gross margin from offering their unique products in niche markets.

Figure 2.5 maps the three strategies to the inventory axis.

Figure 2.5   Mapping Treacy and Wiersema to the inventory axis

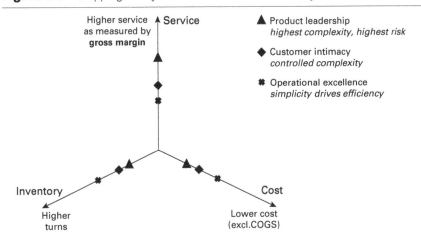

The opex players have the highest inventory turns. Remember from the previous section that simplicity drives efficiency for the opex players. They will avoid complex products and will avoid a long tail of slower moving products. As a result, they will have the highest inventory turns.

As already mentioned, the complexity of customer intimacy players will be in the broader product portfolio required to come to the best total solution. Managing a broader range of products adds complexity, but in our experience, companies have found ways to manage this. If you segment your customers and products in A/B/C and have a good statistical and collaborative forecasting process, you should be able to control the required levels of inventory and cost. Controlling complexity is required, because the premium you command as a customer intimacy player is continuously challenged by the opex players in the market.

In our experience, the toughest inventory challenge resides with the product leaders. Purchasing as a product leader is challenging. R&D has probably forced you to work with niche suppliers in the quest for the newest and the best. Getting consistent quality and service from a wide range of niche suppliers is challenging. Frequent updates and revisions of components and raw materials is common. It is a common cause of obsolete inventories.

On the other hand, for the more common inputs, as somebody more focusing on niches, your volumes may be small compared to the mass market players focusing on cost or a broader offering. If you're small, you don't have leverage, again creating a challenging situation when trying to streamline your supply chain. You may be confronted with long lead times and high minimum order quantities. On the production side, working with the newest, the latest and the most complex is challenging. You're sure to carry higher levels of work-in-process and have higher levels of rework compared to the industry average. From the sales side, predicting how niche markets will react to the newest product is daunting. You easily make mistakes, and half of the mistakes end up in inventory (the other half in lost sales).

This explains why we expect product leaders to have the highest inventories, and have put them as the ones with the lowest inventory turns in Figure 2.5.

Figure 2.6 shows the overall summary.

Different strategies lead to different positions in the Supply Chain Triangle. In their quest to provide the lowest price in the market, opex players will drive out complexity to have the lowest inventory. We believe inventory can be extended to capital employed. They will have lower assets and make sure that the utilization rate is higher, again to ensure the lowest cost as a prerequisite for having the lowest price in the market.

Figure 2.6 Different strategies lead to different positions in the Supply Chain Triangle

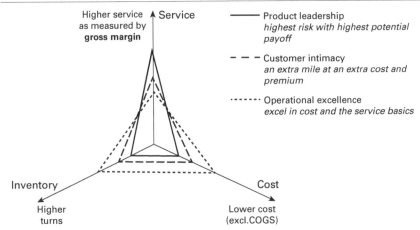

The more difficult discussion is in positioning the customer intimacy players versus the product leaders. The best total solution of the customer intimacy players commands a premium from the customer, but that premium is under a continuous pressure from the opex players. Yes, customers are willing to pay more for a one-stop shop and for the expertise going into the total solution that is fit for purpose, but in the age of internet transparency, they will want the premium to stay in sync with the market. This requires customer-intimate companies to keep control of complexity, and closely monitor their added value. Compared to the opex players, more products require more space in the warehouse, and a more diverse set of tools and machines to deliver the broader range. Again we believe the inventory can be extended into the capital employed.

Product leaders have the unique advantage that their products are simply better than those of the competition. If they find the right applications where the higher specifications translate into a significantly higher value, they are in a good position to charge a superior premium. However, product leaders are also high-risk patients. Delivering superior products is risky. You have to commit the cost of developing and selling the product, but one or two mistakes can bring companies into the danger zone.

We've discussed the fact that in our experience, product complexity is more difficult to handle than product portfolio complexity. This translates into lower turns for product leaders. Again we believe this extends into the capital employed. If you want to make a top-notch product, you need top-notch equipment. Making the highest spec product requires the highest

Figure 2.7 Different strategies lead to different positions in the extended Supply Chain Triangle

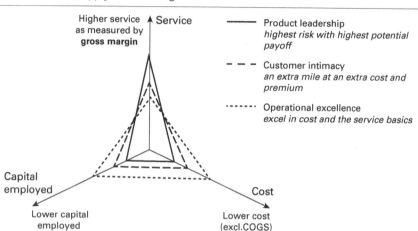

spec infrastructure. The highest spec infrastructure tends to have narrower application. All this drives up the cost of the fixed assets.

So where we started out with discussing inventory as a measure of complexity, as discussed above, we believe it can be extended into capital employed, which is working capital plus fixed assets. That extended version is shown in Figure 2.7.

Linking the three strategies back to ROCE

Now let's link the triangle back to our discussion of the ROCE. As we show in Figure 2.8, the service (which is now measured as gross margin), and the cost (now measured as the costs not going into the cost of goods sold) translate into EBIT. In the previous section, we started with inventory as a measure for complexity and then extended inventory into capital employed.

We have argued why operational excellence leaders require less capital employed. The main driver of simplicity will make sure they require a lower working capital and fewer fixed assets than their customer-intimate and product leader competitors. At the other extreme, we have argued why product complexity is the hardest to deal with, leading to a higher inventory. The highest spec product requires the highest spec infrastructure. As a result, product leaders will have more costly assets and a higher overall capital employed.

The ROCE principle leads to the following. As an investor I will say to the product leader, it's OK if you need more capital, as long as you have a

Figure 2.8   Different strategies lead to different ways of generating ROCE

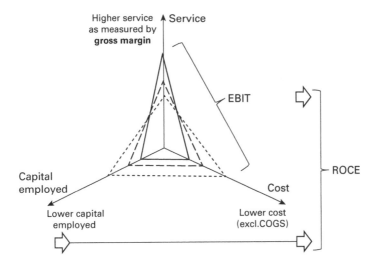

higher EBIT. Or vice versa to the opex leader, it's OK if your EBIT is lower as long as you require less capital. As an investor I will be indifferent, as long as I get the same 'bang-for-the-buck'. As the product leader has a higher risk profile, I may require a kind of risk premium – driving up the EBIT target for the product leader.

In any case, when benchmarking companies – on inventory turns, on working capital, on fixed assets, on cost, or on service metrics like number of products – it is clear that we need to account for the chosen strategy. Though this seems obvious, we have seen many companies blindly benchmarking inventory turns without accounting for the balance with cost and service, and without accounting for the chosen strategy.

We will now look at three example financial benchmarks: two manufacturing companies and one comparison of different companies active in food retail.

CASE STUDY – Barco

Any technology-related sector is a dream for applying Treacy and Wiersema. You can have product leaders, who are continuously on the edge and live for the newer, better, and higher spec technologies. You can have customer intimacy players, who solve the broad technological challenges for their customers. You will have the opex players, who strip down products to their core, work with older but still recent versions of the technology, making products that are 'good enough' and which come at prices you can't possibly beat.

In this section we will look in more detail at Barco, a Belgian company active in high-end projection and visualization equipment. Barco is headquartered in Kortrijk in Belgium, and listed on the stock exchange of Euronext in Brussels. The public listing means financial information is available for over 15 years. The financial reports of the company report on strategy, any acquisitions or divestments and any changes in strategy. Any information we share is drawn from information available to the public.

The interesting aspect of Barco is that it went through a clearly communicated strategy shift. The shift came in response to the significant downturn Barco experienced during the financial crisis. Figures 2.9 and 2.10 show the sales and EBIT (before restructuring and goodwill impairment) in the period 2004–14.

We see at least three distinct periods:

1 2004–07, where EBIT was between €60 and €80 million, and sales between €600 million and €800 million;

2 2008–10, where 2009 was the absolute dip, in both sales and EBIT;

3 2011–14, where sales for the first time in the history of the company exceeded €1 billion, and where the EBIT rebounded to between €80 million and €100 million, except in 2014.

Looking back, 2010 was a year of transition. The data shown in Figures 2.9 and 2.10 has been taken from the publicly available financial reports of Barco.

The shift in strategy was linked to a change in CEO. Eric van Zele became CEO in 2009, at the deepest moment of crisis. As an alumnus of Stanford, he is

Figure 2.9   Barco's sales for 2004–14

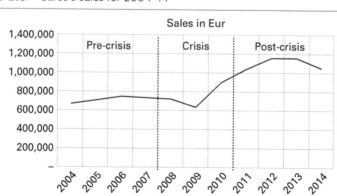

Figure 2.10   Barco's EBIT for 2004–14

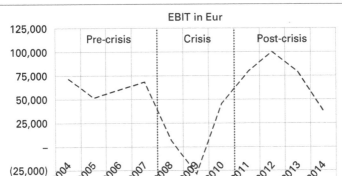

familiar with the model of Treacy and Wiersema. He used the model in public presentations to first of all explain that as a product leader, Barco had fallen behind on operational excellence, so a catch-up had to be done.

Secondly, he announced a shift from product leadership into customer intimacy, borne out of the observation that of all the beautiful technologies originally invented at Barco, not enough were reaching more mass markets.

'Connect', the 2013 annual report, provides the most elaborate documentation of the shift. It discusses the shift from high-end to the mid-segment and of volume markets. High-end remains the roots of Barco. The 2013 report talks about 40% market share in projection solutions for entertainment, 45% market share for diagnostic and modality imaging in healthcare. The claim of the top segment is supported by the mentioning of 223 technology patents and by sustained R&D spending.

The move into mid-segment projection solutions was exemplified by the acquisition of a Norwegian company called 'Projectiondesign', a provider of mid-range projectors. The move into the volume markets is announced through the launch of a 'range of single-chip DLP projectors to facilitate collaboration in meeting rooms'. So the range was extended into business projectors, where Barco started competing with whole new range of competitors like Optoma, Benq, Acer, InFocus, Casio, Viewsonic, Epson, and many more.

'For a smarter tomorrow', the 2012 annual report, talks about customer intimacy and the objective to expand the product portfolio with mid-range products, with a strong focus on a two-tier channel model, as opposed to the direct model in the high-end market. 2012 is the year where Barco launches its 'clickshare' product. By inserting a clickshare dongle into your laptop via USB, you can connect wirelessly to a projector by just a push on the button. It's another illustration that the strategy shift was serious, not just talk.

Connecting the strategy shift to our Supply Chain Triangle, we'd expect the shift to customer intimacy to be accompanied by a drop in gross margins, requiring a drop in spending on R&D and SG&A. If the shift is well organized, we'd also expect an increase in inventory turns, cutting some of the complex products, to make room for expanding the portfolio into the mid-range. Figures 2.11 and 2.12 show the evolutions over the period 2004–14. Table 2.1 shows the averages. The data have again been taken from the publicly available financial reports of Barco.

Gross profit drops from 41% to 32% after the strategic shift. R&D spending drops from 9.5% to 8.4% (a 1% drop). The biggest impact is in the SG&A spending, which drops from 23% to 17.5%. Inventory turns improve from 2.7 to 3.3, which is an improvement, but only a limited one.

The explanation is in the strategy. Instead of a full shift towards customer intimacy, it more seems as though the customer intimacy comes 'on top of' the product leadership – we will keep our positions in the niche markets, and in parallel expand into the mid-range and the volume markets.

Figure 2.11   Barco's gross profit, R&D and SG&A 2004–14

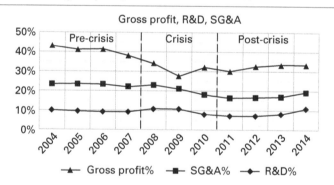

Figure 2.12   Barco's inventory turns 2004–14

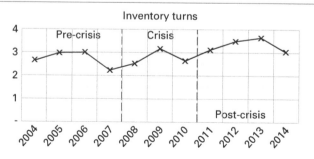

Table 2.1   Barco's key figures 2004–07, 2008–10 and 2011–14 – part 1

	2004–07	**2008–10**	**2011–14**
Gross profit %	40.92%	31.27%	32.34%
R&D spending %	9.51%	9.85 %	8.39%
SG&A spending %	23.16%	20.87%	17.49%
Inventory turns	2.71	2.78	3.32

Connecting back to the ROCE principle in our Supply Chain Triangle, we'd expect a customer intimacy player to generate the ROCE with a lower EBIT, but using less capital employed (in comparison to the product leader). Figure 2.13 shows the EBIT and the ROCE over the period 2004–14. Table 2.2 shows the averages. The average ROCE of 12.25% in the pre-crisis period is based on an average EBIT of 8.82%. The ROCE in the post-crisis period averages 11.25%, which is exactly 1% lower, based on an EBIT of 6.66%, which is more than 2% lower.

Looking at the inventory turns, it seems the company did not cut product complexity sufficiently to make room for the extension into the mid-range. Making tougher choices here would have supported a further reduction of the capital employed, and as such a further increase to the ROCE.

Figure 2.13   Barco's EBIT and ROCE 2004–14

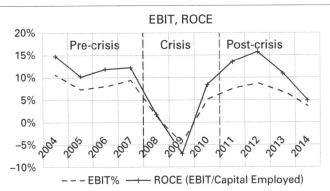

Table 2.2   Barco's key figures 2004–07, 2008–10 and 2011–14 – part 2 (*EBIT before restructuring and goodwill impairment)

	2004–07	**2008–10**	**2011–14**
EBIT, in kEur (*)	63.109	8.167	73.963
EBIT % (*)	8.82%	0.54%	6.66%
Capital employed, in kEur	516.648	493.445	680.973
ROCE %	12.25%	0.98%	11.25%

CASE STUDY – Casio

Some companies will move in the exact opposite direction. A remarkable example is Casio. In its 2016 annual report, Casio claims high profitability through innovative products. With a 12% operating margin and a return on equity of 15.4%, that's a credible claim. Today 85.4% of the net sales are from consumer electronics, 12.1% from system equipment (including projectors) and 2.5% from others.

The report showcases six global 'timepiece brands', including G-Shock (absolute toughness) and Pro Trek (ideal for the field). The strategy talks about 'promoting the introduction to upscale retailers'. The report also talks about 'expanding scientific and localized calculators', 'expanding high-unit-price keyboards featuring high-quality rich tones and rhythms', 'wrist devices for fishing, trekking and cycling', and 'Laser & LED hybrid projectors with 20,000 hours light source lifetime'. This breathes a product leadership strategy – high-end niche products being sold through upscale retailers.

Casio was a completely different company before the financial crisis. As Pierre-Yves Donze describes in his book on the history of the Japanese watch industry (Donze, 2016), the dominant strategy of Japanese watch companies Seiko, Citizen and Casio was to offer high-quality goods cheaply. He describes how they were dominated by a real technological paradigm which had not changed since the 1950s, in which the competitiveness of a firm relied on the quality – hence the necessity to innovate and develop new technologies – and the cost – that is, relocating plants to low-wages countries – of their products.

Their Swiss and Hong Kong-based rivals started from a marketing strategy, constructing brands, carefully positioning their products, and watching the right distribution channels. Contrast that with the 2016 annual report, and it is clear the company has made a shift.

The strategic shift is well documented in the Casio annual report of 2008, 'Changing lives around the world'. It states: 'Fiscal 2008 was our 50th anniversary, and fiscal 2009 is our first year of a new phase of innovation under the name of The Rebirth of Casio'. In the 'Medium and Long-Term Management Strategy' section it declares that efforts will be made to 'ensure high profitability', 'create new strategic businesses' and 'strengthen our financial structure'.

Under 'ensure high profitability', it mentions the goal to achieve an overall operating income margin of 10% or more. The main contributors to this are lowering the cost of sales through improved productivity, and strengthening global market presence to create economies of scale.

Under 'creating new strategic businesses', it states: 'We will have to develop new business areas in addition to our existing segments, drawing strengths from the unique technological base, which other companies cannot match, focusing even more management resources on the development of promising new business areas, creating new business with tough earnings structures and getting them up and running as soon as possible'. In short, cutting edge innovations which nobody else can match.

Where operations has to contribute to the goal of improving profitability, the real strategic choice is in the second goal, which shows a shift to product leadership.

Let's get back to our Supply Chain Triangle. A shift from operational excellence to product leadership should provide a dramatic shift in gross margin. As gross margin increases, this creates more room for spending on R&D and SG&A. It is clear from the above that the Japanese watchmakers may always have had smart R&D, but have underinvested and been weak in marketing and sales.

Finally, as products get more advanced, they may less appeal to the mass markets, which may increase the overall complexity and increase the inventory required or decrease the inventory turns. Figures 2.14 and 2.15 show exactly that.

Table 2.3 shows the average gross profit increase from 29% to 42%. R&D spending remains relatively constant, around 2–3%. SG&A spending increases dramatically, from 19% to 30%. The inventory turns decrease, from an average of 3.5 to an average of 1.3.

Compared to Barco, the 2–3% spending on R&D seems low, and the SG&A of 30% seems high. Also the turns of 1.3 seem low. More extensive benchmarks are required to develop industry standards.

The numbers for Figures 2.14, 2.15 and Table 2.3 have been taken from the publicly available annual reports of Casio.

Figure 2.14 Casio's gross profit, R&D and SG&A 2004–16

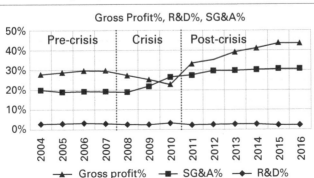

Figure 2.15   Casio's inventory turns 2004–16

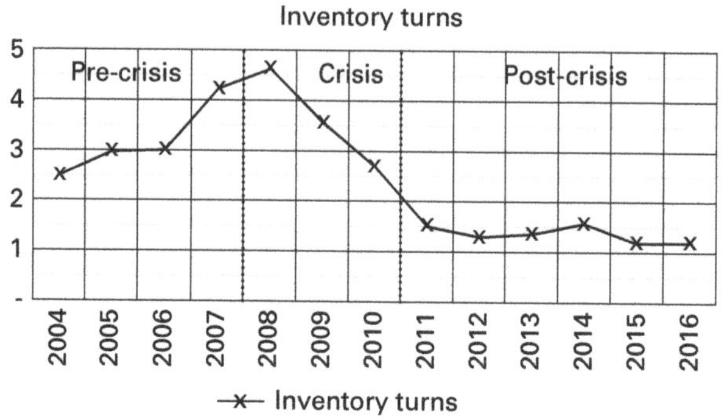

Inventory turns

→×— Inventory turns

Table 2.3   Casio's key figures 2004–08, 2009–12 and 2013–16 – part 1

	2004–08	2009–12	2013–16
Gross profit %	28.66%	29.10%	41.87%
R&D spending %	2.82%	2.60%	2.38%
SG&A spending %	19.15%	26.39%	30.32%
Inventory turns	3.48	2.27	1.31

Let's turn to the expected ROCE impact. If we switch from operational excellence to product leadership, we expect that the EBIT% will significantly increase, but as the complexity increases we need more capital employed. Figure 2.16 and Table 2.4 show that the EBIT% increases from 6.7% to 9.2%, which is a 2.5% increase. The ROCE decreases from 13.1% to 11%, which is a 2.1% decrease.

At first sight the spending on SG&A seems heavy, negatively impacting the ROCE. You have the feeling that just as they may have underinvested for a prolonged period in the 1980s and 1990s, now they are overdoing it. At the same time, looking at the inventory turns, the turns seem below par, even for a product leader. This may be a signal that they have let go of complexity too much, putting a stretch on the capital employed.

The numbers for Figure 2.16 and Table 2.4 have again been taken from the publicly available annual reports of Casio.

Figure 2.16 Casio's EBIT and ROCE 2004–16

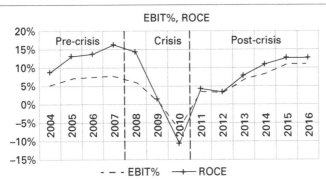

Table 2.4 Casio's key figures 2004–08, 2009–12 and 2013–16 – part 2

	2004–08	**2009–12**	**2013–16**
EBIT, in mio Yen	39.094	(1.047)	30.039
EBIT %	6.69%	0.11%	9.18%
Capital employed, in mio Yen	299.587	277.782	270.894
ROCE %	13.13%	−0.40%	10.97%

Strategies: to change or not to change?

Our two case studies seem to offer some initial proof that a change in strategy does indeed affect the balance in the triangle. There's not enough data yet to derive an industry benchmark, but you feel it's tempting to add more. We will do exactly that in the next three chapters.

A second observation is that both technology companies seem to struggle with generating the same ROCE levels with their new strategy as with their old one. Which is exactly what Treacy and Wiersema predict. They advocate 'once a product leader, always a product leader', and similarly for opex players. The main reason is that 'old habits die slowly'.

In their 1995 book, Treacy and Wiersema take ample time to discuss the importance of 'disciplined execution'. If you want to be an opex player, every fibre in your organization needs to be focused on the lowest cost. In *Strategy Implementation* (2014), Kurt Verweire confirms the importance of the operating model, which comprises the direction and goal-setting processes, operational processes, support processes, evaluation and control processes and organizational behaviour processes. These are pieces of a puzzle that need to fit together. Once they fit together, they are the engine driving the strategic positioning.

For an opex player the targets are related to efficiency and zero-defect quality and service, and the key operational processes are all the operations like purchasing, manufacturing and logistics. Support processes are focused on automation and efficient information flows. The control is centralized, based on detailed metrics and very hierarchical. The dominant culture is centralization and continuous improvement.

Building such an organization takes years. Once it is in place, it is nearly impossible to change. Yes, large organizations are tankers which are difficult to turn. The operating model of an opex player is drastically different from that of a customer-intimate company or a product leader. Looking at Barco and Casio, you can say that both did a reasonable job in changing their operating model, but neither did a perfect job.

It's tempting to change the strategy when it no longer seems to work, which seemed the case for both Barco and for Casio. So what's the alternative? According to Treacy and Wiersema (1995) there is only one alternative, which is to 'just try harder'. If you are a cost leader and not successful: just try harder. Changing the strategy will cost you at least five years and will not necessarily deliver more value. If you are a product leader and under pressure: just try harder. Switching to a customer intimacy strategy means asking your R&D people to design something which is 'good enough' instead of 'top of the bill'. That is awkward. Starting to source on cost instead of quality will lead to issues. You're down a road you've never been down before. You have a lack of experience so you will make mistakes. Making mistakes destroys value.

Changing strategy is tempting, it's exciting and it's popular. But it is not what Treacy and Wiersema advise.

CASE STUDY – Food retail companies

Whereas for manufacturing we found two cases where companies changed their strategy over the last 10 years, we didn't see the same types of examples in retail. The retailers we analysed showed a more consistent strategy and (lack of) performance over a longer period of time.

When looking for 'opex players' or 'cost leaders' in retail, we need to look for hard discounters. Famous examples in Europe are Aldi and Lidl. Unfortunately both companies are privately owned by the German families Albrecht and Schwarz, so they don't publish financial statements. Instead we will analyse the financials of Edeka. In an article entitled 'Supermarkets: Day of the Discounters' published in the *Financial Times* (London), 10 December 2014, Edeka was the third biggest global discount retailer. In contrast to Aldi and Lidl, Edeka is active only in Germany. It consists of several cooperatives of independent supermarkets all operating under an umbrella organization. Headquarters are in Hamburg.

Marc Sachon from IESE defines the key success factors of the German hard discounters as a limited assortment of products, an increased percentage of private labels offered at low prices, maintaining a high quality/price ratio, and super-efficient operations (Sachon, 2010). Sachon mentions that at Aldi 90% of products in the standard catalogue are distributed via cross-docking facilities. Cross docking minimizes the warehousing space required and saves on logistics handling. If you have ever shopped at Aldi or Lidl, you will notice the ample use of pallets in the shop, as opposed to racks or shelves. This saves significantly on handling by in-store personnel. The use of pallets requires a high rotation of the goods, which links back into the limited assortment which focuses on fast moving products.

As Sachon argues, the 'hard-discount model is a prime example of strategic coherence: there is a perfect fit between business strategy, operations strategy and day-to-day operations'. In terms of Treacy and Wiersema, it is operational excellence taken to its extreme.

When looking for publicly listed product leaders, we land on three US companies: Whole Foods Market, The Fresh Market and Sprouts Farmers Market. On its website, Whole Foods Market proclaims itself to be 'America's Healthiest Grocery Store'. It exclusively features foods without artificial preservatives, colours, flavours, sweeteners and hydrogenated fats. It focuses on organic products, which means that crops are grown without toxic and persistent pesticides.

The Fresh Market brands itself as 'your neighborhood food market & premium quality local produce store'. For produce they claim to stock the freshest and tastiest choices all year long, and to have locally sourced seasonal selections. The meat promises to be hand-cut and trimmed by expert butchers, on duty at all times in all stores. The premium choice is claimed to include only the top 10% of all beef in the US. As you read on, the product leadership positioning is clear.

Finally, Sprouts Farmers Market markets itself as the 'neighbourhood grocery store' offering thousands of natural, organic and gluten-free items. Whereas The Fresh Market seems more about the best, Sprouts Farmers, as Whole Foods, is more focused on health. An example is grass-fed beef products. Most grass-fed cattle are leaner than feedlot beef, lacking marbling, which lowers the fat content and caloric level of the meat. Meat from grass-fed cattle also has higher levels of conjugated linoleic acid and omega-3 fatty acids. In short, it's healthier.

Whole Foods Market, The Fresh Market and Sprouts Farmers Market are all heavily focused on fresh food categories. The traditional supermarket will extend the product range into canned and packaged goods, and various non-food items such as cleaning products, personal care, baby items, and pet items. If you're looking for the 'best total solution' as a consumer, you'll have to deal with the traditional supermarket with anywhere from **10,000** to **30,000** SKUs to ensure you get all your shopping for your daily needs done in one place.

We have looked at Ahold, Delhaize, Colruyt Group and Kroger as traditional supermarkets. In 2016, Delhaize was bought by Ahold, but we'll report on the figures up to 2015. Both Ahold and Delhaize had activities in both Europe and the US. Albert Heijn is the biggest brand of Ahold, mainly focused in the Netherlands, and its brands in the US are Stop&Shop, Giant, Martin's and Peapod. Delhaize grew from the Delhaize stores in Belgium and is known in the US through Food Lion. Colruyt Group is the biggest food retailer in Belgium, with limited activity in France. And with $110 billion of revenues, Kroger is one of the biggest food retailers in the US.

Let's try to map the three strategies onto our Supply Chain Triangle. Our first expectation is that we'll see differences in the gross margin, between the product leader, the customer intimacy and the opex leaders, leading to differences in cost, and to differences in EBIT. We expect the EBIT of the cost leader to be the lowest, but for them to generate comparable ROCE, as they are using fewer assets, or, to put it another way, getting more out of their existing assets.

Figure 2.17 shows gross profit, SG&A and inventory turns for the selected food retailers. We show 10-year averages, taken from 2006 to 2015. Table 2.5 shows the underlying figures. For Colruyt Group and Edeka we have derived the underlying data from their publicly available annual reports. For the other companies, we taken the data from amigobulls.com, which provides a free and easy download of the 10-year financials of companies with a public listing in the US.

First of all we notice a difference in gross margins. For our product leaders, Whole Foods Market, The Fresh Market and Sprouts Farmer Market, the range is 29–35%. For our customer intimacy players Ahold, Delhaize, Colruyt and Kroger, the range is 22–26%. Edeka, the opex player, works at a gross margin of only 12%.

The differences in gross margin translate into differences in SG&A. What is less clear is the impact on inventory. Our previous expectations were that the inventory turns would go up as the gross margin goes down, but turns are a bit higher for the product leaders, lower for the customer intimacy players, and then significantly higher for Edeka as our chosen opex player.

Figure 2.17   Gross profit, SG&A and inventory turns for selected food retailers

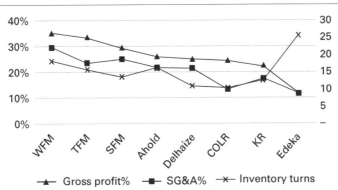

Table 2.5   Gross profit, SG&A and inventory turns for selected food retailers

Company	Gross profit%	SG&A%	Inventory turns
Whole Foods Market	34.99%	29.57%	18.19
The Fresh Market	33.38%	23.46%	15.62
Sprouts Farmer Market	29.31%	25.07%	13.60
Ahold	25.79%	21.72%	16.15
Delhaize Group	25.06%	21.40%	0
Colruyt Group	24.40%	13.28%	10.32
Kroger	22.39%	17.63%	12.60
Edeka	11.63%	11.58%	25.60

Table 2.6 shows the averages for the three strategies (we rounded up the gross profit of Sprouts Farmer Market to bring it in the 30%+ range).

The explanation for the inventory turns lies in the offered product categories. As mentioned, the chosen product leaders focus on fresh food categories. Fresh will always have a higher turn compared to some of the non-food categories carried by the supermarkets.

Secondly, when looking at the capital employed axis of our Supply Chain Triangle, we need to be aware that food retail is drastically different to manufacturing. As is shown in Figure 2.18, food retailers typically have a small or even negative working capital. The reason is that compared to manufacturers, they have a limited amount of inventory. The lowest turns in Table 2.5 are 11, which means approximately one month of stock, compared to the turns of 3 and 1.5 at Barco and Casio, which results in four to eight months of stock.

Table 2.6 Gross profit, SG&A and inventory turn averages for selected food retailers

Company	Gross profit%	SG&A%	Inventory Turns
30%+ gross profit	32.56%	26.03%	15.80
20–9% gross profit	23.95%	17.44%	11.29
<20% gross profit	11.63%	11.58%	25.60

Figure 2.18 Working capital and capital employed in manufacturing vs food retail

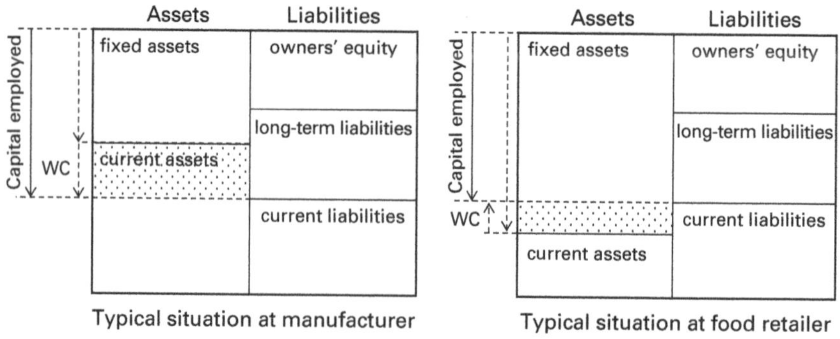

Typical situation at manufacturer   Typical situation at food retailer

Thirdly, where manufacturing companies face payment terms of customers of 30 to 90 days, retailers typically receive their cash immediately. If they accept credit cards, they may receive the cash in 30 days. But the average days of sales outstanding will be significantly smaller compared to production companies, in the range of 5–15 days, versus 30–75 days for manufacturers.

So firstly, retailers carry less inventory, and secondly, their receivables are significantly lower so their current assets are significantly lower. Still, retailers will pay their suppliers in anything between 30 and 75 days. So as Figure 2.18 illustrates, it is common for food retailers that their current liabilities (driven by the accounts payable) exceed the current assets (kept low by lower inventories and receivables), leading to a negative working capital.

Table 2.7 shows the cash conversion cycle (CCC), which we defined in our section on accounting basics in Chapter 1 as the days of inventory on hand (DIOH) + days of sales outstanding (DSO) – days of payables outstanding (DPO). We see a range from +12 for Whole Foods Market to –28 for Edeka.

Table 2.8 shows the averages per type of retailer.

Notice that the mass retailers (20–29% gross profit) carry more inventory, but still end up with a lower working capital (a lower CCC). This can only happen by having longer payment terms to their suppliers, compared to the product leaders.

Table 2.7 Gross profit, SG&A, inventory turns and CCC for selected food retailers

Company	Gross profit%	SG&A%	Inventory turns	CCC
Whole Foods Market	34.99%	29.57%	18.19	12.76
The Fresh Market	33.38%	23.46%	15.62	5.56
Sprouts Farmer Market	29.31%	25.07%	13.60	5.46
Ahold	25.79%	21.72%	16.15	(5.45)
Delhaize Group	25.06%	21.40%	10.95	4.59
Colruyt Group	24.40%	13.28%	10.32	(5.45)
Kroger	22.39%	17.63%	12.60	9.35
Edeka	11.63%	11.58%	25.60	(27.58)

Table 2.8 Gross profit, SG&A, inventory turns and CCC averages for selected food retailers

Company	Gross Profit%	SG&A%	Inventory Turns	CCC
30%+ gross profit	32.56%	26.03%	15.80	7.93
20–29% gross profit	23.95%	17.44%	11.29	2.83
<20% gross profit	11.63%	11.58%	25.60	(27.58)

The mass retailers are significantly bigger in size than the mentioned product leaders. Size does matter. So the size of the mass retailers probably gives them the leverage to extend payment terms towards suppliers. Edeka puts the same pressure on suppliers, combined with turns at 25, which is an average inventory of two weeks, resulting in a negative working capital of 28 days.

The conclusion from Figure 2.18 is that when it comes to capital employed, for retailers, the fixed assets are dominant and the impact of working capital is limited, as it is financed by the suppliers. So when looking for a measurement on the capital employed axis, it'll be better to use something like fixed asset turnover, which is the sales revenue divided by the fixed assets, instead of inventory or working capital.

Figure 2.19 summarizes what you could call the 'Retail Supply Chain Triangle'. Product leaders focus on exclusive product, customer-intimate retailers on serving your broad needs, and opex players give good quality at an unbeatable price.

Figure 2.19   Different strategies lead to different positions in the Retail Supply Chain Triangle

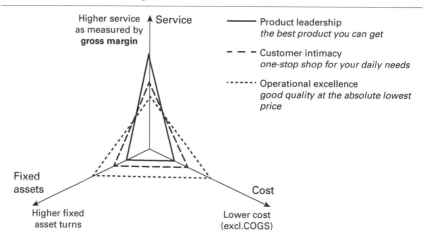

So let's try to continue the story. From a ROCE perspective we'd expect the opex leader to have the lowest EBIT, but to compensate for that by having less capital employed, or to put it another way, by putting its assets to better use, in this case measured as the fixed asset turnover.

Table 2.9 shows the EBIT, the fixed asset turnover and the ROCE for our selected retailers. Table 2.10 again shows the averages.

In general we see that the EBIT goes down as the gross margin goes down, but that we compensate for that by increasing the asset turns. Edeka takes it to an extreme. With an average EBIT of less than 1%, they still manage to generate a ROCE of 12%!

Table 2.9   EBIT, fixed asset turns and ROCE for selected food retailers

Company	EBIT	Fixed asset turns	ROCE
Whole Foods Market	5.15%	3.38	15.40%
The Fresh Market	6.44%	4.20	28.31%
Sprouts Farmer Market	1.79%	2.28	5.12%
Ahold	3.17%	3.31	9.36%
Delhaize Group	2.75%	2.63	7.11%
Colruyt Group	6.65%	5.06	32.85%
Kroger	2.13%	4.96	11.39%
Edeka	0.95%	7.42	12.02%

Table 2.10   EBIT, fixed asset turns and ROCE averages for selected food retailers

Company	EBIT	Fixed asset turns	ROCE
30%+ gross profit	4.46%	3.29	16.28%
20–29% gross profit	3.84%	4.22	17.11%
<20% gross profit	0.95%	7.42	12.02%

The retail examples again stress the importance of thinking in the triangle. Revenue or growth is not a goal in itself, nor is it a profit metric like EBIT. It is all about the EBIT generated over the capital employed, or the 'bang-for-the-buck'. Different strategies lead to different ways of reaching that same goal. The opex leaders will work at lower margins, but compensate with higher efficiency on the capital employed. The product leaders require more capital to lure customers to more high-end products, but they manage to compensate for this by higher margins.

Conclusion

There are two key message so far in the book. The first is that when looking at metrics, you always need to look at a combination of service, as a driver for top-line, cost, as a driver for bottom-line, and capital employed, as a measure for the 'bang-for-the-buck'.

The second is that when setting targets, or comparing across companies, it is vital to account for the strategy. Different strategies are different paths to delivering ROCE. In the next three chapters, we will develop a comprehensive set of metrics, based on the triangle, and show how different strategies lead to different targets and different priorities.

CASE STUDY – Owens Corning

Owens Corning was founded in 1938 and has grown to become a market-leading innovator in glass fibre technology. The company is a world leader in composite and building materials systems, delivering a broad range of high-quality products and services. Products range from glass fibre used to reinforce composite materials for transportation, electronics, marine, infrastructure, wind-energy and other high-performance markets to insulation and roofing for residential, commercial and industrial applications.

The company has three strong business segments: Composites, Insulation and Roofing, accounting for 33%, 30% and 37% respectively of the net sales in 2016. It employs approximately 17,000 people worldwide, operates in 33 countries and has been on the Fortune 500 for 63 consecutive years.

When reviewing the concepts of the Supply Chain Triangle (as shown in Figure 1.5) and how strategy impacts the triangle (as shown in Figure 2.8), Tony Heldreth, the VP of Supply Chain at Owens Corning, comments: 'I recognize from my experience at previous companies that people sometimes go too far in reducing inventory, to the point that it starts hurting business performance. This is not the case at Owens Corning. We talk about improving "inventory quality" instead of plain "inventory reduction". We look at gross profit and inventory turns to manage our product portfolios.

'If both gross profit and inventory turns start to decline, these are candidates for exclusion. This accounts for the three corners of the triangle. It ensures we have the inventory of the "right" product and it will positively impact our turns, ability to serve our customers and deliver business performance.'

When it comes to using 'return' metrics, like ROCE, Tony continues: 'Yes, we look at metrics like the return on capital or the ROCE to evaluate our businesses, and as a guideline when making major investment decisions. And yes, we will for instance account for the cost of inventory when making sourcing decisions. Extending our supply chain may lower the cost of goods, but it will increase the cost of inventory and reduce our ability to service our customers. This needs to be taken into account. Over the last few years we have consistently talked about the total landed cost, which accounts for the cost of inventory.'

When asked whether the triangle or ROCE principle is also used in more operational decision making, Tony states: 'Over the last three to five years, the supply chain team has worked on improving on the three corners at the same time. We have improved the service, while reducing the cost and reducing the inventory.'

Figure 2.20 summarizes some key financials of Owens Corning from the last five years.

We see a 10% improvement in the gross profit, translating into a 10% improvement in the EBIT, which is huge. We see a mild improvement in the inventory turns, from an average of 5.5 in 2012–14 to 6.5 in 2015 and 6 in 2016. We see a comparable pattern in the CCC, which is stable at around 33 days in 2012–2014 and then drops to 22 days in 2015–16. We also see a slight improvement in the fixed asset turns.

As Tony argues, there is an improvement on all of the parameters at the same time, resulting in a dramatic ROCE improvement from around 2% in 2012 to around 10% in 2016. The figures shown are publicly available and have been taken from the website amigobulls.com.

Figure 2.20 Five-year key financials of Owens Corning

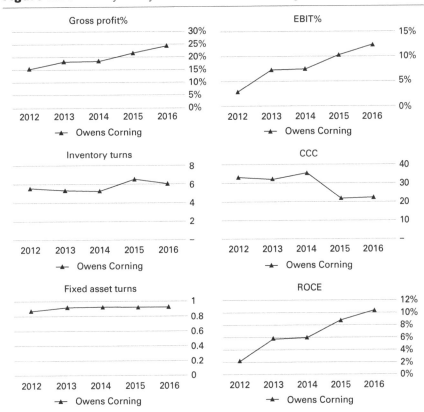

According to Tony, Owens Corning is improving but has room to improve further in each of the corners. Via continuous improvement he wants to keep shifting the boundaries in each of them. Tony comments: 'We believe we can be an AND-AND company: drive service, improve inventory quality, and drive supply chain productivity at the same time. I understand that conceptually you may need to choose a certain strategy [as shown in Figure 2.8], like accepting a lower EBIT% for a lower capital employed, in more commoditizing markets, where you need to play on cost, or vice versa, accepting a higher capital employed for the more high-end niches, but in return for a higher gross profit and a higher EBIT in return. But we're not there yet.'

The improvement in all metrics, as shown in Figure 2.20, is indeed different from a case such as Casio, where an increase in gross profit came at the expense of lower inventory turns, because of a change in strategy from operational excellence to product leadership.

The results of Owens Corning prove that supply chain management, through initiatives like improving the distribution network, improving the health of the product portfolio, improving the inventory quality or improving the planning and the execution, is a key enabler of simultaneous improvements to service, cost and capital, and as such a key driver for shareholder value.

Notes

1 Regardless of your strategy, applying the principles of lean manufacturing will improve operations, in that it will improve service (eg through better quality), at a lower cost (less rework) and with a lower working capital (less WIP). Its principle of 'flow' and techniques including 5S apply to a very broad range of production and administrative processes. In that sense it is what you could truly call a 'best practice'. If operational excellence is my strategy, I will translate the outcome of any lean implementations in a lower price for my customer. If I'm a product leader, the goal may be different, eg reducing throughput times to reduce time-to-market, and any improvements in cost or working capital will be invested in better products instead of lower prices.

2 First pass yield (FPY), also known as throughput yield (TPY), is defined as the number of units coming out of a process divided by the number of units going into that process over a specified period of time. Only good units with no rework or scrap are counted as coming out of an individual process (Prysdek and Keller, 2014).

3 Maintenance, repair, and operations (MRO) involves fixing any sort of mechanical, plumbing, or electrical device should it become out of order or broken (known as repair, unscheduled, or casualty maintenance). It also includes performing routine actions which keep the device in working order (known as scheduled maintenance) or prevent trouble from arising (preventive maintenance).

References

ABB Robotics [accessed 20/07/2017] Maintenance [Online] http://new.abb.com/products/robotics/service/maintenance

Barco [accessed 20/07/2017] Connect – Barco Annual Report 2013 [Online] http://www.barco.com/en/about-barco/investors/company-results

Barco [accessed 20/07/2017] For a smarter tomorrow – Barco Annual Report 2012 [Online] http://www.barco.com/en/about-barco/investors/company-results

Bosch [accessed 20/07/2017] Predictive maintenance solutions [Online] http://www.bosch-si.com/manufacturing/solutions/maintenance/predictive-maintenance.html

Casio [accessed 20/07/2017] Casio Annual Report 2016 [Online] https://world.casio.com/media/files/ir/annual/annual_2016.pdf

Casio [accessed 20/07/2017] Changing Lives Around the World" – Casio Annual Report 2008 [Online] http://http://arch.casio.com/file/ir/pdf/annual_2008.pdf

Colruyt [accessed 20/07/2017] About us [Online] http://www.colruytgroup.be/en/about-us

Colruyt [accessed 20/07/2017] Annual report 2016–17 [Online] http://www.colruytgroup.be/en/annual-report

Crawford, F and Mathews, R (2007) *The Myth of Excellence: Why great companies never try to be the best at everything*, Crown Business, London

Donze, P-Y (2016) *Industrial Development, Technology Transfer, and Global Competition: A history of the Japanese watch industry since 1850*, Routledge, Abingdon

EDEKA [accessed 20/07/2017] EDEKA Unternehmensbericht [Online] http://www.edeka-verbund.de/Unternehmen/de/presse/unternehmensberichte/unternehmensbericht_4.jsp

IBM [accessed 25/10/2017] IBM Tops U.S. Patent List for 20th Consecutive Year [Online] http://www-03.ibm.com/press/uk/en/pressrelease/40124.wss

Kim, W C and Mauborgne, R A (2005) *Blue Ocean Strategy: How to create uncontested market space and make the competition irrelevant*, Harvard Business Press, Boston

Pyzdek, T and Keller, P A (2014) *The Six Sigma Handbook: A complete guide for green belts, black belts and managers at all levels*, New York: McGraw-Hill Education, New York

Sachon, M (2010) The Hard Discount Model in Retailing, *IESE Insight*, PN-465-E

Treacy, M and Wiersema, F (1995) *The Discipline of Market Leaders: Choose your customers, narrow your focus, dominate your market*, Basic Books, New York

Verweire, K (2014) *Strategy Implementation*, Routledge, Abingdon

Womack, J P and Jones, D T (2010) *Lean Thinking: Banish waste and create wealth in your corporation*, Simon and Schuster, New York

Womack, J P, Jones, D T and Roos, D (1990) *The Machine that Changed the World: How lean production revolutionized the global car wars*, Simon and Schuster, New York

Financial benchmarking in two dimensions

03

In the previous chapter we introduced the idea that different strategies lead to a different balance in the Supply Chain Triangle, and as such to different targets for service, cost and capital employed.

In Chapters 3, 4 and 5, we will develop a two-dimensional benchmarking technique which allows you to account for strategy when setting targets. So, more specifically, it allows you to define, for your company in your sector, what your targets would be if you were to be an operational excellence leader, a customer intimacy player or a product leader. Though these chapters are a bit more technical, they develop a new and key capability for supply chains to become strategy-driven.

In this chapter we will introduce the idea of benchmarking in two dimensions. Instead of comparing just one KPI across companies, for instance inventory turns, we look at a combination of two KPIs, for instance EBIT% and inventory turns. We will also explain how benchmarking in two dimensions makes a difference.

In this chapter we will also ask and answer the question 'which KPIs should I benchmark?'. We will use the Supply Chain Triangle to answer this question, analyse different KPIs combining the service and the cost corner into a profit metric, and also analyse different KPIs related to the capital employed corner.

In Chapters 4 and 5 we will extend the two-dimensional benchmark graphs with the so-called 'indifference lines' or 'bang-for-the-buck' lines. These show the combinations of (for instance) EBIT and capital employed leading to the same return on capital employed (ROCE). We know that as an investor we are indifferent to the options on those lines given they lead to the same 'bang-for-the-buck'. They allow us to compare performance and targets across different strategies.

We will analyse the minimum, the median and the maximum 'bang-for-the-buck' performance in a benchmark group, and use that to define the targets for an opex player, a customer intimacy player and a product leader, for a set of KPIs.

Benchmarking in two dimensions

'How much inventory do we really need?' A simple question that is not easy to answer. I see companies try to answer it in two ways. The first is doing a bottom-up calculation. We carry inventory for different reasons (safety stock, cycle stock, anticipation, demo, spares) and across multiple steps in the supply chain (raw materials, intermediates, finished product). Some companies try to estimate each of these composing parts and then add up to get a total. In my experience, only one in 10 companies has ever done this type of bottom-up analysis.

A second and more common way to answer the inventory question is to perform a benchmark. Figure 3.1 shows an example benchmark for six technology companies. We show the inventory turns over the last five years. As we only look at the total inventory, it is called a 'top-down' approach. Moreover, this type of benchmarking and target setting is typically done by the central finance department, which adds to the feeling that this is a 'top-down' approach.

If you are company 1, which target will you get? Companies 2, 5 and 6 consistently realize inventory turns of 6 to 9. If your CFO is gentle, you may land a target of 6. With inventory turns currently between 2.5 and 3.5,

Figure 3.1   Inventory benchmark for six technology companies

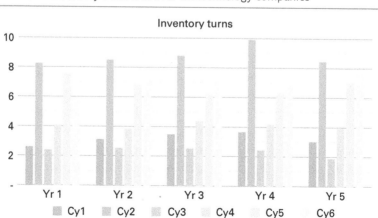

getting to 6 is a huge challenge. Turns of 3 means four months of inventory. Turns of 6 means two months of inventory. Cutting the inventory by half may seem a mission impossible!

So how will we persuade the CFO that turns of 6 are unrealistic? Yes, chances are we will blame the benchmark for comparing apples to pears, that our company cannot be compared with the companies getting inventory turns of 6 to 9. The answer from the CFO might be to drill down to the direct competitors only active in our niche. Unfortunately, as shown in Figure 3.2, Company 2 turns out to be a direct competitor. Instead of landing a target of 6, I probably just landed myself a target of 8 or 9!

While benchmarking in one dimension, as illustrated in Figure 3.1 and Figure 3.2, is common, it is dangerous. We will introduce benchmarking in two dimensions to explain why, and as a better alternative.

We came across the technique of two-dimensional benchmarking in the book *Supply Chain Metrics That Matter* (Cecere, 2014). Figure 3.3 shows the performance of three direct competitors in the period 2004–13 in a so-called 'orbit chart'. Each dot shows the combination of EBIT, as % of sales revenue, and inventory turns, at the end of a fiscal year.

Looking at company 2, this gives a different picture. Company 2 may be leading in inventory turns, but it seems to have a profit problem. The average EBIT over the 10 years is only 1.5%! The company could be in financial distress, and may have aggressively lowered inventories to generate cash, as banks and shareholders are reluctant to provide extra money.

If you look at EBIT%, company 3 has realized EBIT% levels of around 18% in the period 2004–06. If we do a one-dimensional benchmark in inventory turns and a one-dimensional benchmark in EBIT%, we may end up

Figure 3.2   Inventory benchmark for three direct competitors

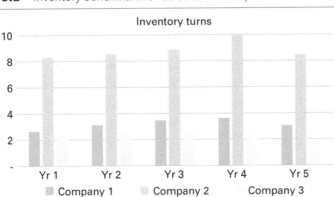

Figure 3.3   Two-dimensional benchmark showing EBIT vs inventory turns for three direct competitors

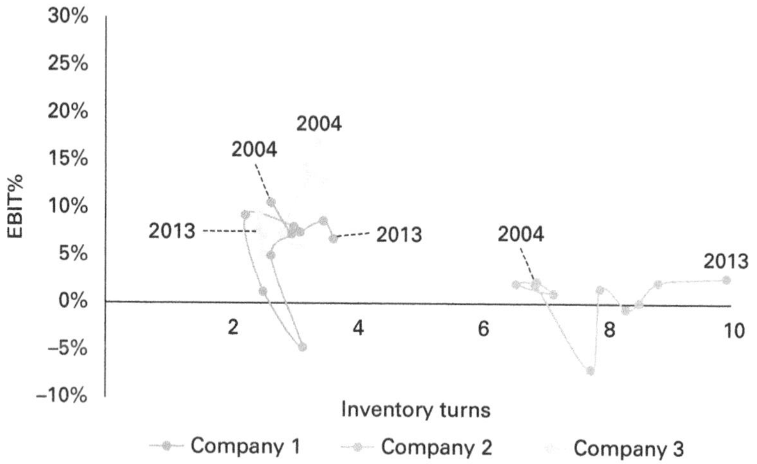

with a target of nine turns and 18% EBIT. That is unrealistic. We may have turns of 9 with an EBIT of 2–3%, or an EBIT of 18% with turns around 3, but no company has ever been near to turns of 9 with an EBIT of 18%.

We hope this simple example shows that benchmarking in one dimension is dangerous. As we do not account for performance in other dimensions, we may land ourselves unbalanced or even unrealistic targets. Next we will further explore which KPIs we should include in our benchmark.

Exercise: One-dimensional vs two-dimensional benchmarking

Identify five key competitors and gather the necessary information to calculate their EBIT% and inventory turns. As explained in our section on accounting basics in Chapter 1, the EBIT% is calculated by dividing EBIT by the sales revenue. Inventory turns are calculated by dividing the cost of goods sold by the inventory.

Make sure to gather the figures for 10 consecutive years. You can manually gather the information from the financial reports of the chosen companies, or if you search the internet, websites such as amigobulls.com offer free Excel downloads of 10 year financials for companies listed in the US.

Plot the inventory turns for your own company and the five key competitors, as shown in Figure 3.1. What do you learn? What inventory target would you derive for your company from this type of one-dimensional benchmark?

Plot the EBIT% versus inventory turns as shown in Figure 3.3. You can use the 'scatterplot with smooth lines and markers' from Microsoft Excel for this. What do you learn? What is the EBIT performance of the company with the highest inventory turns? How does it compare to the performance of your company?

What inventory target would you derive after seeing the two-dimensional benchmark? And what EBIT% target would it go with?

Which KPIs to include in a benchmark

OK, so let's benchmark in two dimensions... but which KPIs? In Figure 3.3 we chose inventory turns on the X-axis and EBIT% on the Y-axis. Why did we choose these? What are the alternatives?

We remember from Chapter 1 that companies struggle in balancing the Supply Chain Triangle of Service, Cost and Cash. Balancing the triangle is important, as it optimizes the ROCE, or the 'bang-for-the-buck'. If we had three-dimensional graphs, we might benchmark in three dimensions, with each dimension taking a metric from service, cost and capital employed. If we can use only two dimensions, it is helpful to combine the service and the cost dimension into a profit metric, as shown in Figure 3.4.

In previous chapters we have frequently talked about EBIT, Earnings Before Interest and Taxes. In this chapter we will also explore gross margin, EBITDA (EBIT before depreciation and amortization), and net profit. We will put the profitability on the vertical axis. That leaves us with the horizontal axis for capital employed metrics.

Figure 3.4   Possible metrics for two-dimensional benchmarking

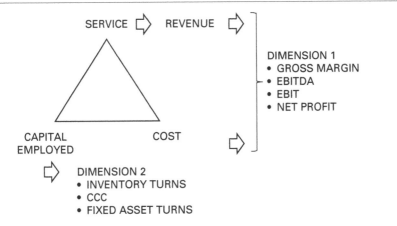

In Figure 3.3 we have looked at inventory turns as a KPI for inventory. We will look at the cash conversion cycle (CCC) as a metric for working capital (the inventory + the accounts receivable – the accounts payable).

Finally we will looked at fixed asset turns, which is the sales revenue / fixed assets. Working capital + fixed assets equals the capital employed. For production companies we believe that inventory is a good measurement of the 'complexity' of a business and 'how well it is run'. For retail companies, as discussed in Chapter 2, working capital is typically very low or even negative. Here fixed asset turns can be a better measure of the capital employed.

Comparing alternative metrics for profit

The first alternative to the EBIT shown in Figure 3.3 is the EBITDA shown in Figure 3.5.

EBIT is derived from EBITDA by subtracting depreciation and amortization, so in general, EBITDA should be higher than EBIT. We indeed see that all companies shift up. Company 2 remains on the right bottom corner. Company 1 and 3 seem to shift a little closer to each other. Where the best EBIT performance of company 1 (in the periods 2004–07 and 2010–12) seems to match the worst EBIT performance of company 3 (in the period 2008–13), the best EBITDA performance of company 1 (in the period 2004–07) seems to match the average EBITDA performance of company 3.

So which one should we use, EBIT or EBITDA? EBITDA does not account for depreciation and amortization. Depreciation and amortization is not a

Figure 3.5 Two-dimensional benchmark showing EBITDA vs inventory turns for three direct competitors

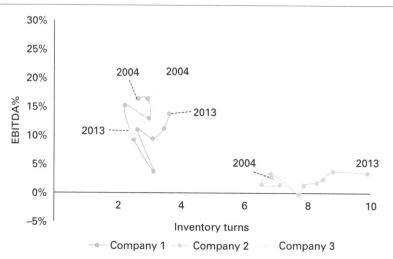

cash-out. As discussed in our section on accounting basics in Chapter 1, an investment is only a cash-out at the time of the initial investment. In that sense companies use EBITDA as a proxy for the cash generated by the operations. EBIT does account for the depreciation and amortization. If a business requires heavy investments and as such carries high levels of depreciation, the EBIT accounts for that, where the EBITDA does not. Based on this, we typically prefer benchmarking EBIT over EBITDA.

Whether comparing EBIT or EBITDA, always try to assure you are comparing apples with apples. Companies may use different accounting rules for their investments. As an example, in accounting, R&D costs can be treated in two different ways. Option 1 is to account for the R&D costs in the year they are incurred. Option 2 is to capitalize the R&D costs and amortize them over the lifetime of the resulting products. If R&D costs are stable, the result on the EBIT will be the same. However, the EBITDA in option 1 will be lower than in option 2, as option 1 has no amortizations, whereas option 2 does. Another reason to be careful when benchmarking EBITDA.

Figure 3.6 shows the gross margin versus inventory turns.

This shows another picture again. Firstly, the gross margin performance of company 2 is more consistent than its EBIT or EBITDA performance. Gross margin is consistently around 30%, while inventory turns have consistently improved from around 7 to around 10 in 2013. In general, investors like consistency, as it reduces their risk.

Companies 1 and 3 seem to have switched position. Where company 3 had a superior EBIT or EBITDA in the period 2004–07, as seen from Figure

Figure 3.6   Two-dimensional benchmark showing gross margin vs inventory turns for three direct competitors

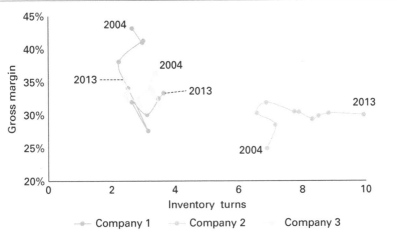

3.3 and 3.5, it is company 1 that has a superior gross margin in the same period. So what explains that switch? And which metric should we look at? EBIT, EBITDA or gross margin?

Let's start with remembering the definition of gross margin. Gross margin equals the sales revenue minus the cost of goods sold (COGS). The COGS includes the cost of purchase, costs of conversion and other costs incurred in bringing the inventories to their present location and condition. Cost of goods made by the business include material, (direct) labour, and allocated overhead (also called indirect labour).

In Chapter 2 we used the gross margin as an indicator for the service dimension in our Supply Chain Triangle. If customers are willing to pay a higher premium over the cost of goods, it implies a higher service. The consistency in gross margin of company 2 implies a consistent service towards its customers. The drop in gross margin of company 1 hints towards a change in business model, to which we will come back later.

We can derive the EBIT from the gross margin by subtracting the selling, general and administrative (SG&A) costs and the depreciation and amortization. If Company 1 and 3 switch positions when looking at gross margin versus EBIT, then it has to do with those costs in between. Figure 3.7 looks at the SG&A (versus the inventory turns). The gross margin of company 3 in the period 2004–07 oscillates between 32%–36%, the SG&A between 16%–20% (as seen from Figure 3.6 and 3.7) – whereas for company 1 the gross margin in that same period goes from 43% to 38%, for an SG&A around 32%–33%.

The SG&A spending of company 3 is significantly lower than that of company 1 – in 2005 the spend was only half (16% versus 32%)! As such, the reason for the superior EBIT of company 3 in the period 2004–07 is not a superior service (as measured by gross margin), but rather a cut back on spend.

For this reason, when setting EBIT targets, we need to exclude the EBIT of company 3 during 2004–07 as 'not sustainable'. In Figure 3.7 we see that company 3 does not sustain those low levels of spending. SG&A grows to 25%, which is more comparable to companies 1 and 2.

From Figure 3.3 we see that the EBIT of company 3 drops as the spending picks back up. This supports the argument that the EBIT% performance of company 3 in 2004–07 should be excluded from a target setting exercise as being 'not sustainable'.

The last profit KPI shown in Figure 3.4 is net profit. Net profit is calculated from the EBIT by subtracting interest and taxes. We consider interest and taxes to be primarily driven by financial optimization. Though important

Figure 3.7 Two-dimensional benchmark showing SG&A vs inventory turns for three direct competitors

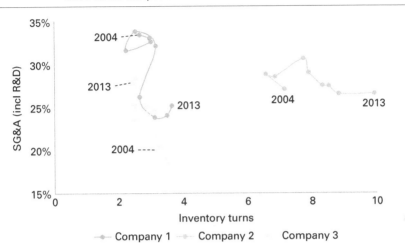

for a company, it has little relation to operations. From that perspective, when setting operational targets, we advise using a combination of EBIT and gross margin as discussed above. Gross margin gives an idea of the premium that customers are willing to pay for the delivered service and as such will help in revealing the chosen strategy. EBIT gives the operational result after accounting for all operational costs and investments.

This concludes our review of possible 'profit' metrics to put on the vertical axis of our two-dimensional benchmark. In the next section, we will review some possible 'capital employed' metrics, as shown in Figure 3.4.

Exercise: Comparing different profitability metrics

Expand the analysis of your company and five key competitors. Collect the necessary data from the financial reports to calculate the gross margin%, the EBITDA%, and the net profit%:

- Gross margin% is calculated as (sales revenue – cost of goods sold)/ sales revenue.

- EBITDA is EBIT before depreciation and amortization. In case it is not separately mentioned in the P&L, you may need to add the depreciation and amortization to the EBIT to calculate the EBITDA. These are typically found in the statement of cash flows.

- EBITDA% is calculated as EBITDA/sales revenue.

- The net profit is really the bottom line of the P&L, and net profit% is calculated as net profit / sales revenue.

Compare the different orbit charts showing gross margin%, EBITDA%, EBIT% and net profit% versus inventory turns. What kinds of observations can you make? Starting with gross margin, which companies are higher, and which are lower? What are the possible reasons for which customers are willing to pay a premium to some of the companies?

What about EBIT versus EBITDA differences – are they consistent? Are some companies more or less heavy on investment and depreciation? Could there be differences in accounting rules that we need to be aware of?

What about the net profit? Any companies that could be in financial distress? Could that translate into a high pressure on inventories to generate cash from operations?

Comparing alternative metrics for 'capital employed'

In all of the above figures, we have shown inventory turns on the horizontal axis. We will zoom out from inventory to capital employed by first looking at working capital, as measured by the CCC, and then looking at the fixed assets as measured by the fixed asset turns. Working capital plus fixed assets gives the capital employed.

As introduced above, and as explained in more detail in the section on accounting basics in Chapter 1, working capital consists of the inventory plus the accounts receivable, minus the accounts payable. As a company we need to finance the inventory and the receivables from our customers. We can subtract the money we still owe to our suppliers. As illustrated in Chapter 2, retailers may owe more money to their suppliers than they have inventory or receivables. They can end up with a negative working capital.

Working capital as defined above is a currency figure, for instance in dollars, pounds or euros. When comparing companies, it is handy to convert the currency figure to a number of days. For the inventory and accounts payable we take the cost of goods sold as the basis; for the accounts receivable we use sales revenue.

The CCC is defined as the days of inventory on hand (DIOH) + days of sales outstanding (DSO) – days of payables outstanding (DPO):

- DIOH = inventory / COGS * 365;
- DPO = accounts payable / COGS *365;
- DSO = accounts receivable / sales revenue *365.

These figures and the CCC can easily be calculated by studying the balance sheet and the P&L of a company. We again refer to the section on accounting basics in Chapter 1 for more details.

Figure 3.8 shows EBIT% versus the CCC for the three competitors.

Our first observation is that where we want inventory turns to be high, we want the CCC to be low. In the previous charts we wanted to be up right, with high inventory turns, and a high EBIT%. In the CCC charts we want to be up left, with a low CCC and a high EBIT. Let's analyze the 10-year performance of companies 1, 2 and 3.

Company 1 has seen huge swings in its CCC. Since 2007, it has made a consistent effort to reduce its working capital, from 200 days down to around 100 days. Company 3 has seen fewer swings, but a gradually degrading CCC, from 130 to around 180. The increase in working capital is in line with the increase in inventory (or the decrease in inventory turns) earlier observed in Figure 3.3.

The strangest behaviour is observed in company 2. Whereas Figure 3.3 showed a consistent decrease in inventory, Figure 3.8 shows a consistent increase in working capital. This implies that any savings in inventory are more than cancelled out by either an increase in receivables or a decrease in payables. This is not a sign of strength. An increase in receivables may

Figure 3.8 Two-dimensional benchmark showing EBIT% vs CCC for three direct competitors

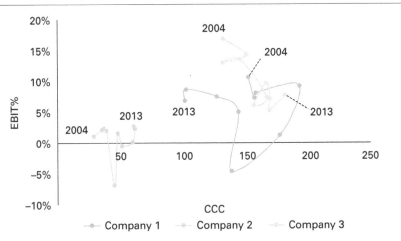

indicate a weak negotiating position. A decrease in payables may indicate suppliers asking for pre-payment, due to a weakening financial position of your company.

All of this indicates that the focus on reducing inventories is not a sign of health, but rather of weakness. Company 2 may be pushing inventories down to try and compensate for the increase in receivables and reduction of payables.

If we are cautious, we may label the inventory turns of company 2 as 'potentially not sustainable'. Just as we identified the EBIT of company 3 in the period 2004–07 to be 'not sustainable', we may exclude any suspicious inventory turns from the benchmark when we come to target setting in the next chapter.

So which one should we use, inventory turns or CCC? As introduced above, we believe that inventory, for production companies, is a good measurement of the complexity and the performance of a company. Companies struggle more with inventory, and setting inventory targets, than with accounts receivable and accounts payable. Receivables and payables are simpler. They are defined by the payment terms and the speed of collection. Payment terms are the result of a negotiation, and are about a trade-off between cost and cash. You can probably extend your payment terms towards a supplier, if you are willing to pay a bit more.

Inventory is more complex. As introduced in the beginning of this chapter, and in the beginning of Chapter 1, there are different types of inventory (safety stock, cycle stock, seasonal stock, demo stock, spares) and we keep it across different steps in the supply chain (raw materials, intermediates, finished products, consignment). Inventory is the lifeblood of your company, or even more likely the cholesterol – some is good, some is bad, you should have enough, but not too much. Measuring it tells us a lot about the health of the patient.

That's why in what follows, we will continue our analysis of inventory, and see how we can set targets for inventory, accounting for the chosen strategy. As illustrated above, doing a check on the CCC will provide a broader view on the overall health of the company, and its direction. So in general both are useful. We will typically first look at inventory turns and then zoom out to the CCC.

Getting back to Figure 3.4, next to inventory, or working capital, we want to take a look at the fixed assets through the fixed asset turnover. The fixed asset turnover is calculated as the sales revenue divided by the fixed assets. A higher ratio implies the company has fewer assets compared to its competitors, or likewise, is getting more use from its existing assets. Likewise, a lower asset turn indicates the need for more assets.

Figure 3.9 shows the EBIT% versus the fixed asset turnover for our three companies. We don't really see what we'd expect or like to see. The ROCE principle says that it's OK to have a lower asset turn as long as the EBIT is higher. The asset turns of company 1 make important swings, from around 2.5 to close to 4 and back. The asset turns of company 3 are consistently and significantly lower with an average around 1.5. In the period 2004–07 that is compensated for by a higher EBIT, but we know from the analysis above that this EBIT was driven by below average spending, and not by superior service or gross margin.

The performance of company 2 is worrisome altogether. For comparable or even higher asset turns, company 1 has a consistently higher EBIT (in eight out of the 10 years).

So which metric should we use? Inventory turns, CCC or fixed asset turns? As mentioned above, we believe companies struggle with setting targets and managing inventory. As such, analysing inventory turns is helpful. Taking the broader view of the CCC will help in gaining a broader understanding of the company performance and where it is going. If we want to understand what drives the ROCE, we also need to understand the fixed assets. Where company 2 was lower on working capital, from Figure 3.9, we feel its asset turns are significantly lagging behind. We can expect this to hurt the ROCE. As we have shown in Chapter 2, for retailers, the asset turns are more important than the working capital, which can be close to zero or even negative.

In conclusion, while for the profitability metrics we were able to select gross margin and EBIT as more relevant than EBITDA or net profit, for capital employed we really need to look at all three metrics if we want to get a complete picture.

Figure 3.9 Two-dimensional benchmark showing EBIT% vs fixed asset turns for three direct competitors

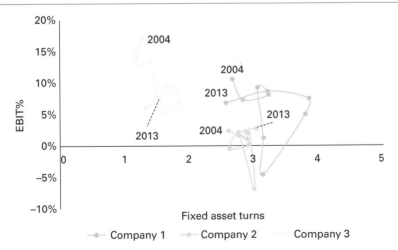

Exercise: Comparing different capital employed metrics

Expand the analysis of your company and the five key competitors. Collect the necessary data from the financial reports to calculate the CCC and the fixed asset turns. The CCC is defined as the days of inventory on hand (DIOH) + days of sales outstanding (DSO) – days of payables outstanding (DPO):

- DIOH = inventory value / COGS x 365;
- DPO = accounts payable / COGS x 365;
- DSO = accounts receivable / sales revenue x 365.

Note that accounts receivable and payable are often referred to as trade receivables and trade payables.

As pointed out before, notice that the inventory and the trade payables are using the cost of goods sold as the reference base. The trade receivables are using the sales revenue as the reference base. The fixed asset turns are easily calculated as the sales revenue / fixed assets.

Compare the different orbit charts showing EBIT% versus inventory turns, versus CCC and versus fixed asset turns. Are the conclusions from the CCC graph in line with that from the inventory turns graph? Any changes of position between the two? Does it tell anything about how inventory is being used? Are any companies lowering inventories to generate cash or to compensate for changes in the receivables or payables?

Can you reach any conclusions from comparing the CCC graph to the fixed asset turns graph? Are companies confirmed in their positions, or do we see differences in how well they manage their working capital versus their assets?

Combining profit and capital employed in the ROCE

Getting back to Figure 3.4, we have taken a look at profitability metrics on the vertical axis, and capital employed metrics on the horizontal axis. Where profitability is the 'bang' and the capital employed is the 'buck', they combine in 'bang-for-the-buck', financially measured as the EBIT/capital employed or, in short, the ROCE. So based on our benchmarks so far, what can we expect as a ROCE performance, and what are the actual results?

We have seen company 2 working at low EBIT levels, pushing inventories down as to compensate for an increase in working capital, and struggling with asset turns. From this we expect company 2 to be working at below average ROCE.

We have seen company 3 with an exceptional EBIT in the period 2004–07 – a result driven by a cutback on spending rather than offering a premium service in the market. The high EBIT may have compensated for the low asset turns throughout the 10 years. EBIT has dropped, as spending has been restored, but the asset turns have stayed the same and the working capital has increased. Altogether, this may result in a high ROCE in the period 2004–07, but a non-sustainable one, as proven by a decrease in the subsequent years.

We have seen company 1 starting with superior levels in gross margin, in the period 2004–07, but dropping back to lower levels in the years after. Company 1 has adjusted its spending on SG&A accordingly and has been able to keep EBIT levels in the higher 5-10% range. Asset turns have been swinging back and forth, but seem OK in relation with EBIT. Since 2007 the company has consistently lowered working capital, which should benefit the ROCE.

The actual results for the ROCE are shown in Figure 3.10. They are quite close to what we expected. Company 2 is struggling. The 10-year ROCE is below the performance of its two competitors. Company 3 is doing well to extremely well in 2004–07, but has reached that level of performance in a non-sustainable way, by temporarily cutting back on spending. It seems to be paying the price in the subsequent years.

Taking that into account, company 1 seems to be leading the pack. With high ROCE levels before and after the crisis. The change in gross margin indicates a big change in strategy, to which we'll come back in Chapter 5. Except for the crisis period, this may act as a reference for the two competitors. How to use it as a reference is something we'll explore in the next chapter.

Figure 3.10 The 10-year ROCE for three direct competitors

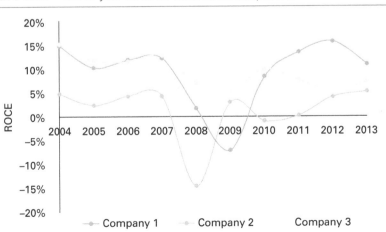

Exercise: Comparing the ROCE

Before making the ROCE graph for your company and its five key competitors, write down what you expect to see as differences in ROCE based on your previous analyses. Which companies will have a higher ROCE, which ones will be lower? Which companies will have improved, and which ones will have slipped back?

Next, calculate the ROCE of your company and its five key competitors. The ROCE is calculated as the EBIT / capital employed, and the capital employed = working capital + fixed assets. Make a graph as in Figure 3.10.

What do you observe? Is what you see in line with what you expected? Which companies are actually higher or lower? Which companies have actually improved or slipped back? What explains any differences between the actual results and what you expected?

Conclusion

In this chapter we started by illustrating how in one-dimensional benchmarking companies compare individual KPIs like EBIT% or inventory turns for key competitors. The typical outcome is that we try to be the best in EBIT% and the best in inventory turns, but the combination of the two is not necessarily realistic.

The ROCE principle tells us that it is OK to have some more inventory as long as your EBIT is higher. Two-dimensional benchmarking better reveals those trade-offs, and as such helps to derive realistic targets.

Once you accept two-dimensional benchmarking as a better practice, the obvious next question is which KPIs to use for the vertical and the horizontal axis. We have combined the service and the cost side of our Supply Chain Triangle into one dimension, being profitability, and plotted different alternatives on the Y-axis: gross margin%, EBIT%, EBITDA% and net profit%. We have used the X-axis for measuring the capital employed side of our Supply Chain Triangle and have plotted inventory turns, cash conversion cycle and fixed asset turns.

The combination of the X-axis and the Y-axis gives insight in the 'bang-for-the-buck' or the ROCE performance.

For profitability we prefer gross margin% and EBIT% over EBITDA% and net profit%. Gross margin% indicates the premium the customer is willing to pay on top of the cost of goods, and as such measures the perceived service. The EBIT% shows what remains after accounting for all relevant costs, which include the SG&A, but also the depreciation and amortization. If your business is heavy on investments, you need to account for them. The EBIT% does, the EBITDA% does not. The difference between the net profit% and the EBIT% is finance driven, where in our benchmarking we want to focus on operational benchmarks. These are the reasons we prefer EBIT% over EBITDA% and net profit%.

For capital employed we always take a look at inventory turns, at the CCC and at the fixed asset turns. Inventory is a good measure for the operational complexity and the performance of a production company. Both aspects are very relevant when benchmarking. The CCC takes a broader perspective in accounting for the accounts receivable and the accounts payable. It tells us more about how inventory is being used in the company. We may see an improvement in both inventory turns and CCC. We may see an aggressive reduction in inventories to counter an increase in the CCC. This helps in understanding the behaviour of your competitors.

Finally, for understanding the ROCE, you need to understand how a company is using its fixed assets, which we have measured through fixed asset turns. The management of working capital attracts a lot of attention, as working capital equals cash. But good management of the working capital does not imply good management of the fixed assets. Both are required to get a full comprehension of what is driving the ROCE.

In the next chapter we will further build on the two-dimensional benchmark graphs. We will add the 'indifference' or 'bang-for-the-buck' lines that show all combinations, for instance of EBIT% and inventory turns, leading to the same 'bang-for-the-buck'. These lines will help us in comparing performance across different strategies.

We will reveal the minimum, median and maximum performance in our group of benchmark companies, which in turn will help us in setting targets for the combined sets of KPIs.

Reference

Cecere, L M (2014) *Supply Chain Metrics That Matter*, John Wiley & Sons, New York

Financial target setting in two dimensions 04

In Chapter 3 we introduced two-dimensional benchmarking as an improvement over one-dimensional benchmarking, better revealing the trade-offs between a profit metric and a capital employed metric.

For profit we analysed and preferred gross margin and EBIT over EBITDA and net profit. Gross margin indicates the premium customers are willing to pay, and as such the perceived service. EBIT is a profitability metric which accounts for all operational costs, including R&D and selling, general and administrative (SG&A), and including any depreciations and amortizations, but excluding any taxes or interest which are the domain of financial optimization.

For capital employed we have argued the need to look at inventory through inventory turns, at working capital through the cash conversion cycle (CCC) and at the fixed assets through the fixed asset turns. Only by understanding the three can we understand what is driving the return on capital employed (ROCE).

In this chapter, we will extend the two-dimensional benchmarks with the so-called 'indifference' or 'bang-for-the-buck' lines. They show the combinations of (for instance) EBIT and inventory turns leading to the same 'bang-for-the-buck'. We know that as investors we are indifferent with respect to the different positions on those lines, as they deliver the same 'bang-for-the-buck'. This helps us to compare performance across different strategies.

We will add the minimum, the median and the maximum performance lines which will help us in deriving targets. Connecting to the maximum performance line will reveal different possible targets. Finally, we will show in Chapter 5 that which target to choose depends on the chosen strategy.

Adding 'indifference' or 'bang-for-the-buck' lines to the EBIT/inventory graph

From Chapter 2 we remember that different strategies are different ways to generate the same ROCE. We have argued that a product leader carries more complexity, and as such requires more inventory or has a higher capital employed. Because product leaders sell high-end products in high-end niches, they are able to offset that higher capital employed with a higher gross margin, allowing for a higher spending on SG&A while still retaining a higher EBIT.

Operational excellence players typically work at lower EBIT levels, as to guarantee the lowest price in the market. They compensate for the lower EBIT by employing less capital. On the one hand, their lower complexity results in less working capital. On the other hand, their focus on efficiency allows them to work with fewer fixed assets, or alternatively make better use of their assets.

To visualize those strategic trade-offs, we will add so-called 'indifference' or 'bang-for-the-buck' lines to Figure 3.3. As an investor I'm indifferent, as long as you deliver the same 'bang-for-the-buck'. More investment for a higher reward indicates a product leadership position. Minimal investment for a minimal reward points towards operational excellence. Based on the discussion in the previous chapter, we will take company 1 as the reference company in our benchmark.

Table 4.1 shows the EBIT (in €K), the inventory (in €K) and the EBIT/inventory for company 1 over the last 10 years. Looking at the ratio of EBIT/inventory, 2004 was the best year, with a percentage of 49.59%. 2009 was the worst year with -20.19%. In 2009 we were at the full depth of the financial crisis. The median performance is 33.5%, which was realized in 2011.

Table 4.1 Company 1 EBIT, inventory and EBIT/inventory for 2004–13

Company 1	2004	2005	2006	2007	2008
EBIT (in kEur)	71,427	52,008	60,687	68,314	8,903
Inventory (in kEur)	144,049	141,364	146,672	204,085	189,107
EBIT/inventory	49.59%	36.79%	41.38%	33.47%	4.71%

Company 1	2009	2010	2011	2012	2013
EBIT (in kEur)	(29,537)	45,135	78,359	100,238	79,024
Inventory (in kEur)	146,264	230,420	233,928	223,677	211,575
EBIT/inventory	–20.19%	19.59%	33.50%	44.81%	37.35%

Let's take the best year, 2004, with an EBIT/inventory performance of 49.59%. Which other combinations of EBIT% versus inventory turns would give that same performance? If we can plot that line, we can create a benchmark for company 1, but also for the other companies. We need a little maths to solve this question. It starts by rewriting:

$$EBIT/inventory = EBIT/sales\ revenue \times sales\ revenue/COGS \times COGS/\ inventory$$

Or stated differently:

$$EBIT/inventory = EBIT\% \times 1/(1\text{-}gross\ margin\%) \times inventory\ turns$$

Or when solving EBIT% from this:

$$EBIT\% = EBIT/inventory \times (1\text{-}gross\ margin\%)\ /\ inventory\ turns$$

It is clear from this equation that as well as the EBIT/inventory and the inventory turns, we also need the gross margin% to be able to calculate the corresponding EBIT%. The gross margin% is the one from the reference year, 2004 in this case. For completeness, we have added the gross margin% in Table 4.2. The gross margin% of 2004 is 43.18%.

So, as an example, for inventory turns of 2, the EBIT% leading to the same EBIT/inventory ratio of 49.59% can be found from the equation as EBIT% = 49.59% × (1-43.18%)/2 = 14.09%. The actual inventory turns for company 1 in 2004 were 2.65 with an EBIT% of 10.63%. Our analysis says that if you need more inventory, and would have turns of only 2, as an investor I'm OK with that, as long as you generate more EBIT, more specifically, as long as the corresponding EBIT is 14.09%.

Table 4.2 Company 1 EBIT, inventory and EBIT/inventory for 2004–13

Company 1	2004	2005	2006	2007	2008
EBIT (in kEur)	71,427	52,008	60,687	68,314	8,903
Inventory (in kEur)	144,049	141,364	146,672	204,085	189,107
EBIT/inventory	49.59%	36.79%	41.38%	33.47%	4.71%
Gross margin%	43.18%	41.03%	41.34%	38.13%	34.11%

Company 1	2009	2010	2011	2012	2013
EBIT (in kEur)	(29,537)	45,135	78,359	100,238	79,024
Inventory (in kEur)	146,264	230,420	233,928	223,677	211,575
EBIT/inventory	–20.19%	19.59%	33.50%	44.81%	37.35%
Gross margin%	27.63%	32.05%	30.05%	32.49%	33.38%

In the same way we can calculate the EBIT% corresponding with inventory turns of 3, or 4, or 4.5. Figure 4.1 shows the resulting curve. It shows all combinations of EBIT% and inventory turns, leading to the same, maximum, EBIT/inventory performance. It is the maximum performance or best-in-class line. That maximum curve is exponential – if your turns drop below 2, we can see that the EBIT% increases rapidly. The equation shows that the maximum performance line is of the form y = a/x, with y the EBIT% and x the inventory turns. A function of the form y = a/x has this exponential form.

In the same way as we have plotted the 'maximum performance' or MAX line, we can also plot the 'median performance' or MED line, and the 'minimum performance' or MIN line. This is done by substituting the median and minimum EBIT/inventory in the above equation, and using the gross margin% of the corresponding years, 2011 and 2009 respectively. The three lines for company 1 are shown in Figure 4.2.

We see that the performance of company 1 is 'bound' by the MIN and the MAX line. The MED line is much closer to the MAX line than to the MIN line. This means that the target performance of company 1, which we can define as median to maximum range, is in a relatively narrow bound.

We also see that company 3 outperforms company 1 in the period 2004–07 – but this is the period that we have taken out in the previous chapter as being not sustainable. In the period 2008–13, company 3 is in the minimum to median zone. Company 2 is also in the minimum to median zone, except for 2013, where the turns of 10 and the EBIT of 5% is in the median to maximum performance zone.

Figure 4.1 Two-dimensional benchmark showing 'bang-for-the-buck' line for EBIT% vs inventory turns, based on the 2004 performance of company 1

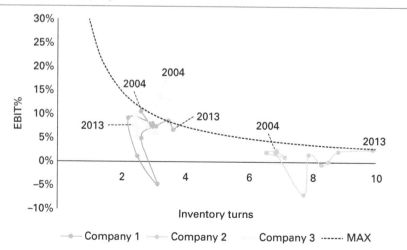

Figure 4.2 Two-dimensional benchmark showing 'bang-for-the-buck' lines for EBIT% vs inventory turns, based on the MIN, MED, and MAX performance of company 1

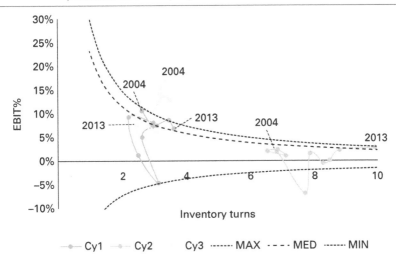

Exercise: Calculating the 'bang-for-the-buck' lines for EBIT/inventory

Let's calculate the 'bang-for-the-buck' lines for the EBIT/inventory. Select a company you'd consider to be best in class from the earlier analyses. A first step is calculating the EBIT/inventory ratio for each of the years, as shown in Table 4.1.

Select the year with the highest EBIT/inventory ratio. This will give us the MAX line. In Excel, make a table with the first column lining up inventory turns, let's say from 0.5 to 10, in steps of 0.5. In the second column, calculate the corresponding EBIT% from the formula 4.1, EBIT% = EBIT/inventory x (1-gross margin) / inventory turns.

Where EBIT/inventory is the ratio for the year you have selected, inventory turns is taken from column 1, and (1-gross margin) is again taken from the year you have selected. You will have a first column with a listing of inventory turns, in the second column the corresponding EBIT. Do the same for the year with the minimum and for the year with the median EBIT/inventory ratio.

Add the three lines, the minimum, median and maximum performance lines to your two-dimensional EBIT% versus inventory turns graph. Is the performance of the chosen company nicely fitting into the minimum and the maximum lines? Do the lines look exponential, like the ones shown in Figure 4.2?

Calculate the three lines in the same way for two or three other companies? How do they compare? Compare the median performance line for all six companies. How close are they? Which companies are leading? Which ones are lagging behind?

Using the 'bang-for-the-buck' lines for setting targets

So how can we use these two-dimensional benchmarks, with the 'bang-for-the-buck' lines, for target setting? We will illustrate that by looking at the 2014 performance of company 1, and setting targets for 2015.

In all of the previous graphs, we have shown the performance of 2004–13. Figure 4.3 has now added the 2014 performance of company 1. We see a drop back on EBIT% and inventory turns. The EBIT% has fallen back from 6.82% to 3.64%. The inventory turns have fallen back from 3.65 to 3.04. That is bad news. This type of bad news typically comes with a lot of pressure when setting targets for the next fiscal year.

So being company 1, and given the bad performance of 2014, what type of target do we set for 2015? In Figure 4.4 we show two basic options.

Figure 4.3 Two-dimensional benchmark showing 'bang-for-the-buck' lines for EBIT% vs inventory turns, adding the 2014 performance of company 1

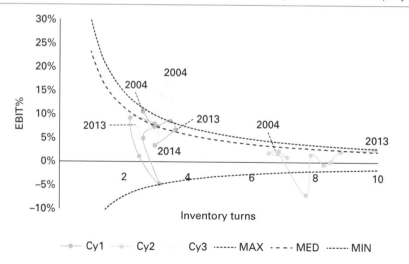

Figure 4.4   Two possible targets for EBIT% vs inventory turns for company 1, based on the MAX performance line

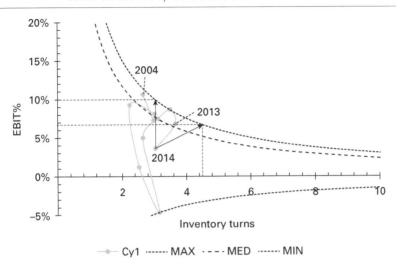

Both come from connecting 2014 to the maximum performance line. Option 1 is to stay at inventory turns of 3, and improve EBIT back to 10%, as in 2004. Option 2 is to improve inventory turns to 4.5 while improving EBIT to around 7%.

If we ask people which option they would choose, most of them go for option 2, as improving on both EBIT% and inventory turns at the same time seems the easiest. In the next chapter we will argue that the choice is not random, but in fact linked to a choice of strategy, between product leadership, and customer intimacy. Before we can do that, let's do another exercise and continue with the plotting the 'bang-for-the-buck' lines in the EBIT% versus CCC graphs.

Exercise: Setting targets using the bang-for-the-buck-lines for EBIT/inventory

Take a look at the EBIT% versus inventory turns for your company. What does the path look like? When did you improve and when did you fall back on which dimension? Take your last year's performance and connect it to the maximum performance line. As shown in Figure 4.4 you may try two ways of connecting: one is a line going straight up, sticking to the current inventory turns and improving on the EBIT, a second is a line going up to the right, improving on both EBIT% and inventory turns at the same time.

What types of targets does that give? How does it compare to the targets you currently have in place? Out of the two options, which one seems the more realistic?

Adding 'bang-for-the-buck' lines in the EBIT% versus CCC graphs

Figure 3.8 showed the EBIT% versus CCC for our three direct competitors. As for the inventory turns graph, we will now try to plot the 'bang-for-the-buck' lines corresponding with the maximum, median and minimum EBIT/working capital performance. As before, we will take company 1 as the reference company.

Table 4.3 shows EBIT/working capital ratio for company 1 for the period 2004–13. We see that the maximum performance is realized in 2012, the minimum performance in 2009. As median performance, we take the 21.40% realized in 2007.

As before, let's start with plotting the maximum performance line for 2012. These are the combinations of EBIT% and CCC, leading to the same EBIT/working capital ratio of 35.90%. To be able to plot that line, we again first need to do some maths. It starts by rewriting:

$$EBIT/working\ capital = EBIT/sales\ revenue$$
$$\times\ sales\ revenue/working\ capital$$

To introduce the CCC we further rewrite as:

$$EBIT/working\ capital = EBIT/sales\ revenue$$
$$\times\ sales\ revenue/(working\ capital/CCC) \times 1/CCC$$

Or when referring to the EBIT% as:

$$EBIT/working\ capital = EBIT\% \times sales\ revenue/(working\ capital/CCC)$$
$$\times 1/CCC$$

Table 4.3   Company 1 EBIT, working capital and EBIT/working capital for 2004–13

Company 1	2004	2005	2006	2007	2008
EBIT (in kEur)	71,427	52,008	60,687	68,314	8,903
Working capital (in kEur)	231,773	258,488	281,743	319,207	290,428
EBIT/working capital	30.82%	20.12%	21.54%	21.40%	3.07%

Company 1	2009	2010	2011	2012	2013
EBIT (in kEur)	(29,537)	45,135	78,359	100,238	79,024
Working capital (in kEur)	213,217	306,050	310,251	279,231	274,909
EBIT/working capital	–13.85%	14.75%	25.26%	35.90%	28.75%

When we solve EBIT% this gives:

$$EBIT\% = EBIT/working\ capital \times (working\ capital/CCC)/sales\ revenue \times CCC$$

We learn from this equation that as well as the EBIT/working capital and the CCC, we also need the sales revenue and the working capital/CCC to find the EBIT% corresponding with a given CCC. The working capital/CCC is the average value of one day of the CCC. Remember that the inventory and the payables are valued at the cost of goods sold, whereas the receivables are valued at the net sales. The working capital/CCC gives an average value of one day of working capital. For completeness, we have included the CCC, the resulting working capital/CCC and the sales revenue in Table 4.4.

Table 4.4 Company 1 EBIT, working capital, EBIT/working capital, CCC, working capital/CCC and sales revenue for 2004–2013

Company 1	2004	2005	2006	2007	2008
EBIT (in kEur)	71,427	52,008	60,687	68,314	8,903
Working capital (in kEur)	231,773	258,488	281,743	319,207	290,428
EBIT/working capital	30.82%	20.12%	21.54%	21.40%	3.07%
CCC	152.97	157.39	158.61	193.88	177.97
Working capital / CCC (in kEur)	1,515	1,642	1,776	1,646	1,632
Sales revenue (in kEur)	671,923	711,992	750,790	736,433	725,288

Company 1	2009	2010	2011	2012	2013
EBIT (in kEur)	(29,537)	45,135	78,359	100,238	79,024
Working capital (in kEur)	213,217	306,050	310,251	279,231	274,909
EBIT/working capital	−13.85%	14.75%	25.26%	35.90%	28.75%
CCC	139.10	144.70	127.30	102.78	102.04
Working capital / CCC (in kEur)	1,533	2,115	2,437	2,717	2,694
Sales revenue (in kEur)	638,066	896,999	1,041,244	1,155,984	1,158,015

From Table 4.4 we now have all the data required to calculate the maximum performance line for 2012. Suppose that the CCC would be 120 days, then the corresponding EBIT% follows from the above equation as:

EBIT% = 35.90% × (2 717)/1 155 984 × 120 = 10.12%

The actual CCC in 2012 was 103 days, the actual EBIT% was 8.67%. The calculation tells us that as an investor I'm OK with a higher working capital of 120 days, as long as the EBIT is going up to 10.12%. As we have calculated for 120 days of CCC, we can also calculate for 140, for 160 and going down for 80, or 60 and so on. If we replace the 35.90%, being the maximum performance for EBIT/working capital, with the minimum of –13.85% or the median of 21.40% (and the working capital/CCC and sales revenue of the corresponding years, 2009 and 2007 respectively), we can also plot the minimum and the median lines. The three lines based on company 1 are shown in Figure 4.5.

To understand how the 'bang-for-the-buck' lines can support target setting, let's again add the performance of company 1 for 2014. That is shown in Figure 4.6.

In 2014 performance dropped back on both the EBIT% and the CCC. EBIT% dropped from 6.82% in 2013 to 3.64% in 2014. The CCC increased from 102 days in 2013 to 128 days in 2014. The performance drop in the EBIT% versus CCC graph is in line with the performance drop seen in the EBIT% versus inventory turns shown in Figure 4.4.

Figure 4.5 Two-dimensional benchmark showing 'bang-for-the-buck' lines for EBIT% vs CCC, based on the MIN, MED, and MAX performance of company 1

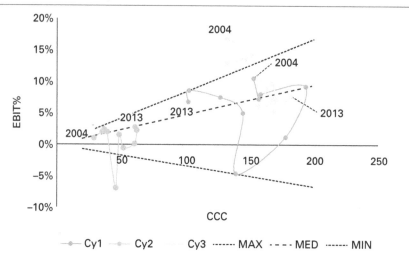

Figure 4.6 Two-dimensional benchmark showing 'bang-for-the-buck' lines for EBIT% vs CCC, adding the 2014 performance of company 1

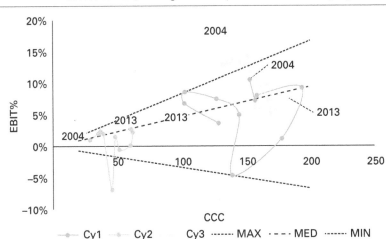

Again, a bad year will increase the tension when setting targets for the next year. Figure 4.7 shows 2 options when setting targets for 2015 (at the end of 2014).

Option 1 could be to go straight up. If we stick to the current CCC of 128 days, the EBIT% would need to improve to around 11%. Option 2 could be to go left up, back in the direction of the 2013 performance, towards an EBIT of around 8%, for a CCC of 95 days.

Figure 4.7 Two possible targets for EBIT% vs CCC for company 1, based on the MAX performance line

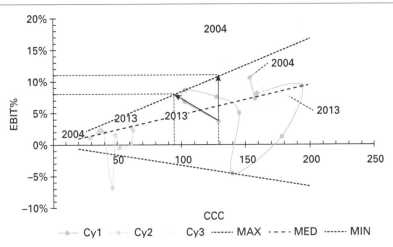

Which option would you prefer? Chances are you'd go for option 2. Improving on the two dimensions at the same time seems more manageable. Getting back to the 2013 performance seems logical. Again, in the next chapter we will argue that the choice is not random, but in fact a choice of strategy. Before we dig into the strategy, let's first do an exercise and then continue with analysing the 'bang-for-the-buck' lines for the EBIT% versus fixed asset turns.

Exercise: Setting targets using the 'bang-for-the-buck' lines in the EBIT% versus CCC graph

In Chapter 3 we have constructed the EBIT% versus CCC graphs for our company and five key competitors. Let's add the 'bang-for-the-buck' lines for the EBIT/working capital.

This starts by summarizing the EBIT, the working capital, and the EBIT/ working capital ratio for your chosen reference company, as we have shown for company 1 in Table 4.3.

Start from the year with the maximum performance. Make a table with different levels of the CCC in the first column, let's say 30 to 150, in steps of five. In the second column, you calculate the corresponding EBIT% using this formula:

EBIT% = EBIT/Working capital x (Working capital/CCC1) / Sales revenue x CCC2

For reasons of clarity I have labelled the CCC as CCC1 and CCC2 respectively. Remember that working capital/CCC1 is the average value of one day of the CCC, for your chosen reference company, in the chosen year. If the working capital was £120 million and the CCC1 was 120, than the ratio is 1 million.

The CCC2 is the CCC for which you want to calculate the EBIT%, which is taken from the first column of your table, and which will be different from the CCC1 (which is the CCC in the reference year for the reference company). The sales revenue is also taken from the reference year of your reference company. The EBIT/working capital is the maximum ratio for the chosen year. Using this expression, you can calculate the EBIT% corresponding with each CCC.

Do the same for the minimum and the median EBIT/working capital years to calculate the minimum and median performance lines.

Plot the maximum, median and minimum performance lines on your two-dimensional EBIT% versus CCC benchmarks, as we've shown in Figure 4.6.

Does the actual performance of your chosen company fit nicely between the minimum and the maximum performance? Do you see straight lines like the ones shown in Figure 4.6? What is your last year performance? How can you connect it to the maximum performance line? What if you go straight up? What if you go left and up? To which types of targets does it lead? How do these targets compare to the targets you currently have in place? Which targets seem the most realistic?

Adding 'bang-for-the-buck' lines in an EBIT% versus fixed asset turns graph

Let's try to plot the 'bang-for-the-buck' lines in the EBIT% versus fixed asset turns graph, as we did in the previous sections for the inventory turns and the CCC. We will again use company 1 as the reference.

Table 4.5 shows the EBIT, the fixed assets and the EBIT/fixed assets for company 1 over the period 2004–13. 2011 has the highest performance, with a ratio of 0.29. It is striking that many years come close to that maximum, 2004 with 0.28, 2006 with 0.26, 2007 with 0.28, and 2012 with 0.28. We will use the 0.21 of 2005 as the median performance, and the –0.15 of 2009 as the minimum performance.

If we want to plot the 'bang-for-the-buck' lines, as before, we'll need to do some maths, though the maths is now relatively easy. We want to find the combinations of EBIT% and fixed asset turns leading to a given ratio of EBIT/fixed assets, for instance the maximum performance of 0.29. We can find those by first rewriting:

Table 4.5 Company 1 EBIT, fixed assets and EBIT/fixed assets for 2004–2015

Company 1	2004	2005	2006	2007	2008
EBIT	71,427	52,008	60,687	68,314	8,903
Fixed assets	251,287	251,340	232,376	240,376	230,565
EBIT/fixed assets	0.28	0.21	0.26	0.28	0.04

Company 1	2009	2010	2011	2012	2013
EBIT	(29,537)	45,135	78,359	100,238	79,024
Fixed assets	203,645	236,431	270,751	359,719	449,702
EBIT/fixed assets	(0.15)	0.19	0.29	0.28	0.18

$EBIT/fixed\ assets = EBIT/sales\ revenue \times sales\ revenue/fixed\ assets$

Which leads to:

$EBIT/fixed\ assets = EBIT\% \times fixed\ asset\ turns$

Or when solving for the EBIT%:

$EBIT\% = EBIT/fixed\ assets \times 1/fixed\ asset\ turns$

Let's apply it to an example. The EBIT% in 2011 was 7.53%, with a fixed asset turn of 3.85. As an investor, I would be indifferent if company 1 needed some more fixed assets – let's say the asset turns would be only 3 instead of 3.85 – as long as that is compensated by a higher EBIT. More specifically, the target EBIT is found by solving the EBIT% from the above equation as EBIT% = $0.29 \times 1/3 = 9.67\%$.

In the same way we can find the EBIT% for turns of 2 or 1, or up to 4 or 5. If instead of the maximum performance of 0.29, we substitute the median performance of 0.21 or the minimum performance of –0.15 this will give us the median and the minimum performance lines. They are shown in Figure 4.8.

We already saw in the previous chapter that the fixed asset turns performance of company 1 is superior to that of company 2 and company 3.

Figure 4.8 Two-dimensional benchmark showing the 'bang-for-the-buck' lines for EBIT% vs fixed asset turns, based on the MIN, MED, and MAX performance of company 1

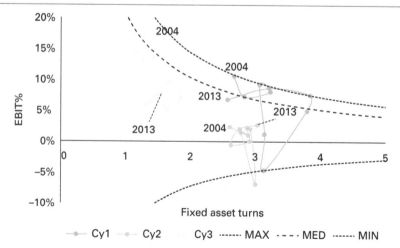

Company 2 has turns between 2.5 and 3, but has significantly lower EBIT% levels. Company 3 has asset turns between 1 and 2, but cannot compensate for that with a higher EBIT, except in the period 2004–07, but as explained in the previous chapter, that performance is non-sustainable, driven by a cut back on spending rather than a superior premium.

Figure 4.8 further shows that company 1 has been quite consistent in its EBIT% versus fixed asset turns performance. Eight of the 10 years are close to or in the median to maximum performance zone, whereas neither of the other two competitors is near to that zone.

Figure 4.9 has again added the 2014 performance of company 1. We see a comparable drop in performance as we have seen with the inventory turns and the CCC. EBIT% drops back from 6.82% to 3.64%. The fixed asset turns drop back from 2.58 to 2.27. This is fully opposite to the direction we'd like to go.

Figure 4.10 again uses the maximum performance line to define two possible targets. 1 is straight up, sticking to the fixed asset turns of 2.27 and increasing the EBIT% to around 12.5%. 1 is right and up, back in the direction of the 2013 performance, with fixed asset turns of 2.9 and an EBIT% of around 10%. Again, improving in the two dimensions at the same time seems the easiest. In the next chapter we will argue that the choice of going straight up or right and up is in fact a choice of strategy.

Figure 4.9   Two-dimensional benchmark showing the 'bang-for-the-buck' lines for EBIT% vs fixed asset turns, adding the 2014 performance of company 1

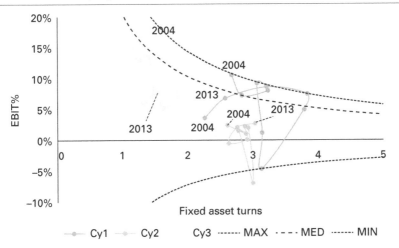

Figure 4.10   Two possible targets for EBIT% vs fixed asset turns for company 1, based on the MAX performance line

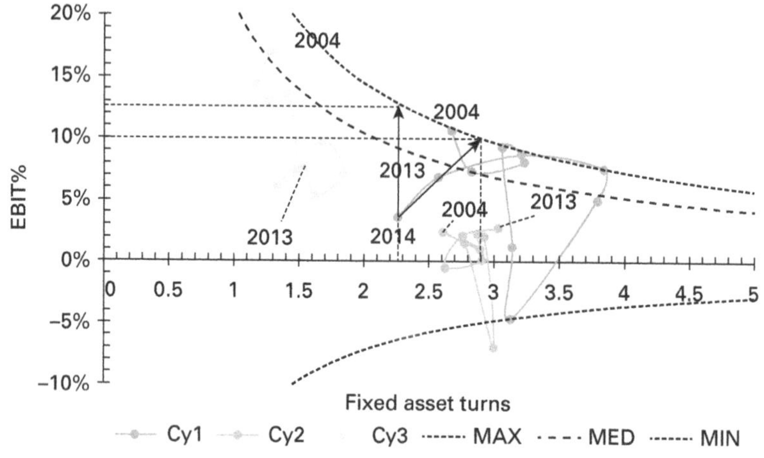

Exercise: Setting targets using the 'bang-for-the-buck' lines in the EBIT% versus fixed asset turns graph

This exercise should have become routine by now! Let's add the 'bang-for-the-buck' lines for the EBIT/fixed assets.

Calculating the 'bang-for-the-buck' lines for the EBIT/fixed assets starts with summarizing the EBIT, the fixed assets, and the EBIT/fixed assets ratio for your chosen reference company, as we showed for company 1 in Table 4.5.

Start from the year with the maximum performance. Make a table with different levels of the fixed asset turns in the first column, let's say 0.5 to 5, in steps of 0.5. In the second column, you calculate the corresponding EBIT% using the formula EBIT% = EBIT/fixed assets x 1/fixed asset turns.

The EBIT/fixed assets is the maximum ratio you've taken from your table. The fixed asset turns are listed in your first column. You calculate the EBIT% in your second column. Do the same for the minimum and the median EBIT/fixed assets years to calculate the minimum and median performance lines.

Plot the minimum, median and maximum performance lines on your two-dimensional EBIT% versus fixed asset turns graphs, as we showed in Figure 4.9. Does the actual performance of your chosen company fit nicely between the minimum and the maximum performance? Do you see exponential lines as the ones shown in Figure 4.9? What was your performance last year? How can you connect it to the max curve? To which types of targets does that lead? Which one seems the most realistic?

Conclusion

In this chapter we have added so-called 'indifference' or 'bang-for-the-buck' lines to our two-dimensional benchmark graphs. We have looked at the combinations of EBIT% and inventory turns, leading to a minimum, median and maximum EBIT per inventory dollar. We have looked at the combinations of EBIT% and CCC, leading to a minimum, median and maximum EBIT / working capital ratio. Finally we have looked at the combinations of EBIT% and fixed asset turns, leading to a minimum, median and maximum EBIT / fixed assets ratio.

Plotting the minimum, median and maximum 'bang-for-the-buck' lines has required some maths, which can seem hard and cumbersome.

The maths is the hard and cumbersome part. The interesting part is that the maximum line can be used as a reference for target setting. In summary, going 'straight up' has led to the following 2015 targets for company 1: stay at inventory turns of 3, improve EBIT% back to 10%; stick to the CCC of 128 days, improve EBIT% to around 11%; and stick to the fixed asset turns of 2.27 and increase EBIT% to around 12.5%. We can of course target only one EBIT level, so a consensus could be to target an EBIT% of 11% and calculate the corresponding inventory turns, CCC and fixed asset turns from the corresponding maximum performance curves.

A second option was to go back in the direction of the 2013 performance. In the inventory turns and the fixed asset turns graph, that was going right and up. In the CCC graph that was going left and up. The corresponding 2015 targets for company 1 are: improve inventory turns to 4.5 while improving EBIT% to around 7%; improve the CCC to 95 days, and the EBIT% towards 8%; improve the asset turns to 2.9, and the EBIT% to 10%. Again, we cannot target multiple EBIT% levels. For a combined improvement, we might fix the 8% EBIT and calculate the corresponding inventory turns, CCC and fixed asset turns from the corresponding maximum performance curves.

What should be clear from this is that we define targets for a set of KPIs, EBIT%, inventory turns, CCC and fixed asset turns in the above. In one-dimensional benchmarking we analyse each of the KPIs individually and set targets individually. Remember from the ROCE principle that it is OK to have some more capital employed as long as the EBIT is higher. Two-dimensional benchmarking contains this type of trade-off, the one-dimensional benchmark does not. In a one-dimensional benchmark the target for the inventory turns may be realistic, but not in combination with the EBIT% target, and vice versa.

In the next chapter we will show that 'going straight up' or 'going right and up' (or 'left and up') is not a random choice, but a choice of strategy. In that chapter we will also use the minimum, median and maximum performance lines to separate the leaders from the average performers and the laggards. Setting targets will be about picking the maximum performance targets that fit your strategy, knowing the leaders in your strategy and trying to apply their best practices to close any performance gap with them.

The impact of strategy on financial benchmarking and target setting

05

In the previous chapter we took the two-dimensional benchmarks from Chapter 3 and added the 'indifference' or 'bang-for-the-buck' lines, showing the minimum, the median and the maximum performance of company 1 as the chosen reference company. We had to do some maths to come to the appropriate equations for the EBIT% versus inventory turns, EBIT% versus CCC and EBIT% versus fixed asset turns. Thanks to the maths, we have been able to plot a maximum performance line on each of the graphs and use that MAX line to derive potential targets for company 1, for 2015, after observing the 2014 performance.

We came up with two options to connect to the MAX line; the first was going straight up, sticking to the current inventory turns, CCC or fixed asset turns and fully improving on the EBIT%. A second option was to go right and up (or left and up for the CCC graph), improving on two dimensions at the same time.

In this chapter, we will show that going straight up versus right and up (or left and up for the CCC graph) is in fact a strategic choice. We will map Treacy and Wiersema's (1995) three strategic options to our benchmark graphs to clarify that, and to show how strategy affects the target setting for a set of financial KPIs.

Mapping Treacy and Wiersema to the EBIT% vs inventory turns graphs

Company 1's choice between product leadership and customer intimacy

Let's start by revisiting the choice of company 1, based on its own 'maximum performance line' for EBIT% versus inventory turns. As shown in Figure 5.1, the choice was to stay at inventory turns of 3, and improve EBIT back to 10%, as in 2004, or to improve inventory turns to 4.5 while improving EBIT to around 7%.

Company 1 is the Belgian technology company Barco, one of our case studies from Chapter 2. As discussed in Chapter 2, Barco went through a shift in strategy from product leadership to customer intimacy. In the period 2004–07 Barco qualified as a typical product leader, focused on high-end visualization products, for specific niches. That position is confirmed by the superior gross margins in that period, as shown in Figure 3.6. The inventory turns in that period were consistently around 2.5 to 3. From that perspective, option 1, staying with turns of 3, and going for a 10% EBIT, is in fact reclaiming that position as a product leader.

As described in Chapter 2, and as seen in their annual reports, Barco had decided to shift from a product leadership into a customer intimacy position, trying to drive value from mid-market products as well as high-end niches.

Figure 5.1 Two possible targets for EBIT% vs inventory turns for company 1, based on the MAX performance line

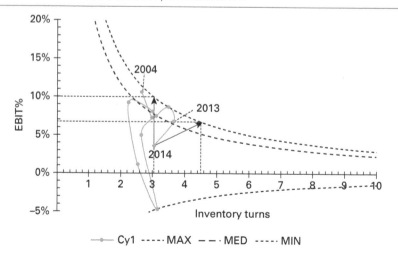

We know that gross margins in the mid-market will be lower, which is confirmed by the drop in gross margin in Figure 3.6. To sustain EBIT, that requires a cut in selling, general and administrative (SG&A) costs, which we saw in Figure 3.7.

To sustain the return on capital employed (ROCE), we needed to cut in inventory or more generally in working capital, which was on the right track till 2013, but on which we took a serious step backwards in 2014.

The danger with the Barco strategy, as presented in its 2013 report, is that we try to be active in both the niches and the mid-market. That means that instead of cutting back on complexity, we keep the complexity of the niche products, and at the same time we further expand it by adding the mid-market products. Expecting inventory to go down in that situation may be unrealistic. Initiatives to reduce inventory may be unsustainable.

A customer intimacy position is based on creating a total solution for the customer. Instead of having only the best, we try to offer a full range. Given that the EBIT drawn from a customer intimacy position is lower than that of a product leadership position, we need to make sure that we can expand the range, while reducing the capital employed, so reducing the inventory. That is challenging.

As such, making the switch really requires cuts in the 'old' business. While Barco still seemed to be struggling to do so in 2014, it did so in 2015. In the beginning of 2015 it divested one of the most complex divisions, its defence and avionics business. Figure 5.2 shows how that helped the 2015 performance. In 2015, the EBIT grew to 4.97%, and the inventory turns to 4.03. This is close to the median 'bang-for-the-buck', but still falls too short on both to classify as a top performance.

Figure 5.2 2015 performance of company 1 vs its two possible targets

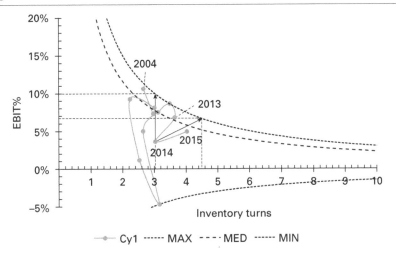

So where option 1, going straight up, was about reclaiming the product leadership position, this example should illustrate that option 2, going right and up, is in fact about continuing the change towards a customer intimacy position. The combined target of 7% EBIT and inventory turns of 4.5 seems to be confirmed by the 2015 figures. The direction is exactly that, though the actual performance is still not there, which may be OK if you're still changing strategy.

In the next section we will generalize the findings from the Barco example and define multiple strategic positions in our two-dimensional benchmark graphs. We will also differentiate the leaders from the laggards, which will help in further refining the target setting.

Visualizing Treacy and Wiersema's three strategies on the two-dimensional benchmarks

Based on the Barco performance we have identified a product leadership position and a customer intimacy position in Figure 5.2. The next step is defining a (potential) operational excellence position. Looking back at Figure 3.6, the logical candidate for the opex position is company 2, as company 2 is working at the lowest gross margins. From the detailed analysis of the working capital in Chapter 3, we still have doubts on how sustainable the inventory turns of company 2 are. Most probably company 2 has been consistently lowering inventories to compensate a growth in receivables and a decline in payables. In pushing for turns of 10, company 2 may have taken inventory turns to an extreme.

Aside from the inventory turns, it is clear that to be a true operational excellence leader, company 2 needs to improve on its EBIT, and get closer to the MAX performance line. Out of the three, company 2 is certainly the most extreme in working at a lower EBIT, and compensating for that by employing less capital, which is what we'd expect an opex player to do.

Figure 5.3 summarizes those three strategic positions.

The product leadership position is 'straight up' (from the 2014 reference point of company 1), aiming for turns around 3 with an EBIT around 10%. The customer intimacy position is 'up right' (again from the 2014 reference point of company 1), aiming for turns around 4.5 with an EBIT around 7%. The operational excellence position is at the far right – it allows an EBIT of 3.5%, which is half the EBIT of the customer intimacy player, but it requires a doubling of the turns from 4.5 to 9.

Let's cross check our model by adding extra companies. In Figure 5.4 we have added three extra companies, coming to a total of six. These are the same six companies shown in our original inventory benchmark of Figure 3.1.

Figure 5.3　Visualizing the three strategic positions on our two-dimensional EBIT vs inventory turns graph

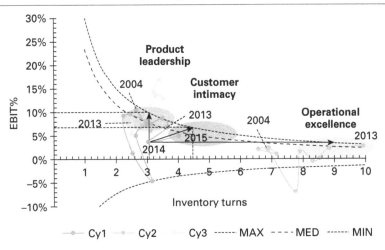

Figure 5.4　Cross-checking the strategic positioning by extending the benchmark to six companies

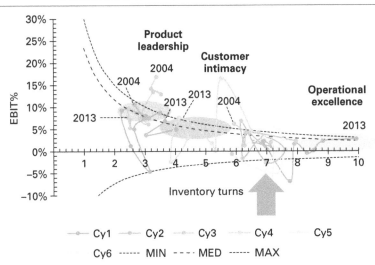

The product leadership and customer intimacy position seem confirmed, with company 4 filling the customer intimacy space and making a shift from the right to the left. The MAX performance curve of company 1 is exceeded three times by company 4 and two times by company 6. That pleads for shifting the MAX curve a little up.

The biggest question mark after adding the extra companies is the positioning of operational excellence. Only after adding the extra companies do we see a clear gap between the opex and the customer intimacy position. Company 5 and 6 have a quite consistent positioning exactly in that gap. Add that to the doubts we had on whether the inventory turns of company 2 are really sustainable it seems logical to shift the target position of the opex player to the left, as shown in Figure 5.5.

So the main adjustment of cross-checking with extra companies is shifting the position of the operational excellence leader. Instead of targeting turns of 9 with an EBIT of 3.5%, we have adapted that to turns of 7.5 with an EBIT of 4%. That seems a better fit with the broader data set.

Let's now take a minute to compare the conclusions of Figure 5.5 with the conclusions from our original inventory benchmark shown in Figure 3.1. Again, when benchmarking in only one dimension, it is attractive to go for the top performance, which in this case would land us a target for inventory turns of around 7 to 8. When accounting for the strategic context, a target for company 3, assuming the chosen strategy remains product leadership, could be target turns of 3. But it is highly unlikely that anyone would pick a target of 3 turns after referring to Figure 3.1. in fact, from Figure 3.1, picking 3 seems like picking the worst performance.

We hope that by reviewing this example, the reader will never, ever again allow a one-dimensional benchmark for the businesses where he or she is involved!

Figure 5.5   Adjusted positioning of the opex player in our two-dimensional benchmark

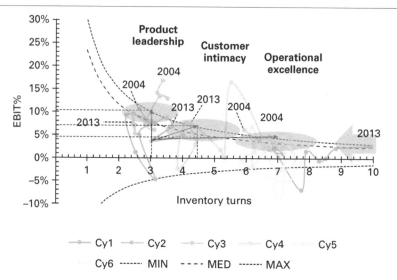

Exercise: Plotting the three strategies on your two-dimensional benchmark

As in Figure 5.5, try to define, on the maximum performance line, which seem the likely EBIT versus inventory turns positions for a product leader, for a customer intimacy and for an operational excellence player.

Remember that the gross margin may be a good indicator of that strategic positioning. The product leader derives the highest premium from offering their unique products to niche markets. That results in a superior gross margin. The operational excellence leader will work at the lowest gross margin and a lower EBIT, and compensate for that by having less working capital and fewer fixed assets.

Do the numbers match with your perception? Are the perceived product leaders really delivering the expected premium? Is the extra complexity visible in the higher working capital and the higher fixed assets? Answer the same questions for the customer intimacy and the operational excellence players.

Separating leaders from laggards

The next step is using the bang-for-the-buck lines to separate leaders from laggards. We show a conservative approach in Figure 5.6, defining a performance between the median and the maximum performance as leading. Any performance with negative EBIT we have classified as a non-performance. We have split the remaining positive EBIT zone into a laggard zone and an average zone.

Regardless of the exact positioning of the zones, we see that most of the companies in our benchmark make big swings. All of them have performed in each of the zones.

In Figure 5.7 we have reduced the variance by taking a three-year average of the EBIT% and the inventory turns. This more clearly shows the course each of the companies is following.

For company 1 we see a deep dip, caused by the financial crisis, a recovery, and then a gradual shift right, where EBIT is clearly lagging below target. Company 2 has been slightly recovering from a lagging performance for almost 10 years. Its current pressure on inventory may be too high and be a risk for the turnover and for the EBIT.

The performance of company 3 has been gradually degrading. Its exceptional performance in the period 2004–07 has been driven by significant

Figure 5.6 Three strategic options in the two-dimensional benchmark graphs, differentiating the leaders from the laggards

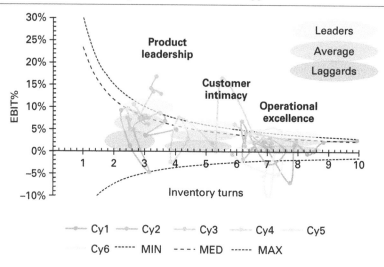

Figure 5.7 Two-dimensional benchmark showing three-year averages

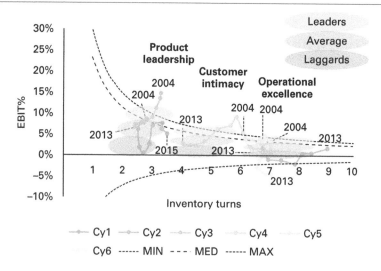

underspending. It may still be paying the price for that period of underinvesting. Company 4 is steadily moving left, but the EBIT is not following suit.

Company 5 has been swinging between turns of 6 to 7. Its EBIT has gradually degraded. Company 6 has been even more consistent in its turns, but has almost literally fallen off the chart, starting from EBIT levels of around 5% to consistently negative EBIT levels. The general picture is one of a sector under pressure. There's not a lot of good news among the six companies!

'Continuous improvement' versus 'experimenting with breakthrough technology' versus 'strategic choices'

When setting targets, it is common for companies to set targets where we improve on all metrics at the same time. We will grow the business, improve profitability, reduce working capital, and better leverage our existing assets. That is possible ... if you are lagging behind. This is illustrated in Figure 5.8.

For laggards or even average performers, it is possible to improve both on inventory turns and on EBIT. Companies do so by adopting so-called 'best practices'. These are practices with a proven benefit. Most of these best practices are applicable regardless of the chosen strategy. Examples are the implementation of sales and operations planning (S&OP), cutting down on 'bad complexity' (SKUs where the margin is not covering the costs for inventory and changeovers), implementing multi-echelon planning (synchronizing different steps in the supply chain), and postponement and modular design (which help in handling more complexity, but with less inventory and less disruption in your operations). If you have not done these, you should, because some of your competitors already have, and if they did, their performance is likely to exceed yours.

Improving on both dimensions at the same time is more difficult for companies that are close to the MAX line. In her book *Supply Chain Metrics That Matter*, Lora Cecere talks about the 'efficiency frontier'. I like to call it the 'best practice frontier'. It is the performance that companies achieve after having implemented all available best practices. It corresponds with the MAX line in our benchmarks.

Figure 5.8 Improving on both EBIT and inventory turns through best practices

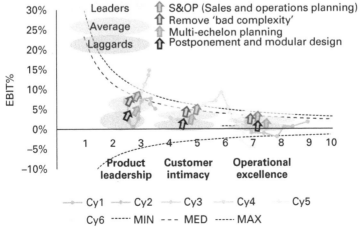

To improve on both dimensions at the same time, companies on that frontier will need to shift it. This could for instance be done by successfully adopting new breakthrough technologies like 3D printing, robotics, autonomous driving or advanced analytics like demand sensing or leading indicator forecasting. New technologies have a higher risk. So the leaders will require a culture of experimentation and innovation to sort out which technologies are really delivering on their promise and which ones don't.

Figure 5.9 shows the best practice frontier and how best-in-class companies shift it by experimenting with breakthrough technologies.

Figure 5.10 shows the difference with strategic trade-offs. A strategic choice makes you shift along the best practice frontier. Instead of improving at both dimensions at the same time, you target progress on one dimension while giving in on a second dimension.

Switching from product leadership to customer intimacy will result in a lower EBIT, but can be compensated by an increase in inventory turns. Or vice versa, switching from customer intimacy to product leadership may require more inventory, which can be compensated for by a higher EBIT.

So where continuous improvement allows improving on both inventory turns and EBIT, at the same time, by the adoption of best practices, a strategic choice will result in an improvement in one dimension at the expense of the other. The only way to avoid that is the application of breakthrough technologies which shift the best practice frontier.

Figure 5.9   Shifting the best practice frontier with breakthrough technologies

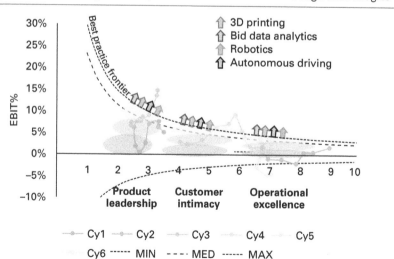

Figure 5.10   Improving on inventory turns at the expense of EBIT, as a consequence of a change in strategy

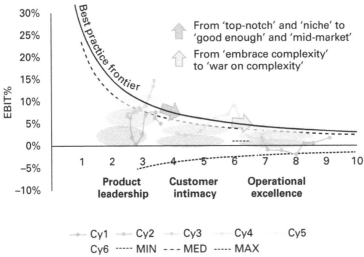

As in Chapter 3 and 4, let's try to make a comparable analysis for the EBIT% versus CCC and the EBIT% versus fixed asset turns.

Exercise: Separating the leaders from the laggards; revealing strategic moves

As in Figure 5.6, try to plot zones for the leaders, the average performers and the laggards. As we did, you may consider the negative EBIT% as a non-performance. As we've done in Figure 5.7, you may use three-year averages for the EBIT% and the inventory turns to reduce some of the variance.

What do you observe? Who are the true leaders? Who are the laggards? Which companies have improved their position?

As shown in Figure 5.10, a strategic move may mean you improve in one dimension and deliberately give in on the second. Do you see any companies shifting strategic position from product leader to customer intimacy, or vice versa? From operational excellence to customer intimacy, or vice versa? Have any of these shifts been announced in financial reports? Are the announced shifts visible in the financial performance?

Mapping Treacy and Wiersema to the EBIT% vs CCC graphs

Let's again start by recapping the choice we were facing in the EBIT% versus CCC graphs for our company 1. As shown in Figure 5.11, at the end of 2014 we had two basic options in setting targets for 2015. Option 1 was to go straight up, sticking to the CCC of 128 days, and improving the EBIT% to around 11%. Option 2 was to go left up, back in the direction of the 2013 performance, towards an EBIT of around 8%, for a CCC of 95 days.

We will plot our three strategic positions, for the product leader, customer intimacy and operational excellence players, by starting from the target EBIT levels of 10%, 7% and 4%, as identified from the analysis of the EBIT% versus inventory turns. Figure 5.12 shows the corresponding CCC positions are 120 days, 75 days and 50 days.

Again, for company 1, going straight up, sticking to the CCC of 128 days, and improving the EBIT% to around 11% corresponds with reclaiming its product leadership position. Option 2, going left and up towards an EBIT of around 8%, for a CCC of 95 days, is claiming the customer intimacy position.

Figure 5.13 shows the 2015 performance of company 1. With an EBIT% of 4.97% and a CCC of 81 days, it has shifted in the direction of the customer intimacy position, in line with the strategy shift described in the previous section and Chapter 2. The CCC has improved significantly, whereas the EBIT% is lagging below the 7% target.

Figure 5.11 Two possible targets for EBIT% vs CCC for company 1, based on the MAX performance line

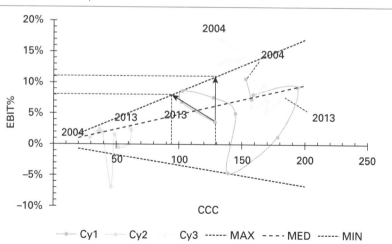

Figure 5.12 Visualizing the three strategic positions on our two-dimensional EBIT vs CCC graph

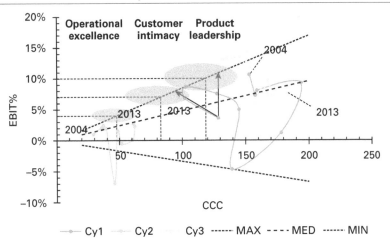

Figure 5.13 Company 1's 2015 performance on the EBIT% vs CCC graph in the direction of customer intimacy

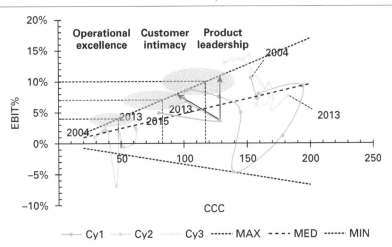

In Figure 5.14 we have again extended the benchmark to our six companies. We see the move from company 1 from product leadership to customer intimacy. We see a move from company 4 from operational excellence to product leadership. We see companies 2, 5 and 6 in the operational excellence area. We see company 3 going in the wrong direction, with an increasing CCC and a decrease in EBIT%.

Figure 5.14 Deriving strategic positions and targets for the three strategies on the EBIT vs CCC graphs

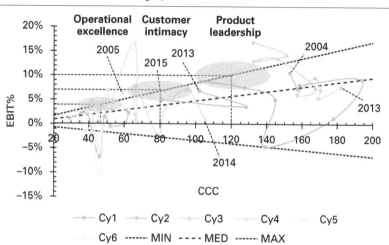

As with the inventory graphs, we can again use the median and the maximum 'bang-for-the-buck' lines to separate the leaders from the rest of the pack. We have again built up from the 0% EBIT to define positions for laggards and average performers, as shown in Figure 5.15.

As in the inventory graphs, we again see important swings in the year-on-year performance of individual companies. All of them have points in the lagging, the average and the leading performance zone. In Figure 5.16 we have again taken three-year averages to take out some of that variance and more clearly identify the underlying trends.

Figure 5.15 Separating leaders from laggards on the EBIT vs CCC graphs

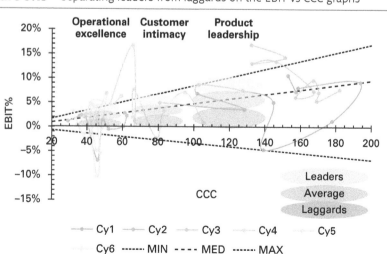

Figure 5.16 Analysing the three-year average performance to reveal trends on the EBIT vs CCC graphs

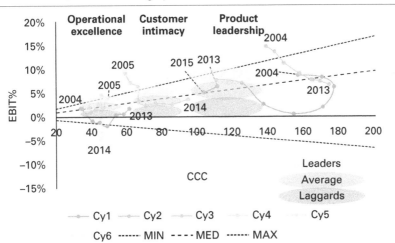

Figure 5.16 confirms our findings from the inventory graph in Figure 5.7. Company 1 is gradually but steadily on its way towards the customer intimacy position. From the CCC analysis it appears that company 2 is doing the same, but from an operational excellence position. The EBIT performance of company 2 has been below target for the last 10 years, so there is a big challenge.

The performance of company 3 seems to be going nowhere. When averaging out, company 4 is seen to gradually shift to a product leadership position, rather than a customer intimacy position. Companies 5 and 6 stay in their operational excellence position, with company 5 making circles around the median performance, and company 6 gradually falling off the chart with a growing EBIT problem.

Looking at these conclusions, we see that the 'trends' identified from the inventory chart are largely confirmed, but at the same time, looking at the CCC identifies nuances. We primarily get a clearer view on the positions of companies 1 and 4. So which one should we use? Which one do we need?

We encourage companies to use both. Certainly as a manufacturer you'll need to define targets for your inventory. The two-dimensional benchmarks for the EBIT versus inventory turns, accounting for the strategy, is the best we have seen. The benchmarks with the CCC take a somewhat broader perspective and will cancel out any games that companies might be playing with inventories versus receivables and payables. Conclusions drawn about where companies are and where they are heading are more solid when having looked from both angles.

However, the work is not yet finished. We still need to look at the fixed assets, which are the third important component of the capital employed. As mentioned in Chapter 4, each of the three – inventory, working capital and fixed assets – are important in understanding the ROCE. We will analyse the EBIT versus fixed asset turns in the next section.

Exercise: Adding strategic positions to the EBIT% versus CCC graphs

Based on your analysis of the EBIT% and the CCC from the previous chapter, now try to define the target position, on the maximum performance line, for the product leader, the customer intimacy and the operational excellence player, as we have shown in Figure 5.12. You may use our trick in starting from the three EBIT levels you have defined in the EBIT% versus inventory turns graphs, and looking at which CCC corresponds with those EBIT levels (10%, 7% and 4% in our case, leading to 120, 75 and 50 days of CCC respectively).

Take your last year's performance, and compare it to the target within the applicable strategy. How challenging is the target? How does it compare to your current target?

Plot three zones for the leaders, the average performers and the laggards, as we did in Figure 5.15. As we did, you may consider a negative EBIT as a non-performance and build from the zero EBIT upward. You may use three-year averages for the EBIT% and the CCC to reduce some of the variance in the year-on-year results, as we have done in Figure 5.16.

What do you see? Which companies are leading and which ones are lagging? Which ones have improved their performance and which have slipped back? Do you notice any changes in strategy, companies moving from the right to the left or vice versa? Are the results in line with the results from the inventory analysis?

Mapping Treacy and Wiersema to the EBIT% vs fixed asset turns graph

Figure 5.17 restates our target setting question for company 1 at the end of 2014.

Option 1 was to go straight up, by sticking to the fixed asset turns of 2.27 and increasing the EBIT% to around 12.5%. Option 2 was to go up and right, improving to fixed asset turns of 2.85 and an EBIT% of around 10%.

Figure 5.17 Two possible targets for EBIT% vs fixed asset turns for company 1, based on the MAX performance line

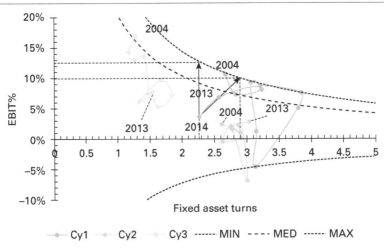

As in the previous section, let's start from the EBIT% targets for the three strategic positions, as derived in the EBIT% versus inventory turns graph. These were 10%, 7% and 5% for the product leader, customer intimacy and operational excellence player. Figure 5.18 shows the corresponding target fixed asset turns to be 3, 4 and 7 respectively.

It also shows that the option 1 and option 2 as laid out above, sticking to the fixed asset turns of 2.27 and increasing the EBIT% to around 12.5%, or improving to fixed asset turns of 2.85 and an EBIT% of around 10%, are both corresponding with a product leadership position. If company 1 wants to go for a customer intimacy position, it would rather need to double its fixed asset turns to 4, for an EBIT or around 7%.

Figure 5.18 Visualizing the three strategic positions on our two-dimensional EBIT vs fixed asset turns graph

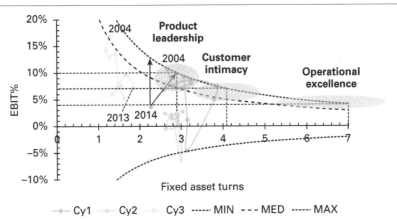

In Figure 5.19 we have again added the 2015 performance of company 1.

We see a step in the direction of the customer intimacy position, but the step is much smaller compared to the step seen in Figure 5.13, showing the EBIT% versus the CCC. Company 1 has been very successful in controlling its working capital, but it has not been able to better leverage its existing assets. Actually, to improve the asset turns it is quite likely you need to sell and shed some of your assets. Remember that the EBIT% comes down when switching from a product leadership to a customer intimacy position. If you need to double your asset turns, with the existing assets, it means you need to more than double the turnover. Selling some of the assets then seems a more realistic scenario.

Figure 5.20, like before, extends our benchmark to the six companies. The analysis is worrisome, as none of the companies except company 1 seems to be close to the median, much less the maximum performance line.

As before, we can cluster the leaders closer to the maximum performance line, and separate them from the average and the laggards, building up from the 0% EBIT line. This is shown in Figure 5.21. This further confirms the important challenge for each of the companies in the benchmark. We'll review and discuss them one by one.

Company 1, on the one hand is doing well, even exceptionally, as it is by far outperforming all other companies in the benchmark. On the other hand, as mentioned above, it will need to get to asset turns of around 4 if it truly wants to claim the position of a customer intimacy player. That challenge is shown in Figure 5.22. That performance is possible, as it is comparable to its 2012 results.

Figure 5.19 Company 1's 2015 performance on the EBIT% vs fixed asset turns graph in the direction of customer intimacy

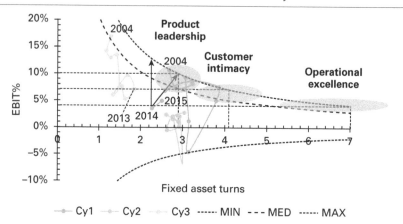

Figure 5.20 Deriving strategic positions and targets for the three strategies on the EBIT vs CCC graphs

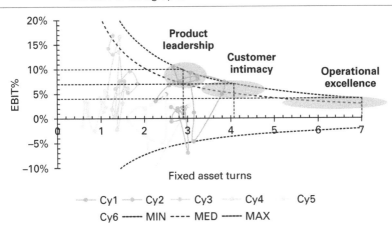

Figure 5.21 Separating leaders from laggards on the EBIT vs fixed asset turns graph

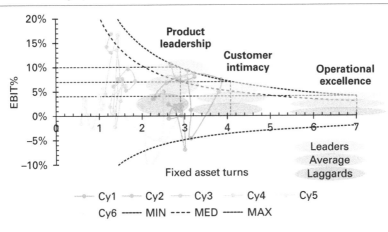

Figure 5.22 The challenge for company 1 on improving in the combined EBIT% and fixed asset turns performance

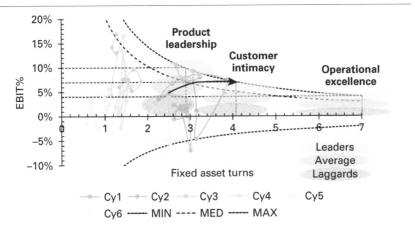

To analyse the challenge for the companies 2 to 6, we have first taken the three-year averages to more clearly indicate the trend for each of the companies, as shown in Figure 5.23.

Company 2 has been quite consistent, with fixed asset turns of around 3. From the EBIT% versus CCC analysis in Figure 5.16, it seemed as if company 2 was gradually shifting towards a customer intimacy position. If that is indeed the target, for its fixed asset turns, it would need to improve to a position of at least 4, which is a step change.

The most logical step for company 3 seems to be to reclaim a product leadership position, which would require an increase in fixed asset turns from around 1.5 to around 3. From the EBIT% versus CCC analysis in Figure 5.16, company 4 was showing progress towards a product leadership position. On the fixed asset turns, that should result in a shift from around 1.5 to around 3.

For companies 5 and 6, really claiming the opex position requires a drastic increase from their current turns of 0.5 and 3 to around 7, while at the same time improving on the EBIT. These companies obviously have the biggest challenge.

The challenge for each of the companies seems so big that we can question whether it is 'correct'. Let's revisit how we came to the benchmark. The benchmark is the maximum performance line of company 1. The maximum EBIT/fixed assets was realized in 2011, as shown in Table 4.5. Remember from Table 4.5 that this level of performance was reached in 2004, 2007, 2011 and 2012. Let's also remind ourselves from Figure 5.21 that these years are all close to or on the maximum performance line. Though a stretch for all of the companies in the benchmark, company 1 has certainly shown some consistency in reaching the target performance.

Figure 5.23   The challenge for companies 2–6 on improving in the combined EBIT% and fixed asset turns performance

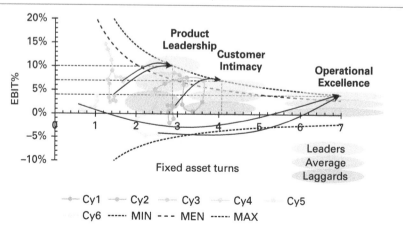

Next, in Figure 5.24 we have recapped the resulting ROCE for companies 1 to 6.

We see that in 2004, 2011 and 2012, company 1 is reaching a ROCE of 14–15%. We consider 15% ROCE as the benchmark we want to put forward. As such, it shows that company 1 will have to improve on its asset turns if it wants to restore its 15% ROCE levels. It also confirms that all other companies in the benchmark do indeed have an important challenge in increasing fixed asset turns, to increase ROCE levels in the direction of the 15% target.

Finally, to get rid of some of the year-on-year variability and be able to show the longer term trends, we have summarized the three-year average ROCE in Figure 5.25. It allows us to summarize the challenges for each of the companies.

Figure 5.24 The ROCE for companies 1 to 6 for the period 2004–14

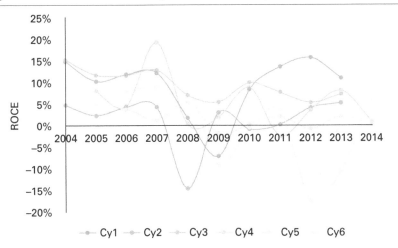

Figure 5.25 The three-year average ROCE for our six technology companies

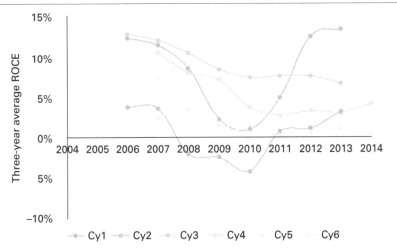

Figure 5.25 shows that companies 5 and 6 probably face the biggest challenge. Looking at Figure 5.7 and Figure 5.16 their inventory turns and CCC seem to be those of an operational excellence player, but their fixed asset turns and their EBIT are significantly below target, and from a ROCE perspective, simply problematic.

We have discussed how company 4 is transitioning from an operational excellence into a customer intimacy or even product leadership position. Its inventory turns and CCC are on that track, but the fixed asset turns and the EBIT% are dragging behind, hurting its ROCE.

Company 3 may have made a mistake by underinvesting in the period 2004–07. It should try to restore its product leadership position by really improving on all fronts at the same time, improving its inventory turns, its working capital, its fixed asset turns and its EBIT. Its current three-year average ROCE is still around 7% so it is still in relatively good shape.

Company 2 has been struggling with its EBIT performance. That may have weighed on its competitive position, and may have led to an aggressive reduction of inventories. We can see a gradual recovery since 2011. It seems positioned to claim a customer intimacy position. Its main challenge there will be improving the fixed asset turns and further improving its EBIT.

And finally, company 1 has been quite successful in changing strategy from a product leader to a customer-intimate company. 2014 saw a drop back in performance, but from the previous sections in this chapter we have shown that 2015 put it back on track to fully claim that customer intimacy position. Its working capital has decreased in line with the targets. The main challenges are improving the EBIT% and improving the asset turns. In all of the analyses performed, it has withstood the test as being the relevant benchmark for this set of companies.

Exercise: Adding the strategic positions to the EBIT% versus fixed asset turns graph

This exercise should have become routine by now! Based on the EBIT% versus fixed asset turns graph and the corresponding 'bang-for-the-buck lines' derived in the previous chapter, now try to define the target position, on the maximum performance line, for the product leader, the customer intimacy and the operational excellence player, as we have shown in Figure 5.18.

You may use our trick in starting from the three EBIT levels you have defined in the EBIT% versus inventory turns graphs, and seeing which fixed asset turns correspond with those three EBIT levels (10%, 7% and 4% in our case, leading to 3, 4 and 7 fixed asset turns respectively).

Take your performance last year and compare it to the target within the applicable strategy. How challenging is the target? How does it compare to your current target? When in doubt on whether the targets are realistic, you may cross-check with the corresponding ROCE performance, as we did in Figure 5.24. What is your target for ROCE performance? What level of fixed asset turns do you require to get to that ROCE level?

Finally, plot three zones for the leaders, the average performers and the laggards, as we did in Figure 5.21. As we did, you may consider a negative EBIT as a non-performance and build from the zero EBIT upward. You may use three-year averages for the EBIT% and the fixed asset turns to reduce some of the variance in the year-on-year results, as we have done in Figure 5.23.

What do you see? Which companies are leading and which ones are lagging? Which ones have improved their performance and which have slipped back? Do we notice any changes in strategy, companies moving from the right to the left or vice versa? Are the results in line with the results from the CCC and the inventory analysis?

Finally, as we have done in Figure 5.25, you may plot the three-year average ROCE performance for a final confirmation of any intermediate conclusions. What are the trends? Who is improving or falling back? Who is changing the strategy? Has that been announced? Is it delivering the same ROCE?

Conclusion

In this chapter we have shown how different strategies lead to different targets. The underlying principle is the ROCE or the 'bang-for-the-buck'. It is OK that as a product leader you require a higher capital employed, as long as you can compensate for it with a higher EBIT. Or vice versa, it is OK that as an operational excellence leader you work at a lower EBIT, as long as you can do it with less capital employed.

The key to accounting for the strategy in the benchmark is identifying relevant examples on the maximum 'bang-for-the-buck line' for a set of chosen companies. In our benchmark company 1 has proven to be the best-in-class. By using the maximum 'bang-for-the-buck line' of company 1, we have been able to identify which combinations of EBIT% and inventory turns, or CCC, or fixed asset turns, are indifferent for an investor. By analysing the different trade-offs that companies make in EBIT% versus inventory turns, we have been able to identify target positions for the product leader, the customer intimacy and the operational excellence leader.

We have used the median to maximum performance line to define the best-in-class zone for each of the strategies. The zones give different directions for the combined EBIT% and capital employed performance. Laggards and average performers can improve on both dimensions at the same time by adopting best practices such as S&OP, the removal of bad complexity, multi-echelon planning and postponement, just to name a few. The best in class will be faced with strategic trade-offs, where they improve on one dimension while giving in on the other, unless they are able to shift what we called the best-practice frontier by experimenting and successfully adopting breakthrough technologies such as 3D printing, big data analytics, robotics or autonomous driving.

When in doubt on whether the derived targets are realistic, link back to the ROCE performance of the reference company in the chosen years. Our derived targets for the fixed asset turns were extremely challenging for some of the companies in the benchmark. Though they seemed unrealistic, we have shown they are required to get the ROCE to a 15% level. Though aggressive, companies should not settle for less. It gives the North Star to which companies can work using a multi-year strategic improvement plan.

In the next two chapters we want to step back to our Supply Chain Triangle to develop a broader KPI dashboard. So far we have focused on a limited set of financial KPIs. We will broaden that and tie in more of the underlying operations. We will also link it back to strategy, and show how different strategies lead to different KPIs and different priorities.

CASE STUDY – Henkel

Henkel is a German chemical and consumer goods company, currently organized around three business units: adhesive technologies, beauty care, and laundry and home care. Global brands include Loctite, Schwarzkopf and Persil, to name just three. 61% of the ordinary shares are still held by the Henkel family. With sales of €18.7 billion in 2016, it is one of the bigger family-owned businesses in Germany.

Figure 5.26 compares some key financials of Henkel and P&G, another major global player in beauty care and laundry and home care. We will review them in the light of the comparisons of the last three chapters.

Figure 5.26   Comparison of the 10-year financials for Henkel and P&G

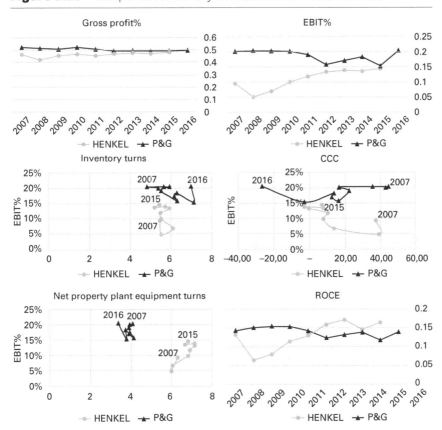

The first chart in Figure 5.26 looks at the gross profit as a percentage of the sales revenue. We see that Henkel has consistently improved its gross profit, from around 40% in 2008 to around 50% in 2015. Looking at the benchmarks in Chapters 2, 3, 4 and 5, a gross profit of 50% indicates a product leadership strategy, which fits its position as a branded goods manufacturer.

The second chart in Figure 5.26, at the top right hand, shows an even more impressive improvement in the EBIT%, from around 5% for Henkel in 2008, to around 15% in 2015. The difference between the gross profit and the EBIT is the SG&A. It means that Henkel has significantly improved its efficiency. Note the consistently high EBIT performance of P&G. With a 15% EBIT, the year 2015 was the worst in the 10-year history.

The third and fourth charts show the inventory turns and the CCC. We see that while P&G improved on its inventory turns from around 5 till around 7 in the period 2007–16, Henkel went back and forth between 5 and 6 in that same period.

The CCC gives a different picture. P&G aggressively lowered their working capital from 40 days in 2007 to around -25 days in 2016. Henkel has also improved, but less drastically, from around 40 days to around 10 days over a comparable period. At P&G lowering the inventory has contributed to this improvement, but, particularly at Henkel, the reduction in the CCC has primarily been driven by a reduction in the accounts payable.

So far, despite the improvement at Henkel, we'd still think of P&G as the better investment. Even if you read financial reports it is common to see such metrics as sales growth, EBIT% and EBIT growth prominently displayed on the first page.

That picture changes when we look at the asset turns. The fifth or bottom left chart shows the EBIT% versus the 'net property plant and equipment turns', which is the sales revenue / net property plant and equipment. First of all we see that Henkel has significantly higher PPE turns than P&G. It means that Henkel reaches its results with significantly fewer assets or vice versa, that it makes better use of its assets. Secondly, we see that whereas Henkel has improved on its asset turns, P&G has dropped back. We'll talk later on how supply chain has delivered a major contribution here.

As shown at the bottom right graph, the higher asset turns translate into a significantly better ROCE for Henkel versus P&G. Whereas gross profit and EBIT are comparable in 2015, we see that the Henkel ROCE has been better since 2012. Looking at the benchmarks of Chapters 3, 4 and 5, the consistent ROCE performance of 15%-18% since 2012 is quite exceptional.

Impact of the supply chain

When asked about how supply chain has impacted the business and the business performance, Dirk Holbach, the CSCO of the Laundry & Home Care division, told us: 'Supply chain impacts the business in two ways. First of all, we need to ensure agility. As an FMCG player demand can change by a factor of two or three over a few days. Secondly, as a branded goods manufacturer, up to 40% of sales are generated from products launched over the last three years. Our ability to launch new products fast and reliably is key to our business strategy.'

When asked which supply chain initiatives have supported the impressive business transformation shown in Figure 5.26, Dirk says: 'In the period 2005–13 we worked on a number of key projects. The first was optimization of our footprint and our efficiency. We nearly halved our factories from 50 to 27, and we reduced our headcount from around 10,000 to around 6,000. Secondly, we optimized our product portfolio. We reduced the number of SKUs by approximately 50%, and by 2013 84% of our sales were generated by the top 10 brands.'

While laundry and home care is only one of the three divisions, it is clear that these types of supply chain initiatives has been key to the dramatic improvement in the years leading up to 2013. All of this of course had to be carried out while not compromising on the required agility as a branded goods and product leadership strategy.

The next question is what the current initiatives are, and how supply chain will continue to support the business results. Dirk says: 'In recent years, Henkel has worked on a centralization of its supply chain activities for all three business units. This should allow a further harmonization and standardization of processes, which should further improve customer service levels and enhance efficiency.

'In fact, some processes like footprint optimization and the target setting and follow-up of key KPIs have been fully centralized in Amsterdam, processes such as net demand planning, production and supply planning have been centralized in six regional centres, and line scheduling is still organized in the factories.'

When asked whether there are significant differences between the three business units, Dirk answers: 'We don't publish these figures in detail on a business unit level. In general, the laundry and home care unit does better on some aspects like the CCC. Our fast movers are quite bulky in nature, so we have to be operationally excellent there. But in general, laundry and home care follows the general trend of the company.

'In 2016 financial report we announced our four new strategic priorities running into 2020. One of them is to "increase agility". Agility remains key and supply chain is key to agility. A second is to "drive growth" and a third is to "fund growth". A further increase of efficiency and the further expansion of the global supply chain organization are key levers to generate the money required to fund our targeted growth.

'The fourth strategic priority is to accelerate digitalization. Supply chain will also play a crucial role here, as we digitalize the relationship with our customers and consumers and translate that into improved agility and efficiency in the supply chain.'

In summary, we can say that the consistent improvement in Henkels's financials is quite impressive. It is also clear from the figures and Dirk Holbach's comments that supply chain is core to both the strategy and the financials. It has been instrumental in the improvements running up to 2013, and it remains core to the strategic priorities that have been announced for 2020.

CASE STUDY – Bekaert

Bekaert is a world market and technology leader in steel wire transformation and coating technologies. To give some examples, every year over 1 billion bottles of sparkling wines are opened via the muselet made of Bekaert wires; one out of three tyres around the world is reinforced with Bekaert tyre cord; every year 8 million cubic meters of concrete is being reinforced with Bekaert steel fibres; and Bekaert sawing wire cuts wafers representing 15GW of annual solar energy capacity in the end markets.

Founded in 1880 in Belgium, Bekaert has grown into a global company serving customers in 120 countries with steel wire solutions for the most diverse industry sectors. The company employs almost 30,000 employees worldwide and generated €4.4 billion sales in 2016.

When asked for the relevance of the Supply Chain Triangle and the ROCE as an overall metric, as shown in Figure 1.16, Ton Geurts, the CPO and SVP for Supply Chain Excellence, comments: 'It feels natural to Bekaert'. The 2016 annual report shows that each of the businesses has targets to improve revenue, profit and ROCE, which perfectly maps to Figure 1.16.

Ton continues: 'In my experience, different entities and different business platforms have a different level of maturity. The ability to balance the triangle depends on the presence and quality of shared and integrated targets. If procurement and supply chain have isolated targets, which are not linked to margin management and to working capital, then people will make biased decisions.

'This has to do with the maturity of the organization. In the more mature parts of the Bekaert organization, we see that S&OP has in fact evolved into Integrated Business Planning, where the supply chain manager brings transparency to the platform, and Regional Management, dealing with where the market is going, which volumes can optimally be produced where, which inventories will be needed to cover seasonality, and which margins will be achieved as a result. If you really want to optimize the business around the three corners of the triangle, you need forward-looking processes and tools and a close collaboration between business, finance and supply chain.'

Figure 5.27 shows the evolution of some key financials for Bekaert over the last five years. The data has been taken from the financial reports for 2016, 2014 and 2012, which are available from the Bekaert website.

Figure 5.27   Five-year financials for Bekaert NV

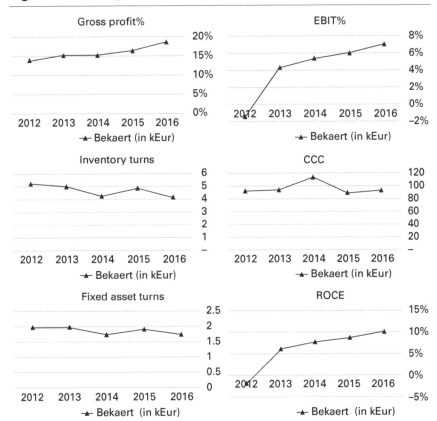

The two graphs at the top show the gradual improvement in gross profit and EBIT. The next two graphs show that while inventory turns have slightly declined from around 5 to around 4, working capital (as measured by the cash conversion cycle) has remained relatively stable around 90 days. At the bottom left we see that the fixed asset turns have slightly decreased. The bottom right graph shows that the ROCE has gradually improved, from being negative in 2012, to 10% in 2016. The combined analysis shows that the ROCE improvement so far has primarily been EBIT-driven.

The EBIT and gross profit improvement can be linked to the major transformation programmes that Bekaert has recently launched. Ton comments: 'Over the last two to three years we have launched in sequence the Bekaert Manufacturing Excellence programme, the Bekaert Customer Excellence programme, and in 2016 Bekaert Safety Excellence and the Bekaert Supply Chain Excellence programme. By reducing complexity in our plants, and better leveraging our scale, manufacturing excellence has been driving an overall lower cost.

'Customer excellence has focused on developing quantified value propositions to our customers, an enhanced product portfolio, and strategic choices in the growth plans of the different segments. The main goal of commercial excellence has been to drive extra value for and from our customers. Safety excellence is key and an essential part of manufacturing excellence and of the value-based corporate culture at Bekaert.'

The combination of both has translated into a gross profit and EBIT improvement, as shown in Figure 5.27.

Ton continues: 'In 2016 we launched the Supply Chain Excellence programme. We started with a focus on processes and organization: ensure clear job descriptions, ensure the right level of maturity at the right level, and get the supply chain managers in the monthly business management meetings.

'A second step was implementing S&OP, with pilots in the US and China. We are switching from an Excel-driven environment to a more integrated tooling platform to enable this. The challenge is bigger in our higher activity platforms with a very diverse product offering, because of the related complexity.

'The third step, which we're piloting in 2017, is managing inventory. We have put targets on the raw materials and on the finished products. In parallel we're also rolling out a functional excellence program called "Fit for Growth", optimizing all support processes in all our global functions. The functions will transform from "supporting" to "co-driving" the businesses. Supply Chain Excellence benefits from the tailwind it is getting by being at the core of this transformation programme.'

As outlined in Chapter 2, we believe supply chain and finance are good allies in ensuring that working capital and fixed assets, in short the capital employed, become part of the overall equation, and that companies become more ROCE-driven, instead of purely top-line, or bottom-line driven. Ton confirms that point: 'Our CFO is teaming up with purchasing and supply chain, as she recognizes that together we will be able to deliver working capital improvement'.

When asked how he explains the relevance of managing working capital to the business, Ton starts with a note on the financing structure of Bekaert. 'Bekaert has grown fast in past years. Not only did the company successfully close the largest acquisition in the history of Bekaert [Pirelli's steel cord acquisition], the Group also realized its largest merger [the Bridon-Bekaert Ropes group deal]. Obviously these large deals had an impact on Bekaert's debt and debt financing positions.

'However, the company didn't change its respective targets and wants to continue to work towards a net debt on EBITDA of 2. In order to do so, cash generation is of the utmost importance, and hence working capital and ROCE have come much more to the forefront. As Bekaert has an explicit growth ambition for the future, financing that growth will remain a challenge. Working capital management is one of the elements that come into the equation. This is how we explain it to the business.'

We agree with Ton that good management of the working capital, or in general, good management of the capital employed, is an enabler of growth. If your EBIT is 15% of the capital employed, let's assume that in the best case your net profit is 10% of the capital employed. Roughly speaking, that 10% can be used – among others – for compensating shareholders through dividends, and the rest can be reinvested in growing the business. If your ROCE is too low, there's not enough head room to self-finance the growth, in which case you'll have to look for debt financing, which in the long run negatively affects the value of your company. We oversimplify here, as the real driver is cash flow, not EBIT, but the conclusion remains the same – if your EBIT is too low, you'll end up with cash problems over the long term.

To manage that growth ambition, Ton also stresses once more the importance of forward looking processes like S&OP and Integrated Business Planning: 'We want to know where our inventories will be going and how this will affect our working capital and cashflow. If sales needs to support the growth of a market segment by temporarily extending payment terms, we should be able to compensate for that in the accounts payable or in inventories, but we want to know it upfront. Whereas financial control was typically more focused on explaining the running numbers, if we really want to balance that Supply Chain Triangle, we need tools which give us a forward-looking view.

'When I became responsible for supply chain excellence, I found some of our businesses looking more at the current month or the current quarter, and less at the longer term. We want to change this to an enterprise type of planning, integrated with financial planning, where we have a horizon of the next five years, where we visualize the cash generated and which type of plans and investments that allows.'

When making the link between the triangle and the chosen business model, as shown in Figure 2.8 and benchmarking-wise in Figure 5.7, Ton recognizes the need to build different teams around different business models from his earlier experience in the chemical industry. He also strongly associates it with the product life cycle of a product. 'In chemicals, companies like DSM have divested commoditized businesses to concentrate on specialities. Being in specialities may deliver higher margins but does not improve ROCE as such.

'A commodity business may be lower margin, but if you streamline your processes and optimize your asset turns, you can easily deliver a comparable ROCE. Though you'll often have to split that off in a separate model. Sales people can be successful in selling specialities and commodities, but not at the same time. It is the same reason why pharma companies often have a separate organization focused on generics, and their more R&D driven businesses under the IP-driven umbrella itself.' All of this aligns with the thinking of Treacy and Wiersema outlined in Chapter 2.

Ton believes that this type of strategic portfolio analysis and management is a key competence which many companies still can develop further. 'Analysing companies and business performance with a short time horizon only is not sufficient. The way operations, finance and the business need to interact and make tough choices, for instance by cutting complexity and refocusing some businesses on a simple price competition, that is a competence which in many companies is still growing.

'Some companies will hire a strategy consultant to get this type of an X-ray every two to three years. Others have organized this capability internally, and have built internal teams to perform this type of analyses on the different businesses on a recurring basis. If you are running the business you risk getting carried away with your short-term issues. With some distance, it's easier to put things in perspective, and ask the right questions, as is done in this book.

'You regularly need to re-evaluate whether the complexity in a business is still delivering the right type of return. Some complexity is "above the skin", which means it can easily be adjusted. If different products have been developed by different engineering teams, there is typically an opportunity to rationalize and reduce the number of raw materials as there can be duplication or overdesign. Other complexity is "under the skin". If you want to change a component in a product or the product itself that you deliver to the aerospace or automotive industry, where you have a long approval cycle, this is more difficult. But you certainly need processes to regularly trim your complexity.'

As much as Ton believes in this type of advanced supply chain thinking, he also sees an important change management challenge. 'Some of this thinking is relatively new and advanced. If we expect our management teams, and the supply chain people in those management teams, to have this integrated focus, and to regularly assess and trim the level of complexity or if necessary make strategic changes, we'll have to invest in our people. Making the top 200 or the top 500 of our organization talk and think in this way is a journey. We'll also have to embed it in our processes and our KPIs, and ensure these things are being put on the monthly agenda. At Bekaert, we are currently building our supply chain academy through which we want to develop this.'

Ton concludes: 'At Bekaert we are convinced that supply chain excellence is a key driver for ROCE improvement and an enabler to co-drive with finance and the business. That is why we have put it as a third firm pillar, next to manufacturing and to customer excellence. The challenge is big from different angles: process and organization, tooling and change management-wise. If I compare where we are versus our peers, I see that many of us have significant improvement potential.

'As well as my role as a CPO, I have gladly accepted the challenge to move Bekaert forward in supply chain excellence and deliver significant contributions to the challenging objectives on growth, EBIT and ROCE improvements that have been put forward.'

References

Barco [accessed 20/07/2017] Connect – Barco Annual Report 2013 [Online] http://www.barco.com/en/about-barco/investors/company-results

Bekaert [accessed 24/08/2017] Annual Report 2016 [Online] https://annualreport.bekaert.com/

Bekaert [accessed 24/08/2017] Financial reports [Online] https://www.bekaert.com/en/investors/information-center/annual-reports [accessed 24/08/2017]

Cecere, L M (2014) *Supply Chain Metrics That Matter*, John Wiley & Sons, New York

Treacy, M and Wiersema, F (1995) *The Discipline of Market Leaders: Choose your customers, narrow your focus, dominate your market*, Basic Books, New York

Redefining the service corner as a value corner   06

In the previous chapters we have discussed financial KPIs, how to set targets based on benchmarking in two dimensions, and how to account for the chosen strategy. Though the answer to those three questions is far more elaborate than one would expect, their importance cannot be understated. Aligned and correctly defined targets give a true compass along which the organization can steer the hundreds or even thousands of people it employs. Unrealistic or unaligned targets will create confusion, and will waste effort and energy, as initiatives may be fighting instead of reinforcing each other.

The challenge though is that so far the metrics used have been very limited. We have focused on gross margin and EBIT on the one hand, and on inventory turns, cash conversion cycle (CCC) and fixed asset turns, as elements of capital employed, on the other. Both combine into 'bang-for-the-buck' metrics, for which we have used the return on capital employed (ROCE), a common financial metric.

In this and the next chapter we will take one step back. Remember that EBIT was the combination of the service and the cost side of the Supply Chain Triangle. Though EBIT is very relevant, it is a high-level metric. We will get back to our underlying triangle and deepen our understanding of the service, the cost and the capital employed corner of the Supply Chain Triangle.

In this chapter, we will use the Treacy and Wiersema strategy model and introduce a new strategy model, Crawford and Mathews, to further analyse and detail the service corner of the triangle. In fact we will rename it as the value corner, list possible value drivers, and define more detailed metrics for those different value drivers.

In Chapter 7 we will use standard financial metrics to further detail the cost side and the capital employed side of the triangle. We will then combine those different metrics on the different corners of our triangle in a supply chain and financial KPI dashboard. We will also show how different strategies lead to different targets and to different priorities in the KPIs.

Redefining the service corner as a value corner using Treacy and Wiersema

Figure 6.1 shows our starting point. It is a recap of Figure 1.9.

Let's start by revisiting the service corner. In Chapter 1 we have already discussed why we should take a 'broad' perspective of service. In supply chain it is common to narrow service to an On-Time-In-Full (OTIF) delivery performance. That is one aspect of service, but there is much more.

Think about the product portfolio. If you deliver a wide range of products, that creates a cost in the supply chain, but it is also a service that you deliver to the customer. In fact, it is one of the unique selling points of a customer intimacy leader. Or consider order flexibility. If customers can order at any time, in any quantity and with any type of delivery requirement, that will again create a cost in the supply chain. Some customers will value that, and will be willing to pay more, as it allows them to lower their inventories and still be responsive to their customers. If you are an operational excellence player, you will try to avoid these costs, to guarantee the lowest price. If you are a customer intimacy player, responsiveness may be part of the 'best total solution' you deliver to your customer.

Figure 6.1 Starting point for building the supply chain and financial KPI dashboard

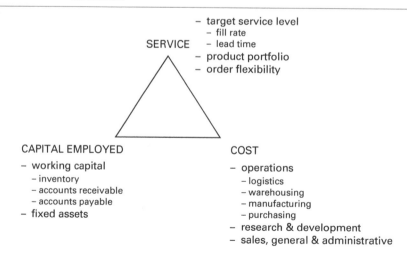

From these examples, it is easy to make the connection to the three strategic options of Treacy and Wiersema (1995). From a customer perspective, we know that some customers will only value the lowest price. They will expect a basic set of services, the qualifiers, but will not be tempted nor be willing to pay for any extra services. Think about flying a low-cost airline. You will not be interested in drinks or quality snacks on the flight. You just want the lowest price. These needs are of course best served by the operational excellence players in the market.

Some customers will value a total solution, a one-stop shop. They will be best served by the customer intimacy players. That total solution will exist of a combination of a broad product portfolio and any 'value-added' services. An example of a value-added service could be an onsite technical service manager, or the supplier analysing their customers' problems and defining appropriate solutions. Whereas for a product leader the service comes on top, for a customer intimacy player the service is really an essential part of the total customer solution.

Finally, some customers will value product quality and specifications. They are best served by the product leader. He or she works with the best of the best to deliver the best of the best. A premium product comes at a premium price, and typically has some premium services included. Your reason to buy is the product – the services come on top, whereas in customer intimacy, the service may be your reason for buying.

From the three strategies we have just derived four possible 'value drivers': the price, the product quality, the product portfolio and value added services. Figure 6.2 summarizes how the three different strategies create value for the customer in three different ways.

The opex player will dominate on price, and can have an average product quality and product range, and even the absolute basics when it comes to service. The product leader and the customer intimacy player take a different position.

We remember from the previous chapters that different strategies come at a different cost and with a different level of capital employed. Instead of only showing 'service' in the narrow definition of the 'service corner', we suggest listing the four value drivers above. If we know our current and our target performance on each of the four value drivers, then we better understand our strategic position, and the resulting balance in the Supply Chain Triangle. If I'm aiming for a product leadership position, I know I will carry more inventory compared to an opex player. This idea is illustrated in Figure 6.3.

Figure 6.2   Different ways to create value based on Treacy and Wiersema using four value attributes

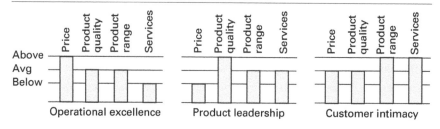

To avoid any confusion about the 'narrow' versus 'broad' definition of service, we have renamed the service corner as the value corner, as it is listing possible value drivers.

Our finding from Figure 6.2 about value drivers and different strategies as different positions or priorities on those value drivers is comparable to the findings and the work of Crawford and Mathews. In their book *The Myth of Excellence* (2007) they arrive at five possible value drivers, and argue that a 5-4-3-3-3 profile is optimal if you want to reach excellence. In the next section, we will introduce their model, and map it to what we have derived so far. It will allow us to further refine our definition of the 'value' corner of our triangle.

Redefining the service corner as a value corner using Crawford and Mathews

Crawford and Mathews have studied the value propositions of manufacturing and retail companies. Their finding was twofold. Firstly, any value proposition is based on the five primary value drivers shown in Figure 6.4: price, product, access, service and experience.

Secondly, they argue that a 5-4-3-3-3 profile is optimal, meaning that you can dominate on one attribute, you can differentiate on a second, and you will (at best) be at par for the other three.

Let's discuss the five attributes in more detail, revisit the 5-4-3-3-3 argument, and then link the findings back to the model of Treacy and Wiersema and to our Supply Chain Triangle.

Figure 6.3 The three strategies of Treacy and Wiersema are different ways to create value

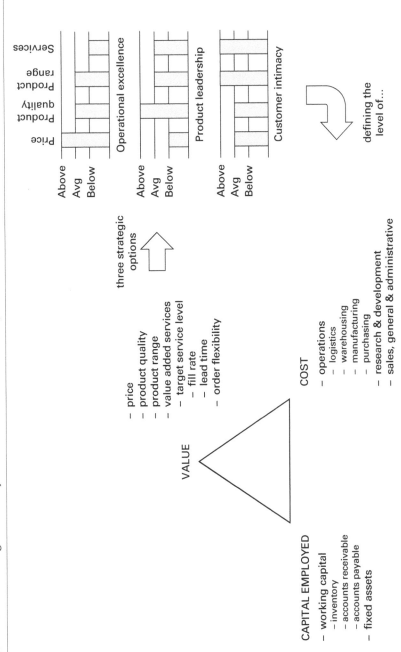

Figure 6.4   An example optimal profile for the five value drivers of Crawford and Mathews

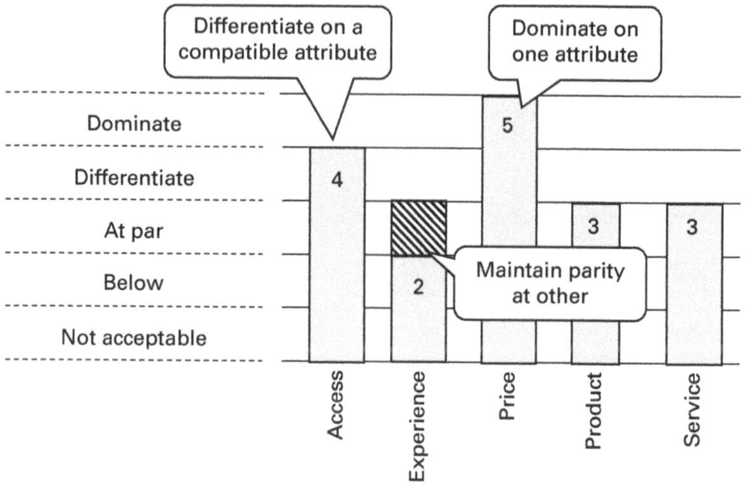

Exploring the five value drivers of Crawford and Mathews

Let's start with *price*. Dominating on price means customers buy from you because you have the lowest price in the market. Next to having the lowest price, Crawford and Mathews stress the importance of honesty and consistency. They even argue that you don't necessarily need to have the lowest price. As long you have a consistently low price, and are honest in your pricing, you will create a loyal customer base around that low-price proposition.

Consistency means you will continuously monitor and adapt your prices to remain in sync with the market. Honesty means you will not try to exploit your customer, for instance by reducing prices on one product while making complementary products more expensive.

An example of consistency and honesty is a so-called 'everyday low price' pricing strategy, as practised by Walmart, and as opposed to a so-called 'high-low' pricing strategy. In an everyday low-price strategy , a company, typically a retailer, guarantees to continuously keep prices down, as opposed to a 'high-low' strategy where the price is low during a period of promotion, and high when not running a promotion.

Crawford and Mathews argue that low-price customers prefer the consistency and honesty of the 'every day low price' to the lack of transparency of high-low pricing. We wouldn't go that far. Low-price retailers like Aldi and Lidl do use promotions to further enhance their image. They will typically do it on temporary products or assortments, while ensuring an everyday low price on their base assortment.

However, companies like Lidl have been attacked by their customers for not carrying enough inventory of the lower priced promo products. Customers feel tricked if they arrive the first morning of the promo to find only three of the discounted flat screen TVs left in stock. It confirms that honesty and consistency is important, but lowest price definitely comes first. The hard discounters will keep exploring the limits on how to grow market share while keeping costs down to ensure the lowest price. Linking back to Treacy and Wiersema, it is clear that the lowest price ties seamlessly into operational excellence.

Let's take *product* next. Crawford and Mathews talk about three aspects in the product dimension: quality, depth and breadth. The quality ties into the product leadership strategy of Treacy and Wiersema. Customers buy from you because you simply have the highest quality product. That's why people buy a Ferrari or a Lamborghini when they want to buy a sports car. As well as having an exquisite design, it is above all a fabulous sports car, the reference in its category.

Depth and breadth are two aspects of the product portfolio or assortment. Breadth refers to the one-stop shop of customer intimacy. Many DIY chains try to offer a full range of tools and consumables for any type of work you want to do in your home. As well as the full range players, you have specialist stores. If I'm a specialist in power tools, my assortment will be less 'wide', but I have more choice than any of my competitors in the specific assortment of power tools. We call that 'depth'. We will link depth to a product leadership position, as in 'I either have the best product, or the best selection of products for a specific application or from a specific type'. Depth links into specialization and the premium we can drive from that, as opposed to breadth, which links into the total solution of the customer intimacy player.

Let's explain *access* as a third value driver. Crawford and Mathews talk about physical access and psychological access. In a retail world, physical access means the average distance to one of your stores, as exemplified by McDonald's or Starbucks. Take an average city around the world, count the number of McDonald's or Starbucks outlets, and you'll know what physical access means. For a manufacturing company it will be the number of distributors or distribution centres across the globe and the resulting customer order lead time.

Increasing the physical access comes at a cost, so conflicts with a low-cost focus. An operational excellence player will never be dominant on physical access. A product leader doesn't need to excel on physical access. Customers are willing to wait or to travel for their products, because of the difference in quality. As a result, we link physical access to the customer intimacy position of Treacy and Wiersema. Proximity is part of the total solution that is being delivered.

Psychological access means 'how easy it is for me to find what I'm looking for'. In a retail environment it means 'easy in and out', which is supported by relatively compact stores, where you have an easy overview of the store with the same layout across different stores, so you more easily find your way in each of the stores belonging to the same chain. Psychological access in retail is focused on 'efficiency for the customer'. From that perspective it matches well with an operational excellence proposition at the side of the retailer.

In a manufacturing environment 'efficiency for me as a customer' could be something like e-ordering. Instead of calling into a customer service desk, faxing or e-mailing, an EDI connection will make my life easier. It will be more efficient for me as a customer. It will also be more efficient for my supplier. If I do need to call a customer service manager, the question could be 'how long does it take to get it done?'. The shorter the call, the more efficient for both the customer and the supplier.

In general, hassle-free service at the customer side goes well with efficiency at the supplier side, so we will link psychological access to the operational excellence position of Treacy and Wiersema.

The fourth value driver is *service*. Service is the broadest and the hardest attribute to explain. Crawford and Mathews start by talking about 'knowledgeable sales persons providing helpful advice'. This breathes 'customer intimacy'. We have an intimate knowledge of the customer's problem and are there to help him or her with advice on how to solve it. That easily translates from a retail world into a manufacturing world, and vice versa.

A second example from Crawford and Mathews is 'customization' or 'tailoring'. A retail example could be a counter service, where a consumer can order a specific portion size of his favourite product. The manufacturing example is customer-specific products, designed to tackle a customer-specific challenge. This again breathes 'customer intimacy'.

Other aspects mentioned are 'hassle-free return', with no complicated procedures for returning products, but trusting the client and sending a replacement without questions. This type of returns policy is easier if there is some kind of long-term relationship and if there is some margin in that relationship. An operational excellence player has to control all of his costs as to guarantee the lowest price, including any returns. If you get grounded with a low-cost airline, don't expect quick and efficient customer service to help you with rebooking or returning your money.

A product leader will probably provide a hassle-free return, though the price of their products may justify maintenance contracts or insurances, which will cover the costs. It is probably the customer intimacy player who needs to earn this from the relationship rather than any maintenance contracts or insurances.

A fourth element we want to add to the service dimension is 'availability'. For Crawford and Mathews availability, ie the fact that you have the product available, is part of the product dimension. We like to classify it as a service. Zara is a product leader, focused on a fast time-to-market and a high innovation rate. They deliberately limit the number of pieces of an individual item. Consumers know that if they return next week the inventory may be depleted, so they buy what they like here and now. If a retailer of your favourite brand of shirts or shoes always has availability of common sizes, then it will require them to take extra inventory. This is an extra cost they hope to win back by your loyalty because of this service.

Availability is not in the product, it is in the way the company organizes its supply chain and in the cost and inventory it is willing to carry to deliver that service. All of these service attributes best tie into the customer intimacy position of Treacy and Wiersema.

The last value driver to discuss is *experience*. In a retail environment, Crawford and Mathews talk about the attractiveness of the store, how employees dress to reflect the atmosphere, or how music and video are used to enhance the experience. As well as providing the best quality products, shopping at Harrods in London is an experience. If you buy a Ferrari, you can expect to discover it under a (Ferrari) red cover, accompanied by a bottle of exquisite champagne and an invitation for a series of driving lessons on a racing circuit.

Experience is ideally suited to further enhancing the value of the products of product leaders. The cost of creating the extra experience can be small compared to the cost of the product. The experience has a high chance of appealing to the vanity of the buyer, significantly increasing the emotional value and as such the willingness to pay the premium price. In theory, you can offer the same products with the only differentiation being the experience. With an average product, consumers will be more price-sensitive and will more easily skip the experience factor as to get the same product at a lower cost – certainly these days, where the internet has made prices very transparent.

For a manufacturer, experience may be more difficult to create, but it could for instance be done by sending sales people or technical service people over to the customer to celebrate the delivery or the installation of the actual product. Even when not strictly necessary, doing this will create a level of excitement that can be classified as experience rather than service. Again, an operational excellence player will avoid this type of cost as to guarantee the lowest price. It is typically the product leaders who can further enhance the perceived value of the product and are in a position to provide this type of experience.

Figure 6.5 summarizes the five attributes of Crawford and Mathews and the main characteristics discussed. Figure 6.6 summarizes our mapping of the five attributes to the three strategic options of Treacy and Wiersema.

Figure 6.5   The five attributes of Crawford and Mathews

Price	Access	Service	Product	Experience
Lowest price Consistency Honesty	Physical	Advice Customization Availability	Quality Depth	Attractiveness Excitement
	Psychological		Breadth	

Figure 6.6   Mapping the five attributes of Crawford and Mathews to Treacy and Wiersema

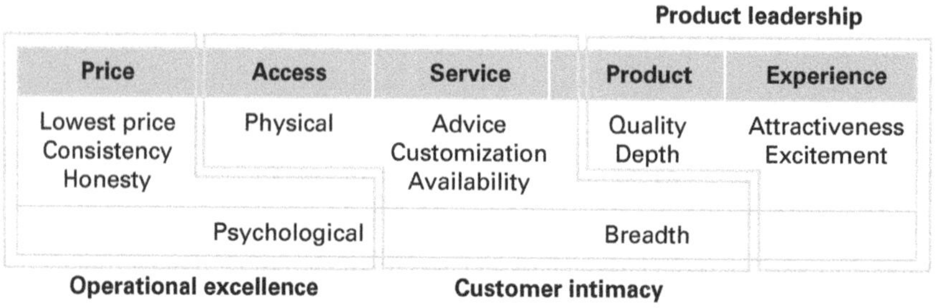

			Product leadership	
Price	**Access**	**Service**	**Product**	**Experience**
Lowest price Consistency Honesty	Physical	Advice Customization Availability	Quality Depth	Attractiveness Excitement
	Psychological		Breadth	
Operational excellence		**Customer intimacy**		

Integrating Treacy and Wiersema into Crawford and Mathews

As shown in Figure 6.4, Crawford and Mathews argue that a 5-4-3-3-3 profile is optimal. This means that you can dominate in one of the dimensions, differentiate on a second, and be at par with competitors on the remaining three. From that perspective their messaging is comparable to that of Treacy and Wiersema: 'you have to make choices'. If you try to be the best in all of the dimensions, you may find yourself outcompeted on each one by different competitors, each focusing on one dimension only. A sharper focus also gives a clearer message to the customer about who you want to be, and a clearer message to your employees who need to execute your promise.

As companies we hate to make choices. We think that choosing is losing. We stand with the message that strategy is about making choices, and that making choices is required if you truly want to be a market leader.

There are two important differences though in the two approaches. Firstly, Crawford and Mathews advocate that any combination of 5-4-3-3-3 can give a competitive edge. So you could have 5-4-3-3-3, 5-3-4-3-3, 5-3-3-4-3 or any other of the 20 possible combinations. Treacy and Wiersema stick to only three possible strategies. From that perspective Crawford and Mathews have a broader palette to paint the competitive situation. Some of them are helpful, and we will give one example.

In one of my strategy sessions with a food retailer, it was helpful to take a look at product leaders. The product leaders focus on delivering the highest quality meat, fish, vegetables, dairy products and so on. When screening a selection of product leaders in more detail, we saw that some of them were more focused on combining the product with experience, while others combined it with service. The 'experience' players had attractive stores with nice decor, an eye-catching display of products, ample opportunity to taste the products and an in-house restaurant allowing you to discover the best and the newest. In a certain sense this was attracting the wealthier consumer looking for inspiration and willing to pay some more for a premium product in an attractive setting.

The 'service' players had basic stores, a somewhat broader assortment and even more knowledgeable personnel, delivering the necessary advice to ensure the product is used and appreciated in the best possible condition. These competitors were more focused towards professionals, for instance restaurant owners looking for the best product and professional advice. These customers don't want to pay for fancy store decor. They want the best product at the lowest possible price, and with some professional advice on what to try and how to combine.

This is just one example where we believe the approach of Crawford and Mathews allows more nuance in the strategic positioning of yourself and your competitors, in comparison to Treacy and Wiersema.

A second difference between Crawford and Mathews and Treacy and Wiersema is in how the dimensions combine as shown in Figure 6.6. From our perspective, it is problematic to combine product quality/depth on the one hand, and product breadth on the other hand, into one 'product' dimension. The two serve very different purposes, as shown by the product leadership versus customer intimacy positions in the model of Treacy and Wiersema.

We like the principle of the 5-4-3-3-3 and having more than three possible strategic options; however, we do believe that any strategy model should contain the three strategic options of Treacy and Wiersema, as 'archetypes'. These archetypes have proven their value in strategy formulation over the last 20 years.

Likewise the combination of physical access and psychological access into one 'access' dimension is problematic. Where psychological access as 'efficiency for the customer' combines very well with an efficiency mindset or an operational excellence position on the suppliers' side, improving physical access increases the cost, which is more a service improvement, which better ties into customer intimacy.

To combine the best of both worlds, and to make the model of Treacy and Wiersema fit nicely into that of Crawford and Mathews, we suggest splitting the five dimensions of Crawford and Mathews into seven dimensions, as shown in Figure 6.7. These seven dimensions then easily combine into the three strategies of Treacy and Wiersema as shown in Figure 6.8.

A 5-4-3-3-3 profile now becomes a 5-4-3-3-3-3-3 profile. Figure 6.9 shows our definition of the three 'archetypes' of Treacy and Wiersema.

Figure 6.7 Extending Crawford and Mathews from five to seven attributes

Price	Psycho-logical Access	Physical Access	Service	Product Breadth	Product Quality/ Depth	Experience
Lowest price Consistency Honesty	Easy Hassle free Successful	Location Number of stores	Advice Customi-zation Availability	One-stop shop Broad range	Highest spec Speciality	Attractive-ness Excitement

Figure 6.8 Linking the seven attributes to Treacy and Wiersema

Price	Psycho-logical Access	Physical Access	Service	Product Breadth	Product Quality/ Depth	Experience
Lowest price Consistency Honesty	Easy Hassle free Successful	Location Number of stores	Advice Customi- zation Availability	One-stop shop Broad range	Highest spec Speciality	Attractive- ness Excitement

Operational excellence		Customer intimacy		Product leadership		

Figure 6.9 The 5-4-3-3-3-3-3 profile for operational excellence, customer intimacy and product leadership

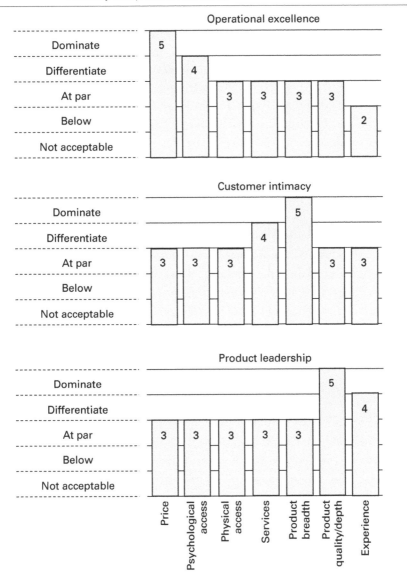

An opex player dominates on price and will differentiate on psychological access. In a recent exercise with an opex player, the experience dimension was actually ranked 'below par'. Once a company is below par it needs to 'mind the gap', as falling too far behind may compromise its leadership position.

The archetypical customer intimacy players dominate on product breadth and differentiate on service. They deliver the one-stop shop, and bring the expertise to assemble the products into the best total solution. The archetypical product leaders dominate on product quality, and differentiate on experience. They deliver the newest and highest specification products, and turn it into an experience, commanding a superior premium from their customers.

The good thing about the Crawford and Mathews model is that it easily allows the definition of variants, like the one described above, where a product leader was focusing on service instead of experience as a differentiator. Having seven value attributes is more complex... but you can't have it all. If you want to put nuance in the strategy modelling, and have multiple options, you'll have to carry some complexity in your strategy model.

As discussed before, showing all of the value drivers on the value corner of the triangle, showing where we are today and where we want to be, gives a better understanding of the current and targeted strategic position of our company. The strategy is essential in understanding the related and required cost and capital employed. The strategy defines the balance in the triangle. If I want to be a product leader, I know I will carry more inventory and a higher cost than the operational excellence player. This is summarized in Figure 6.10. It nicely summarizes how we have used the model and approach of Crawford and Mathews to extend our original result based on Treacy and Wiersema as shown in Figure 6.3.

In the next section we will define KPIs on each of the seven value 'attributes' or drivers derived above. When building a dashboard, we know that we want to dominate and differentiate on the 5s and the 4s, while being on par (at best) for the remaining attributes. Showing the full set of KPIs helps in revealing the chosen strategy and better understanding the impact on the cost and the capital employed. If we need to summarize or collapse our metrics overview, we will first check the attributes where we want to dominate (5) or differentiate (4). This helps in building comprehensive dashboards, while accounting for the chosen strategy.

Figure 6.10 Mapping Crawford and Mathews to Treacy and Wiersema and the
Supply Chain Triangle using seven value drivers

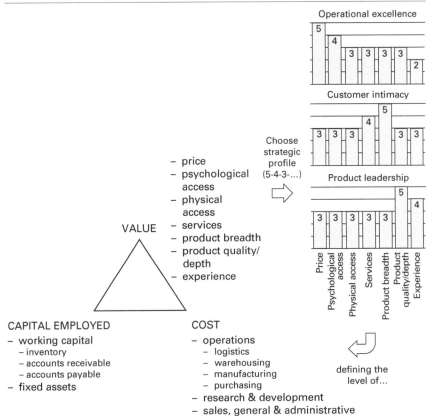

Defining metrics for each of our value drivers

When defining metrics, we will distinguish between retailers, B2C and B2B.
While the seven value drivers are equally relevant for each of these industries, the metrics often require a slightly different definition to make them fit
well. As shown in Figure 6.4, each of the metrics will ask for a comparison
with the market and with key competitors. This is required to know whether
we are dominating, differentiating, or playing at par.

Let's now review the seven value drivers one by one.

Price

For price, the price point is an important KPI. It compares the price of your product to the price of comparable products. As an opex player you want to have the lowest price, so you want to be below the market price. As a product leader you want to get a premium for the premium quality you deliver, so you want to be above the market price.

It is common to compare prices to a set of key competitors. You may either buy this information from market research firms like Nielsen, or you can do your own market research, by shopping at or buying from competitors.

Psychological access

This is a somewhat more abstract concept. It is about 'how easy it is for the customer to do business with us'. It is focused on the 'efficiency for the customer'. In a retail environment we can measure it through the median time a customer spends in your shop. The shorter the time, the more efficiently you have organized the store layout, so the better the psychological access. Bigger shops and a broader assortment will weigh on the shopping time, but that is logical, as it will indeed reduce the psychological access. It will create the stress of choice and having to walk long distances before getting out.

From that perspective a second metric could be the median size of a shop. The equivalent in B2C or B2B could be the time it takes for a customer to place an order through your customer contact centre, or the time between an incoming order request, via e-mail or a website, and its confirmation by your customer service. Again, as we did for price as a metric, all of the above metrics should be compared to the average in the market or to a set of key competitors.

Physical access

For a retailer, physical access could by measured by the number of stores compared to the competition. Or we might be more specific and define the penetration in different types of areas, like rural versus cities. The penetration might be defined as the percentage of consumers within a certain distance of one of your stores. For a B2C company the number of distributors or point-of-sales where the product is offered can be a metric. Again, if we want to differentiate on physical access, we want to be able to compare that to the competition.

For a B2B company, customer order lead time may be an important metric, which is the time between the customers placing the order and receiving the product or service. Again, how does it compare to the competition? We may calculate regional differences as your distribution network may be more or less dense than that of the competition in certain regions. If you want to dominate on physical access, this is crucial information.

Service

Remember that Crawford and Mathews mention at least four aspects of the service attribute. The first is helpful advice by knowledgeable sales persons. For a retailer this could be measured in terms of the number of in-store personnel, or more specifically the number of qualified in-store personnel (eg butcher, bachelor in electronics).

An opex player will have fewer personnel as to cut costs and guarantee the lowest price. A product leader may require skilled personnel to ensure customers select the right products and use it in the correct way. However, as mentioned, for a product leader the product will be leading, and he may differentiate on service, or on experience. For the customer intimacy player, either the service or the product breadth will be leading. Where one is leading, the other will typically be differentiating. In a B2C or a B2B company the metric could be the number of technical service people, or the number of qualified technical service people – those who come to your home or company to analyse your problem and define an appropriate solution.

A second aspect of service is tailoring or personalization. Metrics in retail could include the number of products with service at a counter. In a B2C or B2B environment it could be the number of order lines with customization at the point-of-sale, the distributor or your distribution centre. If we go deeper in the supply chain, we could measure the number of SKUs with customer-specific packaging, the number of customer-specific products (meaning there is some customization other than in the packaging) or the number of customer-specific raw materials or components. If your company works 'engineer-to-order', meaning each product is designed and engineered for one customer, there is a high degree of tailoring, which will be confirmed by ranking high on each of the mentioned metrics.

A third aspect of service mentioned by Crawford and Mathews is hassle-free returns. This could be measured by the median time to register a defective item, or the median time to return a defective item. As a customer we probably want a smooth reporting process and fast return for any defective items. Companies that swap a defective item with a replacement or a new one will score well on the return metric, which is good, as they are indeed delivering an excellent returns service at that point. These same metrics apply to retail, B2C and B2B.

A fourth aspect which we added to service is availability. In retail the key metric is on-shelf availability (OSA). It calculates the number of products available on the shelf versus the total number of products. It can be a snapshot of today, or an average over a given number of days, or even weeks. You may zoom into specific assortments or groups of products like promotions.

Always having stock of promotional items is an exceptional service to deliver. Hard discounters may run promos but typically with limited inventory. They make sure all of it is sold to control the extra costs of running the promo.

In B2C and B2B it is more common to talk about OTIF, defining the number of orders, or order lines, that are delivered on time and in full with respect to the requested delivery date or the confirmed delivery date. Calculating the OTIF requires orders to be logged, which is not the case in a retail operation – hence the difference between this and OSA.

While the four service aspects mentioned are logical and relevant in many industries, service can be much broader and deeper. If as a building contractor you want to stand out on tailoring and customization, you may deliver so-called 'turnkey' projects, where you take care of everything for the customer, including fittings, furnishings and decor. If as an equipment manufacturer you want to stand out on returns and availability, you could offer preventive maintenance, or just guarantee a certain uptime of the delivered machines. Instead of selling machines, you may lease or rent them on a pay-per-use basis.

And this is only sticking to the four attributes mentioned. Many companies offer financial services to their customers, like credit lines, consignment stocks, contracts with fixed or variable pricing that provide some hedging for the customer. You may organize training and coaching for the customers' personnel, or you may actually deliver the personnel in an outsourcing type of solution.

From these examples it should be clear that the service attribute is the richest and the most complex. To separate the customer intimacy leaders from the product leaders and the operational excellence players, you will most probably need to refine the service attribute and the appropriate key metrics.

Product breadth

The fifth attribute, after price, psychological access, physical access and service, is the product breadth. For a retailer we can look at the median number of SKUs per store. To deliver a total solution, a customer intimacy player will need more of them compared to an operational excellence player. However, we need to make sure a large number of SKUs goes into breadth rather than depth. That can be done by adding a second metric median number of assortments per store. If you are a food retailer, think about any assortments carried by food retailers around the world. Than rank yourself against key competitors to see whether you dominate, differentiate or play at par.

For B2C and B2B we will more likely measure the number of SKUs in the product catalogue, complemented by the number of assortments in portfolio, to make sure the SKUs are used to create breadth instead of depth.

Product depth/quality

Firstly, product depth. For a retailer we will look at the median number of SKUs per store, and we may look at the median number of SKUs per assortment to measure the depth we reach. Again, compare yourself to the market to see whether you dominate, differentiate or play at par. For a B2C and a B2B it will be more logical to look at the number of SKUs in the product catalogue, complemented by the median number of SKUs per assortment to make sure the SKUs are used to create depth instead of breadth.

If your assortment is well defined, eg the spare parts for a specific car or a specific brand of cars, then you may also define coverage as the % of the total available products that you carry in your product catalogue. For many assortments, it may be impossible to define the number of total available products.

Online retail is redefining the boundaries of product breadth and depth. By building online transaction platforms and connecting suppliers, companies like Amazon or Alibaba are redefining the breadth and depth that can be delivered by one single company. When doing this type of metrics benchmarking and target setting, as a retailer you may have to make the split between the online world and physical stores.

Related to this is product quality, the dominating attribute for product leaders. The metric here is the maximum product performance or the median product performance in your product portfolio. If you're in the projection business, you may measure the light output in lumens, if you're building monitors or cameras it may be the number of megapixels, if you're in cars it may be the horsepower per gram of CO_2 emitted, and if you're in the food business it may be the number of months your meat has aged.

Experience

The seventh and final value attribute is experience. Of all the value attributes, experience is the most subjective. It is the excitement generated at the consumer or customer side, and the influence it has on his or her buying intention and the perceived value of the product. As it is subjective, we will need to ask the customer to give a score.

If we take increased buying intention and perceived value as the ultimate goals, these are the two questions we'll need to ask. For a retailer we will ask 'Has the atmosphere in the shop increased your willingness to buy?' and 'Has the atmosphere in the shop increased your appreciation of the products bought?'. An alternative could be to look at online forums that publish ratings, or to compile your own rating by analysing the number of positive or negative tweets about the shopping experience at your company compared to that at your competitors.

As a B2C company you will need to extend into your distributor network to be able to compile this type of information. As a B2B company, you need to intentionally design the creation of an experience as mentioned above, for instance by sending over sales people or technical service people to celebrate the delivery or the installation of your products or big orders. If you do so, it is probably best to then test the impact of those initiatives on future willingness to buy, and on appreciation of the products bought.

We have summarized the different value attributes and the underlying metrics in Table 6.1. As mentioned above, this is a starting point. At least for the service attribute you will need to study what is being offered in your market, what is 'playing at par', what is 'differentiating' and what is 'dominating', to separate the customer intimacy players from the opex players and the product leaders.

Conclusion

In this chapter we have essentially redefined the 'service' corner of our Supply Chain Triangle as a 'value' corner. We started by deriving four possible value drivers from the model of Treacy and Wiersema: price, product quality, product range and value added services. We married that to the

Table 6.1 Value attributes and related key metrics

Value Attribute	KPI	Definition	Measurement	Relevancy
Price	Price point vs median market price	your price versus median market price	in absolute terms, in %	Retail, B2C, B2B
Price	Price point vs key competitor(s)	your price versus price of key competitors	in absolute terms, in %	Retail, B2C, B2B
Psychological access	Median time in shop (vs median market or key competitors)	median time a customer spends in your shop (versus median of the market or key competitors)	in absolute terms, in %	Retail
Psychological access	Median size of shop (vs...)	average size of your store, versus...	in absolute terms, in %	Retail
Psychological access	Median time of CCC contact (vs...)	median time a customer talks to your customer contact centre for placing orders, asking questions,...	in absolute terms, in %	B2C, B2B
Psychological access	Median response time between order request and order confirmation (vs...)	median time to respond to a customer order request, eg via e-mail or a website	in absolute terms, in %	B2C, B2B
Physical access	Number of stores in target areas (vs...)	number of stores you have (versus...)	in absolute terms, in %	Retail
Physical access	Penetration of target areas (vs...)	customers within a given physical distance of one of your stores	in absolute terms, in %	Retail
Physical access	Number of distributors/point-of-sales in target areas (vs...)	number of distributors you have (versus...)	in absolute terms, in %	B2C, B2B

(continued)

Table 6.1 (Continued)

Value Attribute	KPI	Definition	Measurement	Relevancy
Physical access	Penetration of target areas (vs...)	customers within a given physical distance of one of your distributors/point-of-sales	in absolute terms, in %	B2C, B2B
Physical access	Median customer order lead time (vs...)	median time between placing of the order and receipt of the goods	in absolute terms, in %	B2B
Service – advice	Number of in-store personnel (vs...)	number of people available in store for help and advice	in absolute terms, in %	Retail
Service – advice	Number of qualified in-store personnel (vs...)	likwise... but with with specific qualifications (eg butcher)	in absolute terms, in %	Retail
Service – tailoring	Number of products with service at a counter (vs...)	number of products that can be ordered in custom portions at a counter	in absolute terms, in %	Retail
Service – returns	Median time for registering a defect item (vs...)	median time for registering a defect item, in the store, or via the CCC	in absolute terms, in %	Retail
Service – returns	Median time for returning a defect item (vs...)	median time between delivering a defective item and receiving it either repaired, receiving a replacement, or receiving a reimbursement	in absolute terms, in %	Retail
Service – availability	On shelf availability (OSA) (vs...)	the number of products available on the shelf versus the total number of products	in %, today, over the last x days, over the last x weeks,...	Retail

			Retail
Service – availability	On shelf availability (OSA) for specific assortments or groups of products (vs…)	availability of specific assortments or groups of products like promotions	in %, today, over the last x days, over the last x weeks,…
Service – advice	Number of technical service people (vs…)	number of technical service people available to analyse customer specific challenges and appropriate solutions	in absolute terms, in % B2C, B2B
Service – advice	Number of qualified technical service people (vs…)	likewise… but with specific qualifications	in absolute terms, in % B2C, B2B
Service – tailoring	Number of order lines with customization at point-of-sale, distributor or distribution centre (vs…)	the number of order lines with customization (eg split packaging, customer specific configuration of product,…)	in absolute terms, in % B2C, B2B
Service – tailoring	Number of customer specific packaging (vs…)	the number of stock keeping units (incl. the type of packaging) that sells to only one customer	in absolute terms, in % B2C, B2B
Service – tailoring	Number of customer specific products (vs…)	the number of products that has a customer-specific bill-of-material or formulation (regardless of the packaging)	in absolute terms, in relative % B2C, B2B
Service – tailoring	Number of customer specific raw materials/ components (vs…)	the number of raw materials, used in only one customer-specific bom or formulation	in absolute terms, in % B2C, B2B
Service – returns	Median time for registering a defect item (vs…)	idem as for retail	idem as for retail B2C, B2B

(continued)

Table 6.1 (*Continued*)

Value Attribute	KPI	Definition	Measurement	Relevancy
Service – returns	Median time for returning a defect item (vs…)	idem as for retail	idem as for retail	B2C, B2B
Service – availability	On-Time-In-Full (OTIF) (vs…)	the number of orders, or order lines, delivered on time and in full with the requested or the confirmed delivery date (which may be on-the-shelf in case of distributors and point-of-sales)	in %, today, over the last x days, over the last x weeks,…	B2C, B2B
Service – availability	On-Time-In-Full (OTIF) for specific assortments (vs…)	availability for specific assortments like spare parts	in %, today, over the last x days, over the last x weeks,…	B2C, B2B
Product breadth	Median number of SKUs per store (vs…)	the median number of products per store	in absolute terms, in %	Retail
Product breadth	Median number of assortments per store (vs…)	the median number of assortments per store	in absolute terms, in %	Retail
Product breadth	Number of SKUs in product catalogue (vs…)	the number of products in portfolio	in absolute terms, in %	B2C, B2B
Product breadth	Number of assortments in portfolio (vs…)	the number of assortments in portfolio	in absolute terms, in %	B2C, B2B
Product depth	Median number of SKUs per assortment (vs…)	the median number of products per assortment, which should be high for a speciality retailer	in absolute terms, in %	Retail

Category	Metric	Description	Measurement	Applicability
Product depth	Number of SKUs in product catalogue (vs…)	the number of products in portfolio	in absolute terms, in %	B2C, B2B
Product depth	Median number of SKUs per assortment (vs…)	the median number of products per assortment, which should be high for a speciality provider	in absolute terms, in %	B2C, B2B
Product depth	Coverage in specific assortments (vs…)	the % of the total available products in portfolio (eg % of replacement parts covering a specific car or brand)	in % of total available	B2C, B2B
Product quality	Maximum/median product performance (vs…)	maximum or median product performance, eg lumens for a projector, hp for an engine, months ripened for meat,…	in absolute terms, in %	Retail, B2C, B2B
Experience	Impact of atmosphere on willingness to buy	score on a scale of 1-5	in absolute terms, in %	Retail, B2C
Experience	Impact of atmopshere on appreciation of the products bought	score on a scale of 1-5	in absolute terms, in %	Retail, B2C
Experience	Impact of targeted actions on willingness to buy	score on a scale of 1-5	in absolute terms, in %	B2B
Experience	Impact of targeted actions on appreciation of the products bought	score on a scale of 1-5	in absolute terms, in %	B2B

model of Crawford and Mathews, but splitting their five value drivers into seven value drivers: price, psychological access, physical access, service, product breadth, product quality/depth and experience.

We adopted the approach of Crawford and Mathews to look for a 5-4-3-3-3-3-3 profile when defining a strategy. You can dominate on one driver, differentiate on a second, and at best be on par at the remaining drivers.

By splitting the five value drivers into seven, we can still derive the three strategic options of Treacy and Wiersema, though we are no longer limited to only three. From that perspective you can say we have extended the model of Treacy and Wiersema by using an extension of the model of Crawford and Mathews.

Secondly, we have defined a list of KPIs to monitor each of the seven value drivers. In the next chapter we will continue our definition of KPIs for the cost and the capital employed side of the triangle and we will build a KPI dashboard around our Supply Chain Triangle.

We recommend taking another look at the seven value drivers. Understanding where you are and where you want to be reveals the strategy of the company and the resulting trade-off with the cost and the capital employed side of the triangle. If you need to collapse your KPI dashboard, you will first focus on the value drivers where you want to dominate or differentiate. All this helps in creating a dashboard that is complete, comprehensive and strategy-driven.

References

Crawford, F and Mathews, R (2007) *The Myth of Excellence: Why great companies never try to be the best at everything*, Crown Business, London

Treacy, M and Wiersema, F (1995) *The Discipline of Market Leaders: Choose your customers, narrow your focus, dominate your market*, Basic Books, New York

Building a strategy-driven KPI dashboard

07

In the previous chapter we defined a list of metrics around seven value drivers, derived by combining the strategy models of Treacy and Wiersema (1995) and Crawford and Mathews (2007). In this chapter we will continue our definition of key metrics for the cost side and the capital employed side of the triangle. To do so, we will base ourselves on common financial metrics.

Once we have gathered the relevant key metrics for each of the three corners, we will assemble a KPI dashboard around our Supply Chain Triangle. We will show how the value metrics support the top-line and its growth. We will show how the value and the cost metrics combine into profitability metrics like gross margin or EBIT, and how the profitability metrics and the capital employed metrics combine into 'bang-for-the-buck' metrics like return on capital employed (ROCE). Next we will add metrics for core processes as so-called 'diagnostic' metrics, and we will show how the strategy of a company changes the set of metrics on which we focus and the targets we set.

We will conclude the chapter by comparing our KPI dashboard with the KPIs of the Supply Chain Operating Reference (SCOR) model. SCOR is a well-known reference model for supply chain processes and KPIs. We will argue that it misses out key metrics to visualize the chosen strategy, and that without knowing the strategy, it is difficult or even dangerous to benchmark and set targets for the cost and the capital employed.

Defining financial metrics for the cost side and the capital employed side of the triangle

Let's start by completing the financial metrics on the cost side of our triangle, and then take a look at the financial metrics on the capital employed side of the triangle.

Defining financial metrics for the cost side of the triangle

Let's start by recapping our latest version of our Supply Chain Triangle, showing the seven value drivers to which we have linked the different KPIs to measure the value corner of the triangle. It is shown in Figure 7.1.

The cost side shows the different operational costs like logistics, warehousing, manufacturing and purchasing. It also shows the cost of inventory write-offs, which links an excess inventory or an obsolete inventory from the capital employed back to the cost dimension. It also shows the R&D and the selling, general and administrative (SG&A) costs, which we need to derive the EBITDA from the gross margin. And finally, we have mentioned the depreciation and the amortization needed to derive the EBIT from the EBITDA.

Figure 7.1   Mapping Crawford and Mathews to Treacy and Wiersema and the Supply Chain Triangle using seven value drivers

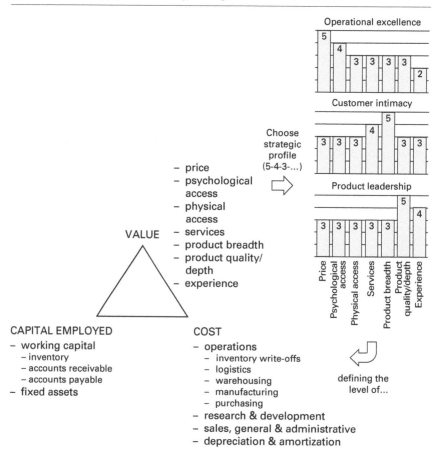

In financial terms, when controlling operations, it is common to distinguish between direct and indirect costs. Direct costs are directly linked to a production order. For instance, if I make a batch of 500 kg of dough, I know the cost of the ingredients and the cost of the personnel hours needed to insert the ingredients, start the mixer and release the batch to an intermediate stocking point or to the next step in the production process. Indirect costs are typically allocated to the product based on allocation rules. If I have three maintenance engineers, with a yearly cost of 300k, I can allocate the cost of the engineers to the product – for instance by saying 'I make 3,000 tons per year', so the maintenance cost per kilogram is €300,000/3,000,000kg = €0.1/kg.

In financial terms we also differentiate between fixed costs and variable costs. The material going into a product is a direct cost, but is typically also a variable cost. If I produce less, I consume less, so the total cost will be lower. The cost of my maintenance engineers may be a fixed cost. If instead of 3,000 tons, I produce only 2,000 tons, the maintenance cost will still be 300k. I may not be in a position to do with only two maintenance engineers, perhaps because of backup reasons. In this case the maintenance engineers are a fixed cost.

Managing the costs that are direct and variable is easier than managing those that are indirect and fixed. Of the two possible dimensions, direct versus indirect is more common in financial reporting. Fixed versus variable may be more important in budgeting, as this is where you ask for and commit extra fixed resources.

To reflect the above, we suggest accounting for direct versus indirect in the cost corner, as shown in Figure 7.2.

Compared to Figure 7.1 we are no longer talk about purchasing or manufacturing, but rather about direct/indirect material versus labour. These typically absorb all the purchasing, the manufacturing and the inbound logistics costs and lead to the so-called cost of goods sold (COGS). Having COGS as a metric is handy, as net sales minus the COGS gives the gross margin, and we know from previous chapters the gross margin is an important indicator of the strategy followed by the company.

Another change in Figure 7.2 versus 7.1 is that we have split the SG&A into its underlying components. In most companies SG&A includes the R&D costs, the sales costs, the outbound logistics costs, the inventory write-offs and what is called 'general and administrative', such as the finance and IT departments. Having details of the SG&A is relevant. As an example, knowing the split between the R&D versus the sales costs can tell us something about a product leadership versus a customer intimacy orientation. If we

Figure 7.2   Refining the financial KPIs on the cost side of the Supply Chain Triangle

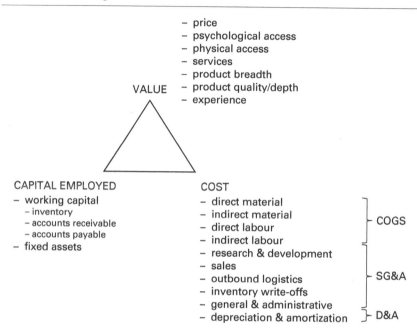

subtract the SG&A and the depreciation and amortization from the gross margin, we get to the EBIT, which is the second key profitability metric used in the financial benchmarking of the previous chapters.

Defining financial metrics for the capital employed side of the triangle

Figure 7.3 shows the refined metrics for the capital employed side of the triangle. We measure the inventory using the days inventory on hand (DIOH), the accounts receivable via the days of sales outstanding (DSO) and the accounts payable via the days of payables outstanding (DPO). We refer to the section on accounting basics in Chapter 1 for more details on how to calculate each of these metrics.

Working capital can be measured via the cash conversion cycle (CCC), which is the DIOH + DSO – DPO. Capital employed consists of working capital plus fixed assets. Looking at the fixed assets, it is probably relevant to look at how these evolve – have we made any new investments in fixed assets over the last year, what has the depreciation been, and what is the result in terms of net fixed assets (accounting for investments and depreciation)?

Figure 7.3   Refining the financial KPIs on the capital employed side of the
Supply Chain Triangle

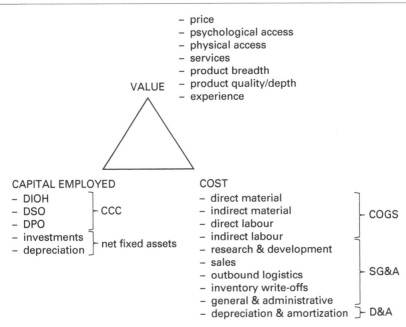

Metrics summary for a retail versus a manufacturing operation

Let's now add back the detailed metrics for the seven value drivers we described in the previous chapter. Figure 7.4 shows the resulting key metrics for a retail operation. Figure 7.5 shows the same but for a manufacturing operation, either B2B or B2C.

In Figure 7.6 we have again added the strategic dimension. A strategy implies a choice between the different value drivers. The choice we make on the value corner will have an impact on the cost and the capital employed corners.

Building our strategy-driven KPI dashboard

In this section we will use the derived KPIs on each of the corners of our triangle to build a KPI dashboard around that triangle. We will build the dashboard in three layers.

Figure 7.4 Metrics summary for a retail operation

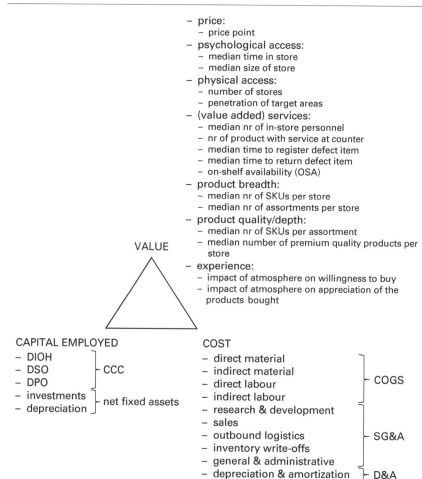

- price:
  - price point
- psychological access:
  - median time in store
  - median size of store
- physical access:
  - number of stores
  - penetration of target areas
- (value added) services:
  - median nr of in-store personnel
  - nr of product with service at counter
  - median time to register defect item
  - median time to return defect item
  - on-shelf availability (OSA)
- product breadth:
  - median nr of SKUs per store
  - median nr of assortments per store
- product quality/depth:
  - median nr of SKUs per assortment
  - median number of premium quality products per store
- experience:
  - impact of atmosphere on willingness to buy
  - impact of atmosphere on appreciation of the products bought

VALUE

CAPITAL EMPLOYED
- DIOH ⎤
- DSO ⎬ CCC
- DPO ⎦
- investments ⎤
- depreciation ⎦ net fixed assets

COST
- direct material ⎤
- indirect material ⎬ COGS
- direct labour ⎦
- indirect labour ⎤
- research & development ⎬ SG&A
- sales
- outbound logistics
- inventory write-offs
- general & administrative ⎦
- depreciation & amortization ⎬ D&A

Building layers 1 and 2 of the dashboard, the result metrics

Figure 7.7 shows the first layer of KPIs, built on the three corners of the triangle.

The top side of the triangle, the value drivers, are supporting the so-called 'top-line'. For an opex player, further improving the price point will help in attracting more customers and support the top-line and its growth. Likewise, for a customer intimacy player, further expanding the product portfolio and the solution set will support its market position and grow the top-line.

If we combine the top-line and the cost, we get to the so-called 'bottom-line'. Different strategies lead to different levels of complexity and to

Figure 7.5 Metrics summary for a manufacturing operation

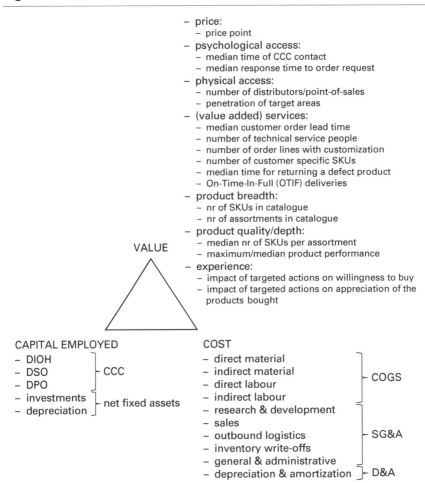

- price:
  - price point
- psychological access:
  - median time of CCC contact
  - median response time to order request
- physical access:
  - number of distributors/point-of-sales
  - penetration of target areas
- (value added) services:
  - median customer order lead time
  - number of technical service people
  - number of order lines with customization
  - number of customer specific SKUs
  - median time for returning a defect product
  - On-Time-In-Full (OTIF) deliveries
- product breadth:
  - nr of SKUs in catalogue
  - nr of assortments in catalogue
- product quality/depth:
  - median nr of SKUs per assortment
  - maximum/median product performance
- experience:
  - impact of targeted actions on willingness to buy
  - impact of targeted actions on appreciation of the products bought

VALUE

CAPITAL EMPLOYED
- DIOH ⎫
- DSO ⎬ CCC
- DPO ⎭
- investments ⎫ net fixed assets
- depreciation ⎭

COST
- direct material ⎫
- indirect material ⎬ COGS
- direct labour
- indirect labour ⎭
- research & development
- sales
- outbound logistics ⎬ SG&A
- inventory write-offs
- general & administrative ⎭
- depreciation & amortization ⎬ D&A

different levels of cost. A product leader will have a higher cost than an opex player, but will still have a higher EBIT. As its products are unique, the product leader can drive superior prices and EBIT from niches that benefit the newest and the highest specification.

If we combine the bottom-line with what is invested, we get to return metrics, or 'bang-for-the-buck' metrics. So far we have used the ROCE, but we will give more examples below. The top-line, the bottom-line and the return are a second layer of KPIs, as shown in Figure 7.8.

Typical top-line metrics used in companies are net sales and gross sales. Net sales is derived from gross sales by subtracting any rebates given in the sales process. You could think of market share or price as top-line metrics, but actually they are value drivers. Price has to do with the price attribute.

Figure 7.6 Metrics summary for a manufacturing operation, linking to strategy

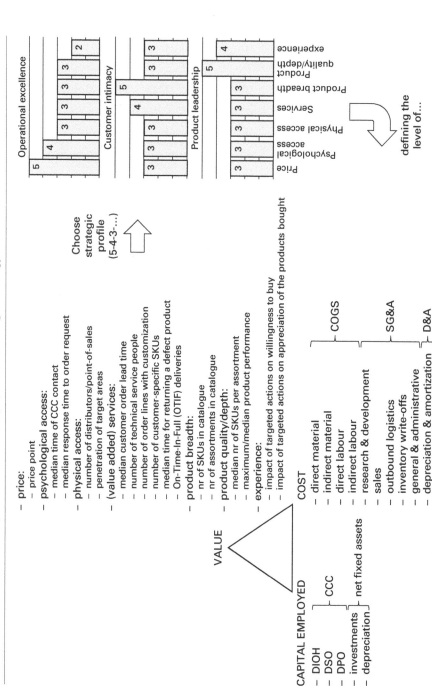

Figure 7.7 Layer 1 of the KPI dashboard: value, cost and capital employed

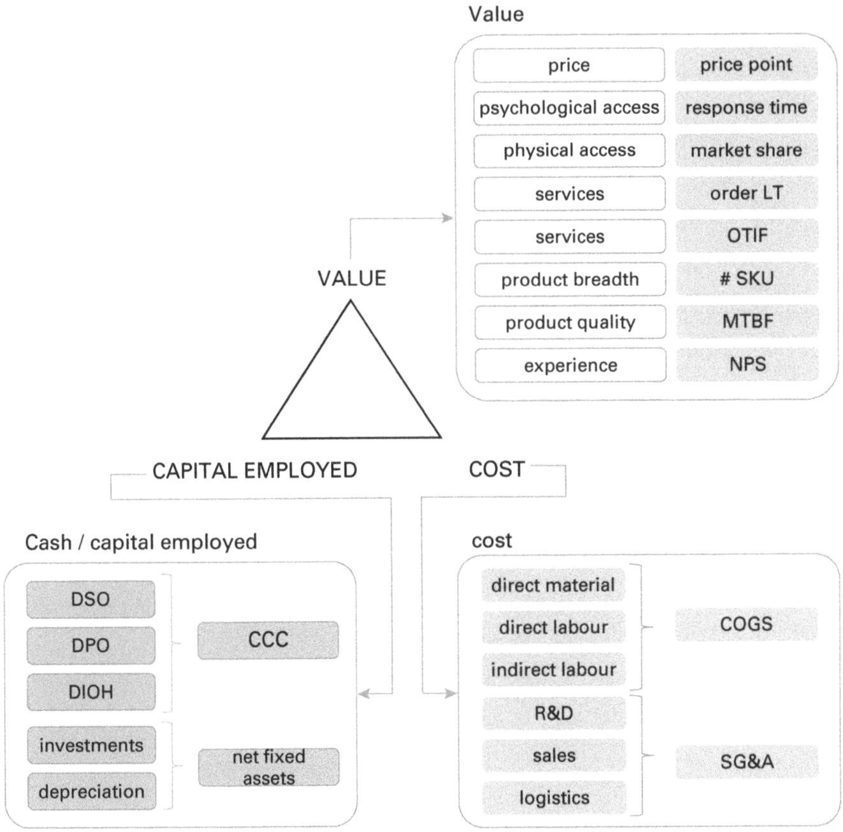

Market share can be linked to physical access – how easy is it for customers to 'physically' do business with me, how many regional sales offices, regional DCs or distributors I have. The bigger my market share, the closer I will be to my customer.

Many companies have growth objectives. Growth is a top-line objective. We have added growth as a top-line KPI in the overview in Figure 7.8.

In Chapter 3 we reviewed different bottom-line metrics: gross margin, EBITDA, EBIT and net profit. In that chapter we retained gross margin and EBIT as the two primary KPIs. Remember that gross margin was an indication of the chosen strategy. A product leader will have a superior gross margin, where an opex player will work with a minimal gross margin as to have the lowest price in the market.

The difference between EBIT and EBITDA is the depreciation and the amortization. These are not cash-outs – the cash-out happened at the time

Figure 7.8   Layer 1 and layer 2 of the KPI dashboard: top-line, bottom-line and return metrics

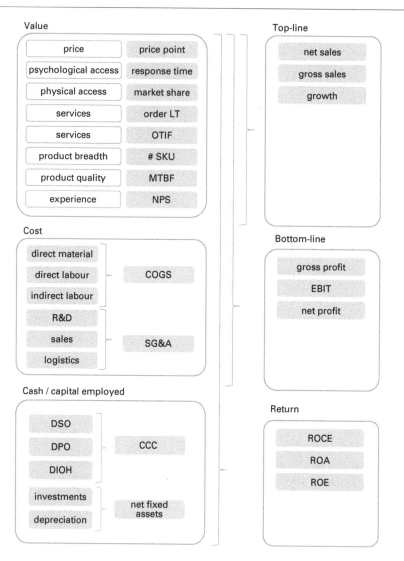

of the initial investment. As a result, EBITDA is a better indication for cash flow. However, every investment needs to be replaced in the long run, so from that perspective it is an overestimate of the real profitability of the company. Moreover, different accounting rules for treating R&D costs may make EBITDA comparisons across companies difficult, so for these two reasons we preferred EBIT when doing the benchmarking in Chapters 3 to 5.

Net profit is the EBIT after interest and taxes. As these are primarily financially driven, we have considered it to be less crucial in the supply chain context.

For the return metric, we have so far focused on the ROCE. While we believe ROCE is helpful, as it includes working capital and fixed assets, some companies look at alternatives such as return on assets (ROA), or return on equity (ROE), or return on average capital employed (ROACE).

ROA looks at the net profit / total assets. The total assets covers fixed assets and current assets, which include the cash, the inventory and the accounts receivable. A challenge we see is that assets can go up or down, for instance as the accounts receivable go up and down. That will affect the ROA. However, as long an increase in accounts receivable is compensated by an increase in accounts payable on the liabilities side of the balance sheet, there is no real change for the shareholder. The ROCE does a better job here, as in this situation the working capital will stay the same and so will the ROCE. This is illustrated in Figure 7.9.

As the accounts receivable increase, the total assets increase, but the capital employed can stay the same if it is compensated by an increase in accounts payable.

ROE looks at the net profit / owners' equity. As shown in Figure 7.10, the capital employed is in fact the owners' equity plus long-term liabilities. We consider the capital employed to be a 'physical' thing – we need certain assets and we need an amount of working capital to be able to run our

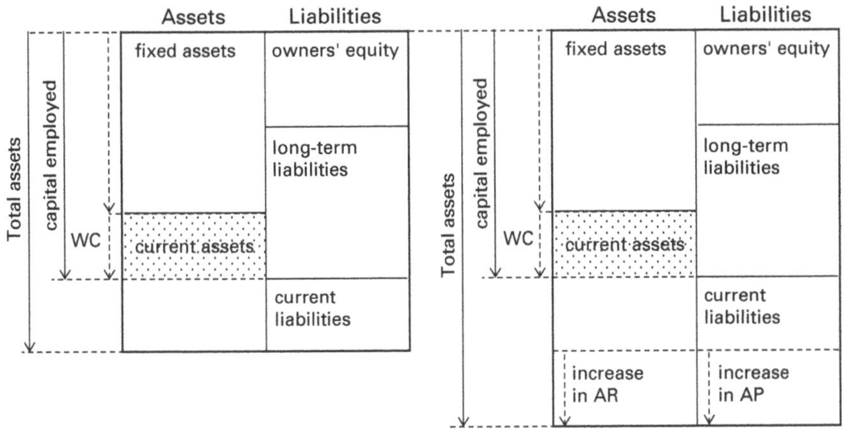

Figure 7.9 Comparing (the return on) capital employed with (the return on) assets

operations. How that capital is financed, and what percentage comes from equity versus loans, is a finance thing. Increasing or decreasing the long-term liabilities will increase or decrease the interest to be subtracted from the EBIT to get to the net profit.

On the other hand, equity is not free either. Equity is rewarded through dividends and by an increase in its value. An example of rebalancing equity versus long-term liabilities is shown in Figure 7.10.

The example shown reduces the so-called 'leverage', the percentage of liabilities that are not equity-financed. It could be the result of a capital increase, where some of the long-term loans are converted into equity. This operation may negatively impact the return on equity (we have lower interest, but there is a significant increase in equity), whereas the ROCE remains unchanged.

In summary, whereas the ROE is an important financial measure, as it measures the returns to the shareholder, we prefer the ROCE as a more operational return metric. The ROCE can be influenced via improving fixed asset turns and reducing the working capital – two elements on which supply chain has a key impact.

Adding layer 3, the diagnostic metrics

The main problem with the metrics in Figure 7.8 is that they are result metrics. We observe only after the fact that the top-line did not grow as planned, costs were higher than expected leading to inferior EBIT, or working capital increased more than planned. If possible we'd like to have metrics

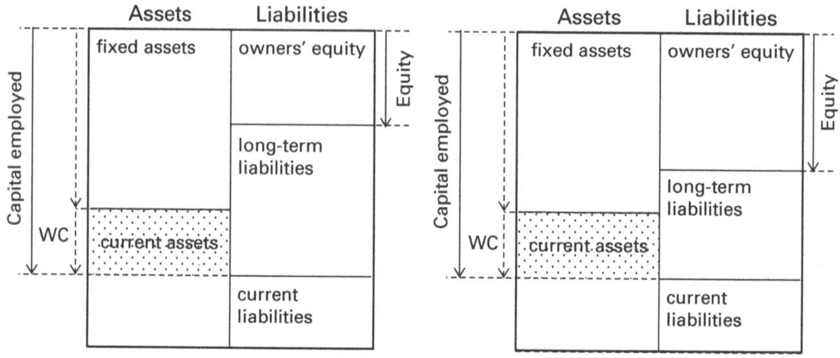

Figure 7.10 Comparing (the return on) capital employed with (the return on) equity

that tell us upfront where the net sales will be going, or what will happen to the direct material cost.

The drivers for the result metrics are the internal operations. We can define KPIs for each of our core processes: product development, order generation, order fulfilment, and after sales service. An example set is shown in Figure 7.11. They are 'causal' or diagnostic metrics.

Just as one example: if the order book is going up or down, that predicts where the revenue will be going. Or if the supplier On-Time-In-Full (OTIF) is going down, it may negatively affect our delivery performance which may lead to lost sales and negatively affect EBIT. Each of the operational metrics impacts the result metrics, typically with some delay.

The dependencies between the diagnostic and the result metrics are not straightforward. Lora Cecere (2014) likes to state that supply chains are complex and non-linear systems. We agree with that. Take the example of the supplier issue. We may have inventory buffers of raw materials, of intermediates and finished products which protect the top-line and the bottom-line. As we temporarily dig into the inventories, it may even positively impact working capital and boost the ROCE.

On the other hand, if inventories are already low, we may start expediting raw materials and increase costs to protect the top-line. Our top-line and delivery performance will stay the same, but our EBIT will be lower.

Finally, when problems are structural, there may be no way to avoid a shortage for customers, leading to lost sales and possibly a long-term effect on customer churn. Modelling all of these relationships is complex, near impossible. That's not our ambition in this book. It is however important to have all the metrics in one table as to see what is happening and being able to make these connections. We will rely on the human brain and the experience of the seasoned managers to make the connections. They will make mistakes, but having all the data at a glance will certainly lead to a better result compared to not having it.

Let's now look at the example KPIs for the different core processes shown in Figure 7.11. Critical KPIs for product development are the number of new product introductions (NPIs) and the number of end-of-life products (EOLs). Many companies are biased towards the top-line. Stopping old products will lead to lower revenue. However, older products typically have lower sales, a lower margin, and require a relatively high inventory to support the target service levels. Stopping old products, from that perspective, typically increases the ROCE. Having some targets for the minimal margin per inventory £, or more simply the maximum size of the product portfolio, can help to keep the complexity and the ROCE under control.

Figure 7.11 Layer 1, 2 and 3 of the KPI dashboard: process or diagnostic metrics

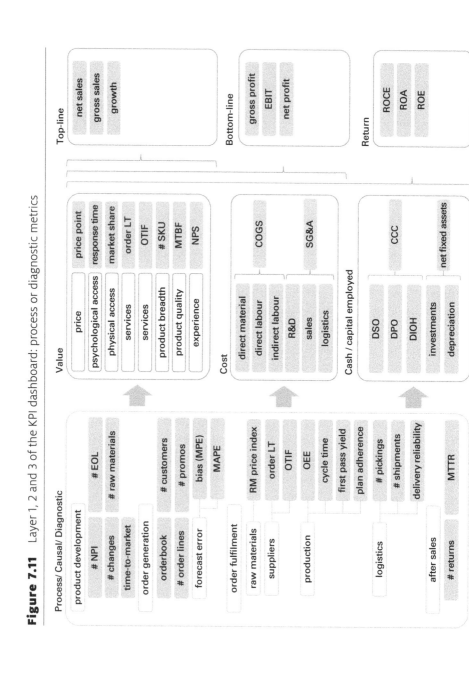

A second key metric for product management is the number of raw materials or components. In general, complexity on the demand side has grown. Even an opex player will have to deliver a more diverse set of products compared with 10 years ago. To remain the price leader, this needs to be done at a minimal cost and with minimal inventory. One of the ways to accommodate that is to design the products 'for supply chain'. Instead of having each product use separate raw materials or components, using 'platforms' with a common base can help in delivering more diversity, while keeping the number of suppliers and the raw material inventory low.

Likewise we can look for postponement opportunities. Instead of applying customer-specific packaging or finishes at the SKU level, it may be more cost-effective to store products in a 'basic', undifferentiated format and then apply last-minute customization based on actual customer orders, either in the plant or in a regional DC. This is another example of how we can deliver a broader customization in the market while reducing the cost and the inventory needed.

Again, the product may need to be designed in such a way that this can actually be done in practice. For this reason, tracking the number of raw materials and components can be a second key causal metric, affecting the cost and the inventory.

Other possible metrics for product management are the number of product changes, or the time-to-market, being the average time between idea and launch in the market. For a product leader it is essential that its products are always up-to-date, requiring a high number of product changes to flow through the supply chain. The supply chain will need to organize for this. It is also essential for a product leader to be first to the market with a new technology, and to continuously be first to the market. Compressing the time from idea to launch is essential to get that done. As a result, measuring that as a key metric, and improving on it, is essential for a product leader.

Example KPIs for order generation or the sales process could be the size of the orderbook, the number of order lines, the number of customers or the number of promos run. The number of order lines per customer may differentiate the customer intimacy player from other strategies, and from that perspective could go on the 'product breadth' under the value drivers.

We have also added forecast error under the order generation process. For many companies the customer order lead time is shorter than the supply chain cycle time, and as a result they need to forecast what customers are going to buy. That forecast will always be wrong – the question is, how wrong, and how to minimize both the bias (the tendency to over- or under-forecast) and the absolute error (how accurately we predicted the quantity in that period). If we can reduce error on the forecast, we can typically work with a lower inventory, we will have lower 'firefighting' costs making up for unexpected orders, and we will improve the OTIF as for some surprises we simply can't address by firefighting. This is another illustration of the causal or diagnostic relationship between the process KPIs and the result KPIs.

Figure 7.11 also shows a selection of KPIs for the order fulfilment process. Many companies follow raw material indexes that tell them something about the cost of their raw materials going up or down. Some companies have their customer prices directly linked to a raw material index, like the ICIS Global Petrochemical Index (IPEX) which provides a capacity-weighted measure of the average change in petrochemical prices over time. In this case, their revenue will go up or down with the price of their raw materials. If you can't charge an increase in raw materials to your customers, or at least not directly, it will be the EBIT that goes up or down.

For many industries the cost of raw materials is an important part of the cost of the product. Especially for opex players, controlling the raw material cost is essential to guarantee the lowest price in the market.

Next we can look at supplier and supplier reliability metrics. Just as we looked at the number of raw materials, we can look at the number of suppliers. A product leader will have more raw materials and suppliers than an opex player. However, for any strategy, reducing the number of suppliers will help in pooling volume and negotiating better prices. For any strategy, design for supply chain and postponement will help in reducing the cost, the inventory and the number of suppliers while delivering a broader set of services to the customer. So in any case, tracking the number of suppliers is relevant.

As well as number of suppliers, supplier reliability is a key metric – their lead time and reliability. Six Sigma teaches to 'first reduce the variance and then shift the mean'. In general you want suppliers to deliver on their promise. If suppliers are frequently late, you either have to add an extra inventory buffer on your side to compensate for that, or it will disrupt your operations and drive up the direct and indirect cost.

Once you have reliable supply, you will try to reduce the lead time. Some companies impel suppliers to reduce lead times, which may shift the inventory burden to the supplier and force them to open a regional stocking point for you. A better alternative could be to see if you can apply postponement at the supplier side. Maybe you can commit to certain volumes eight weeks upfront, and try to specify the exact variant two weeks upfront. In any case, reducing the lead time will reduce the inventory required on your side, and as not all surprises can be covered with inventory, it will also reduce fire-fighting costs and eventually improve the OTIF to the final customer.

The same holds true for your production. Reducing the cycle time will help reduce work in process and finished goods inventories, reduce firefighting costs and eventually improve the OTIF to the customer. In production you'll also need quality metrics such as the first pass yield. The first pass yield defines the percentage of products that come to the end of the production line without any defects. In a five-step assembly process, a yield of 10% on an individual step, meaning 90% of the products are defect-free, will result in a first pass yield of 90%*90%*90%*90%*90% = 59%. Not only does that mean that 41% require rework, significantly impacting the cost of production, it also creates a risk for quality problems in the market. If the quality level is that low, one can question how certain we are we have spotted all potential quality issues in the remaining 59% that will be sent to the customers. It is quite likely we will have extra quality issues there, further increasing the cost burden.

Another common and important metric in production is the operational equipment efficiency (OEE). The OEE is calculated as availability × performance × quality. Availability is the percentage of time that a machine or an operation is really available for production. It accounts for any losses due to planned and unplanned down time, for instance to carry out maintenance. Performance looks at the actual production rate versus the target production rate, and quality looks at the percentage of units produced that are without defect. An OEE of 100% means there is no down time, we continuously keep running, we run at the target production rate and there is no quality loss. If we can run above the target rate, the OEE can even be higher than 100%. The OEE has an important impact on the product cost.

An important metric for supply chain planning is the 'plan adherence' of production. Is production making what it has promised to make? In some companies the quality process is so delicate that it is difficult to predict what percentage of the production will actually be good enough to be sold. Think about any type of growing process, where the output and the quality of the process depends on environmental factors. A significant variability in supply requires an extra buffer stock if you want to keep the next step in the supply chain running. Reducing this variability will allow to reduce those buffer inventories, will lower firefighting costs and ultimately improve the OTIF towards the customer.

Finally, Figure 7.11 shows some logistics and after-sales metrics. The real OTIF should be measured on the actual versus promised delivery date at the customer's site. In this case the delivery performance is an integral part of the OTIF. We already talked about quality issues in production triggering quality issues in the field. The number of issues or product returns may be a key metric for after-sales, as may be the mean time between failure (MTBF) or the mean time to repair (MTTR).

What you should feel after this review is that understanding the key metrics in your operations and how they affect the result metrics is important to ultimately understand and drive your ROCE.

Understanding the impact of strategy on the dashboard

The dashboard essentials

Figure 7.12 shows the three layers and seven blocks that summarize the essence of our KPI dashboard. The three corners of our Supply Chain Triangle in the middle explain the top-line, the bottom-line and the return on the right. The process metrics serve as causal or diagnostic metrics.

Adding Treacy and Wiersema to the dashboard essentials

Figure 7.13 recaps how the three strategies of Treacy and Wiersema are in essence different ways to come to the same ROCE. In the figure OE stands for operational excellence, CI for customer intimacy and PL for product leadership. Remember from Chapter 2 and 3 that the level of service, or

Figure 7.12   The three layers and seven essential blocks of our KPI dashboard

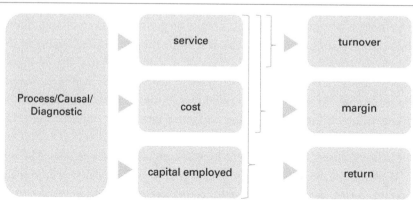

'value' as we came to call it, can be measured by the gross margin. It is the premium the customer is willing to pay, on top of the cost of the goods sold, for the product and the service delivered.

In those chapters we argued at length, and demonstrated, that product leaders can drive the highest gross margin from their unique products delivered to niche markets. The gross margin of the opex players will be the lowest. To have the lowest price in the market they will give away as much gross margin as possible. To still earn a reasonable EBIT, they need to keep the SG&A costs as low as possible. The customer intimacy players have an average gross margin. Their one-stop shop and total solution command a premium from their customers, who will lower their total cost of ownership by going with one solution provider instead of coordinating many themselves. However, those customers will closely monitor whether the premium charged by the customer-intimate supplier exceeds the value derived from it. If it does, the customer will revert to designing the solution in-house and shopping for the components from low-cost suppliers.

To deliver the newest and highest specification product, the product leaders, compared to the other players, will have a higher cost and a higher capital employed. That is OK as long as the EBIT is higher, which is possible as their superior gross margin allows for a higher cost while still landing a higher EBIT compared to the other players in the market. For comparable volumes, the higher price will also inflate the net sales higher compared to the other players. All of this is once more summarized in Figure 7.13.

Looking at it from the perspective of the opex players, for the same volume the turnover will be lower (lower price), the gross margin will be

Figure 7.13 The three strategies from Treacy and Wiersema are different ways to generate the same ROCE

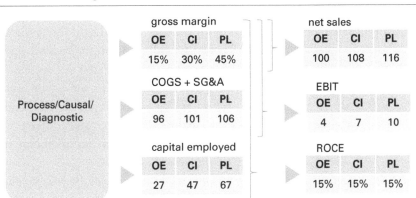

lower and the EBIT will be lower. However, we still come to the same ROCE by employing significantly less capital. We will have fewer assets that are put to better use and will have less working capital.

The customer intimacy players are somewhere in between. They command a premium from their customers for carrying more complexity and adding more services. That gives them a somewhat higher revenue, gross margin and EBIT. They do require some more capital to get their business running. Their customers will keep a close watch on whether the higher price is in sync with the cost reduction and the value creation on the customer side. That keeps the pressure on the customer intimacy players. Again they are in the most difficult position as they are attacked on both sides.

The product leaders bring new products to the market which may disrupt their current offerings, and the opex players are continuously undermining their margin by further cutting costs and lowering prices.

Adding Crawford and Mathews to the dashboard

In the next step we will again map the findings of Treacy and Wiersema to those of Crawford and Mathews, as in the previous chapter. To achieve this we extended the number of value drivers to seven by splitting psychological access (more linked to operational excellence) and physical access (more linked to service), and by splitting out product breadth (more linked to customer intimacy) from product quality and depth (more linked to product leadership).

As well as the value drivers, a second core concept of Crawford and Mathews is the creation of 5-4-3-3-3(-3-3) profiles. In fact we had to extend it from five to seven value drivers. You can choose one driver on which you want to dominate, one driver on which you want to differentiate, and you'll have to be at par at the remaining drivers. We have argued that an opex player dominates on price and differentiates on psychological access, that a customer intimacy player dominates on product breadth and differentiates on service, and that finally the product leader will dominate on product quality/depth, and will differentiate on experience. As illustrated in Figure 6.9, different strategies correspond with different settings for the seven value drivers, it is like an equalizer on a stereo. Trying to boost all of the attributes will not change the sound. You have to make choices to create a difference.

In Figure 7.14 we have added those different settings to our dashboard of Figure 7.11. They reflect the settings shown in Figure 6.9.

The first bar shows the setting for operational excellence, the second and the third for customer intimacy and product leadership. For the first value driver, price, this is where an opex player dominates, and where a customer intimacy player and product leader are at par (or potentially even below par for a product leader). Likewise you'll see that product quality is the dominating attribute for the product leader (the third bar), whereas this is on par for the opex and the customer intimacy player. In Figure 7.14 we have also repeated the tables that explain how the different strategies are different ways to generate ROCE.

We can extend those equalizers to the process or causal metrics. Going back to the explanation of the product leader in Chapter 2, we know that R&D and marketing are the most important internal processes. If you want the have the newest and the highest specification and be able to drive superior margin from niches, than these two core processes are key. If you want to dominate on product, you'll have to dominate on these processes. That doesn't mean that operations (or cost) is not important, it needs to be on par. That's exactly what is shown in Figure 7.14. The right bar is the one of the product leader, it is 5 for product development and 3 for the others.

Likewise, we have discussed at length in Chapter 2 that an operational excellence leader is all about efficient operations – we simply have to do it cheaper than the competition if we want to provide a lower price. It's not that innovation or marketing are not important, but they will be more basic – you'll just have to play at par. If you want to dominate on price, you'll first of all have to dominate in the operational processes. That's again what is shown in Figure 7.14. The left bar is the one for the opex player – it is 5 for the operations processes and 3 for the others.

A customer intimacy player will have to dominate in sales, or the order generation process as it is called in Figure 7.14. After-sales is also a form of service, so we've added the same profile there – a 5 on sales and service processes and a 3 on the others. This is the middle of the three bars in Figure 7.14.

If you want to get the full picture, you'll need to look at all of the KPIs. The targets for the level 5 KPIs will be the highest, whereas for the level 3 KPIs you'll play at the market average. The targets on the KPIs define the way you want to drive value, as measured by ROCE, from your customer base. Treacy and Wiersema described three archetype strategies. and in Chapters 3, 4 and 5 we showed how to use two-dimensional benchmarking to derive targets for gross margin, EBIT, inventory, working capital, fixed asset turns and ROCE for each one. From Chapter 6 we know that Crawford and Mathews argue that any 5-4-3-3-3-3-3 profile is a possible differentiating strategy. That may lead to still other positions on our bang-for-the-buck lines. As an investor we don't mind which strategy is used, as long as the 'bang-for-the-buck' or the ROCE remains the same.

Figure 7.14 The KPI dashboard with the 'equalizer' from Crawford and Mathews and the three Treacy and Wiersema archetypes

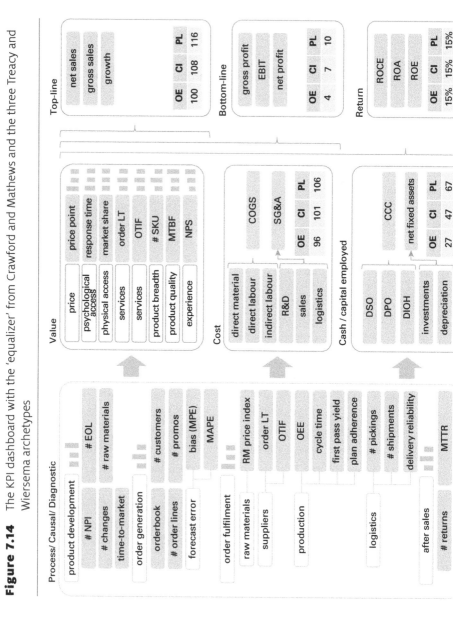

If you need to collapse your dashboard, it is quite logical that you look at the level 5 and 4 metrics first. Any deviation on those is more harmful than a deviation on the 3. Whereas a deviation on the 3 needs to be controlled, as it can erode the advantage derived from the level 5 and the level 4, a deviation of a level 5 is simply considered a major failure which can create a long-term perception issue. Consider an opex player which fails to deliver the lowest price. If he doesn't deliver on his core promise, customers are more likely to stay away for a longer period, compared to the opex player falling behind on experience. You didn't come or buy for the experience right, so you'll be more willing to forgive, unless it becomes worse and pertains.

The same for product leader delivering a crappy product to the market, such as when Samsung had issues with its S7. You don't mind the Apple iPhone being more expensive than its closest competitors, but you would mind if its performance were significantly below that of competitors.

So not only do the 5-4-3-3-3-3-3 guide the way in setting targets, for the process metrics and for the result metrics, they also show the way when trying to collapse the dashboard to its essentials. We'll next show an example of how to use this method to build an iPad metrics dashboard.

An example iPad dashboard

Figure 7.15 shows how to translate the model of Figure 7.14 into an operational dashboard. You can see the process metrics in the first column, the value, cost and capital employed metrics in columns 2 and 3, and you have the net sales, EBIT and ROCE in the column to the right.

From the dashboard we see that sales is at £1,041 million, up £144 million from last year, and £41 million above budget. The EBIT is at 7.53%, up 2.49% versus last year, but 0.47% below budget. Let's try to understand why.

From the value drivers (percentage of sales coming from new products, price point, OTIF, lead time) we learn the following. We see that good results are driven by a booming new product. The company we are looking at is a product leader. It has percentage of sales coming from new products at 33%, which is 8% higher than expected. We see the price point is 23% above the average market price, which is 2% lower than the 25% target. The recent closure of a number of big deals has boosted the turnover, but we have had to give in a little more on the price to sweeten those deals and get the volumes in.

The worrying drivers are the OTIF and the lead time. We see our lead times are up to three weeks, which is two weeks longer than the target of one week. We also see we are bad at delivering on our promise. The realized

Figure 7.15 Example iPad dashboard for a product leader

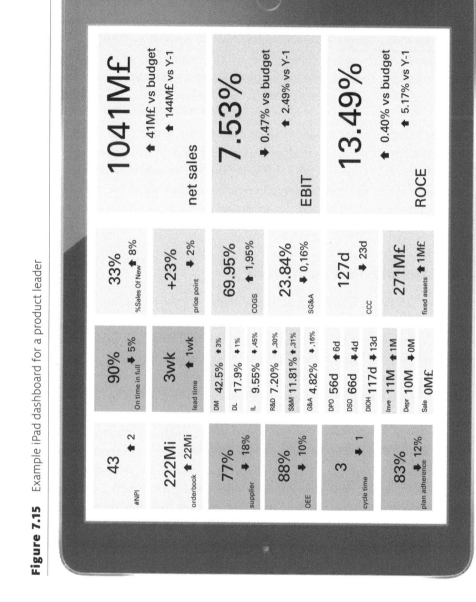

OTIF of 90% is 5% lower than the 95% target. If we scroll to the process metrics, we see the issue is driven by supplier performance. As our business is booming, we have overlooked the fact that some key suppliers are currently unable to keep up, as demonstrated by the supplier OTIF of 77% which is 18% down from the 95% target.

Those supplier issues are also hurting our OEE and our cycle time in production. As materials are coming in late and infrequently, we have multiple changes to the production plan. We start pre-assembling some of the final products and then have them wait for extra material to come in to be able to finish them. All of this weighs on the direct material cost, which weighs on the cost of goods sold, which together with the slightly lower price explains the lower EBIT.

At the bottom right we see that, despite the lower EBIT, the ROCE is actually 0.4% above target and 5.17% up from last year. This is due to the work we've done on reducing the working capital. We can see the CCC has been reduced by 23 days down to 127 days. We also see this is the result of an improvement on all three of the underlying components, the days of payables outstanding, the days of sales outstanding and the days of inventory on hand.

So despite the challenges we have in speeding up suppliers to restore OTIF, this reads as an excellent result. However, if we were able to boost the supplier OTIF, we'd probably be able to push our sales even higher, improve the EBIT, and take the ROCE towards 15%!

Comparison with the SCOR model

As already introduced in Chapter 1, the Supply Chain Operating Reference (SCOR) Model was initially developed by PRTM, now part of PWC, and AMR Research, now part of Gartner, and endorsed by the Supply Chain Council, now part of APICS. SCOR is a process and KPI reference model for supply chain. The model is continuously enhanced and expanded. We will use the v10 as our reference.

The five key processes of SCOR

Figure 7.16 summarizes the five key processes for which SCOR is well known: Plan, Source, Make, Deliver and Return.

Some companies name their divisions after these processes. They have a 'plan' organization, a 'make', a 'deliver' and a 'source' instead of 'production' or 'purchasing'. SCOR also promotes the extended view of the supply

Figure 7.16 The five core processes of the SCOR model

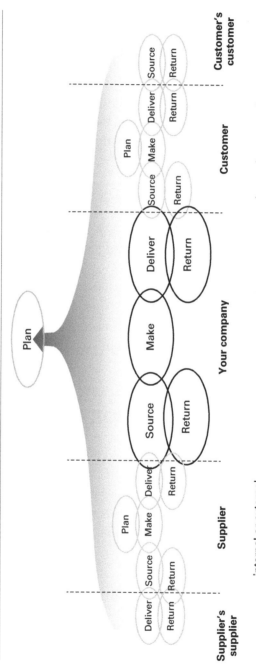

chain, from the customer's customer to the supplier's supplier. We will not show it here, but SCOR offers a great deal of detail on how to organize each of these key processes. We refer to the quick reference guide on SCOR on the APICS website for more information.

SCOR performance attributes and metrics

That quick reference guide will introduce us to the so-called 'performance attributes' and level 1 metrics of the SCOR framework. In SCOR, a performance attribute is a grouping of metrics used to set a strategic direction. There are five, and they are listed in Table 7.1.

Reliability, responsiveness and agility can be linked to the value corner of our triangle. Cost can obviously be linked to the cost side of our triangle, and we will see where to link the asset management efficiency when we talk about the underlying metrics.

Table 7.1   The SCOR model's five performance attributes

Performance attribute	Definition
Reliability	The ability to perform tasks as expected. Reliability focuses on the predictability of the outcome of a process. Typical metrics for the reliability attribute include: on-time, the right quantity, the right quality.
Responsiveness	The speed at which tasks are performed. The speed at which a supply chain provides products to the customer. Examples include cycle-time metrics.
Agility	The ability to respond to external influences, the ability to respond to marketplace changes to gain or maintain competitive advantage. SCOR agility metrics include flexibility and adaptability
Costs	The cost of operating the supply chain processes. This includes labour costs, material costs, management and transportation costs. A typical cost metric is cost of goods sold.
Asset management efficiency (assets)	The ability to efficiently utilize assets. Asset management strategies in a supply chain include inventory reduction and in-sourcing vs outsourcing. Metrics include: inventory days of supply and capacity utilization.

Each performance attribute has one or more Level 1 metrics, supported by Level 2 and Level 3 metrics. Level 2 metrics serve as diagnostics for level 1 metrics. This means that by looking at the performances of the level 2 metrics, I can explain performance gaps or improvements for the level 1 metrics. Table 7.2 lists the level 1 metrics.

Metrics are coded. The coding starts with the performance attributes: Reliability – RL, Responsiveness – RS, Agility – AG, Cost – CO, and Asset Management – AM. Each metric starts with this two letter code, followed by a number to indicate the level, followed by a unique identifier. For example: Perfect Order Fulfilment is RL.1.1 – a level 1 metric within the Reliability attribute. It is defined as 'the percentage of orders meeting delivery performance with complete and accurate documentation and no delivery damage'. The underlying diagnostic metrics are:

- RL.2.1 Percentage of Orders Delivered in Full. An order is considered perfect if the products ordered are the products provided and the quantities ordered match the quantities provided.

- RL.2.2 Delivery Performance to Customer Commit Date. A delivery is considered perfect if the location, specified customer entity and delivery time ordered is met upon receipt.

- RL.2.3. Documentation Accuracy. Documentation supporting the order line is considered perfect if it is all accurate, complete, and on time.

- RL.2.4. Perfect Condition. The product condition is considered perfect if the product is delivered / faultlessly installed (as applicable) on specification, with the correct configuration, with no damage, customer ready, and is accepted by the customer.

Likewise, all other level 1 metrics can be broken down or are supported by level 2 and even level 3 metrics. Example level 3 metrics are:

- RL.3.36 Fill Rate. 'The percentage of ship-from-stock orders shipped within 24 hours of order receipt.'

- RL.3.37 Forecast Accuracy. 'Forecast accuracy is calculated for products and/or families for markets/distribution channels, in unit measurement. Common calculation (Sum Actuals – Sum of Variance) / Sum Actuals to determine percentage error.'

- RL.3.49 Schedule Achievement. 'The percentage of time that a plant achieves its production schedule. This calculation is based on the number of scheduled end-items or total volume for a specific period. Note: over-shipments do not make up for undershipments.'

- RL.3.58 Yield. 'The ratio of usable output from a process to its input.'

Table 7.2 The SCOR model's level 1 metrics

Attribute	Index	Name	Description
Reliability	RL.1.1	Perfect order Fulfilment	The percentage of orders meeting delivery performance with complete and accurate documentation and no delivery damage. Components include all items and quantities on time using the customer's definition of on-time, and documentation – packing slips, bills of lading, invoices, etc.
Responsiveness	RS.1.1	Order Fulfilment cycle Time	The average actual cycle time consistently achieved to fulfil customer orders. For each individual order, this cycle time starts from the order receipt and ends with customer acceptance of the order.
Agility	AG.1.1	Upside supply chain flexibility	The number of days required to achieve an unplanned sustainable 20% increase in quantities delivered.
Agility	AG.1.2	Upside supply chain adaptability	The maximum sustainable percentage increase in quantity delivered that can be achieved in 30 days.
Agility	AG.1.3	Downside supply chain adaptability	The reduction in quantities ordered sustainable at 30 days prior to delivery with no inventory or cost penalties.
Cost	CO.1.1	Supply chain management cost	The sum of the costs associated with the SCOR Level 2 processes to Plan, Source, Deliver, and Return
Cost	CO.1.2	Cost of goods sold	The cost associated with buying raw materials and producing finished goods. This cost includes direct costs (labour, materials) and indirect costs (overhead).

(continued)

Table 7.2 *(Continued)*

Attribute	Index	Name	Description
Asset Management	AM.1.1	Cash-to-cash cycle time	The time it takes for an investment made to flow back into a company after it has been spent on raw materials. For services, this represents the time from the point where a company pays for the resources consumed in the performance of a service to the point that the company receives payment from the customer for those services.
Asset Management	AM.1.2	Return on Supply Chain Fixed Assets	Return on supply chain fixed assets measures the return an organization receives on its invested capital in supply chain fixed assets. This includes the fixed assets used in Plan, Source, Make, Deliver, and Return.
Asset Management	AM.1.3	Return on Working Capital	Return on working capital is a measurement which assesses the magnitude of investment relative to a company's working capital position verses the revenue generated from a supply chain. Components include accounts receivable, accounts payable, inventory, supply chain revenue, cost of goods sold and supply chain management costs.

Mapping the SCOR level 1 to our SC KPI dashboard

Figure 7.17 maps the level 1 metrics of SCOR to our SC KPI dashboard. We have hidden the sections that are not touched by SCOR.

As already mentioned, the reliability and agility metrics are easily linked to the value corner of the triangle. In fact, order fulfilment cycle time is the same as what we have called the order lead time, and perfect order fulfilment is comparable to what we have called OTIF. Upside and downside flexibility and adaptability can also be linked to the service attribute. It is a service to your customer.

The supply chain management cost and cost of goods sold link into the cost side of the triangle. Supply chain management cost is not a common financial metric. As already argued, we prefer common financial metrics like the cost of goods sold, direct and indirect labour and material cost.

The cash-to-cash cycle time is the same as our CCC, and links into the cash or capital employed metrics. The return on supply chain fixed assets and the return on working capital link into the return or 'bang-for-the-buck' metrics, but again, they are not common financial metrics. We prefer the use of something like ROCE, which will easily be understood by a broader audience and the whole finance community, as opposed to a return on working capital or a return on the supply chain fixed assets only.

On the one hand, we see that SCOR maps nicely into our KPI dashboard. On the other, we also see it clearly misses metrics, as shown in Figure 7.18.

On the value side, we see that SCOR in fact only has service metrics. It does not have the price, the access, the product or the experience dimension. This implies SCOR is blind to strategy. That is a problem, especially given the fact that SCOR is frequently used to do benchmarking. How can you compare companies on order lead time or OTIF, or even worse on cost, if you don't know whether they are operational excellence, customer intimacy, or product leaders? Likewise, it is impossible to compare the CCC of two companies if you can't compare their product breadth! Though SCOR seems a de facto standard for benchmarking, we see a huge issue and urgently advise companies to complement SCOR with extra metrics when doing such an exercise.

On the cost side, we see that SCOR is focused on the supply chain costs, but ignores important costs such as R&D or sales. When setting targets for supply chain costs, it is important to balance these against the sales and the R&D costs, and relate them to the chosen strategy. Think of our example in Chapter 2 of the company switching from a product leadership to a customer intimacy strategy. As supply chain, you'll need to look

Figure 7.17 Mapping the SCOR level 1 metrics to our supply chain KPI dashboard

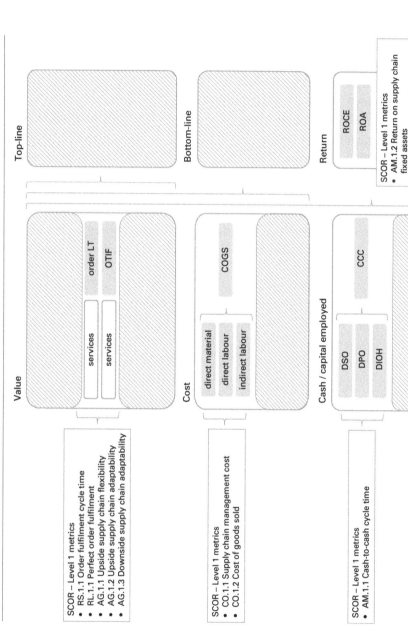

Top-line

Bottom-line

Return

Value

Cost

Cash / capital employed

order LT

OTIF

services

services

COGS

direct material

direct labour

indirect labour

CCC

DSO

DPO

DIOH

ROCE

ROA

SCOR – Level 1 metrics
- RS.1.1 Order fulfilment cycle time
- RL.1.1 Perfect order fulfilment
- AG.1.1 Upside supply chain flexibility
- AG.1.2 Upside supply chain adaptability
- AG.1.3 Downside supply chain adaptability

SCOR – Level 1 metrics
- CO.1.1 Supply chain management cost
- CO.1.2 Cost of goods sold

SCOR – Level 1 metrics
- AM.1.1 Cash-to-cash cycle time

SCOR – Level 1 metrics
- AM.1.2 Return on supply chain fixed assets
- AM.1.3 Return on working capital

Figure 7.18 The SCOR level 1 metrics vs the full supply chain KPI dashboard

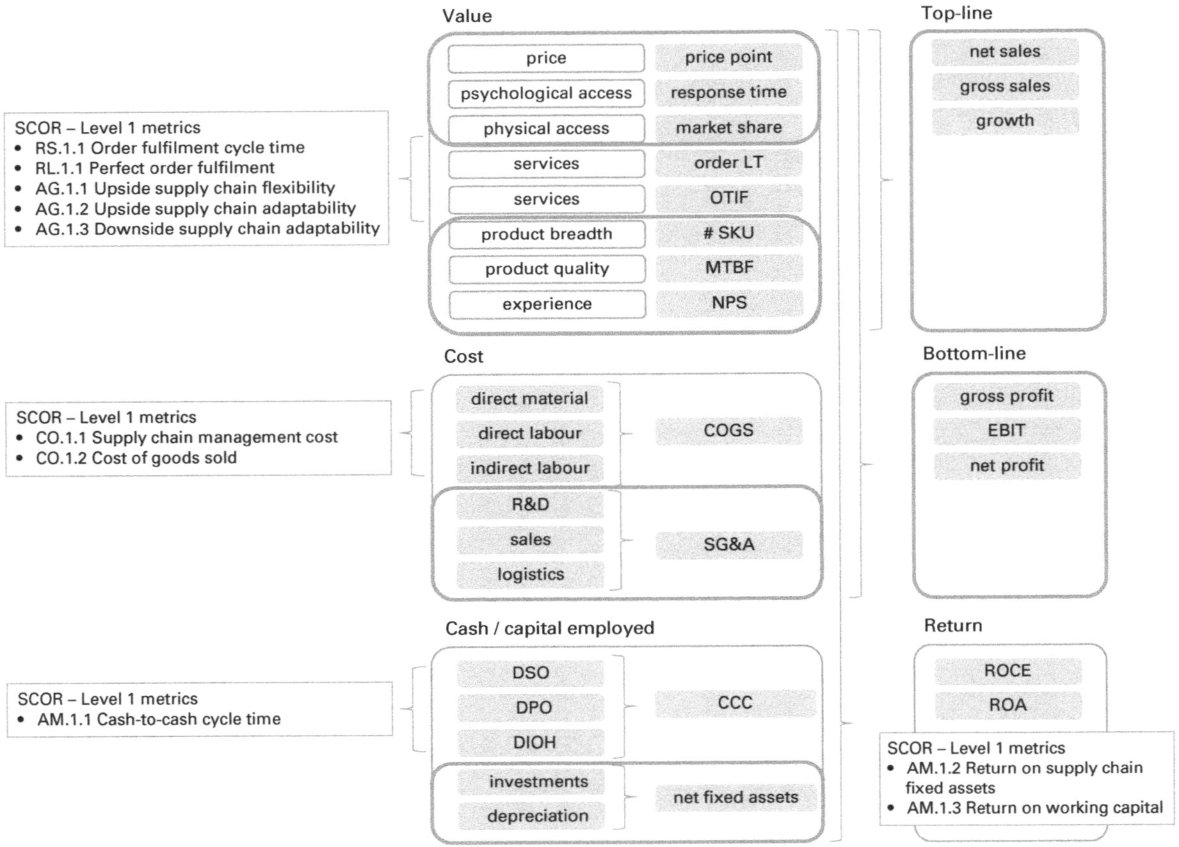

Top-line
- net sales
- gross sales
- growth

Bottom-line
- gross profit
- EBIT
- net profit

Return
- ROCE
- ROA

SCOR – Level 1 metrics
- AM.1.2 Return on supply chain fixed assets
- AM.1.3 Return on working capital

Value
- price → price point
- psychological access → response time
- physical access → market share
- services → order LT
- services → OTIF
- product breadth → # SKU
- product quality → MTBF
- experience → NPS

SCOR – Level 1 metrics
- RS.1.1 Order fulfilment cycle time
- RL.1.1 Perfect order fulfilment
- AG.1.1 Upside supply chain flexibility
- AG.1.2 Upside supply chain adaptability
- AG.1.3 Downside supply chain adaptability

Cost
- direct material / direct labour / indirect labour → COGS
- R&D / sales / logistics → SG&A

SCOR – Level 1 metrics
- CO.1.1 Supply chain management cost
- CO.1.2 Cost of goods sold

Cash / capital employed
- DSO / DPO / DIOH → CCC
- investments / depreciation → net fixed assets

SCOR – Level 1 metrics
- AM.1.1 Cash-to-cash cycle time

at reducing the supply chain cost, but only at the expense of significantly cutting product complexity, and only when R&D also significantly lowers its cost.

In too many companies, supply chain just bears the consequence of what others are willing or not willing to carry. That may easily lead to a mission impossible. If you don't cut the product complexity it may be impossible to make a step change in the cost. Yes, you should make your contribution, but you should demand others do the same. If you are switching from product leadership to customer intimacy you can expect the sales costs to rise. Instead of the product selling itself by its newest and highest specification, you'll need a highly trained and technical sales force that is able to define integrated solutions to customer-specific problems.

The fact that SCOR misses some key value drivers and the R&D and sales costs makes the VP of supply chain very vulnerable. If you want to be part of the executive team, you'll need a broader perspective to be able to challenge for the good of supply chain and for the good of the company.

On the capital employed side, we see that SCOR is missing the fixed assets. It has the 'return on supply chain fixed assets', but not the fixed assets themselves. We are in favour of having both. If the return on assets improves, it can be due to an improved EBIT or net profit, or to a decrease in the fixed assets. You need the underlying components to understand what's happening.

Likewise we do believe you need the top-line and the bottom-line metrics. You know as supply chain that top-line and bottom-line are higher up the agenda of sales. As we have explained at length, it is often wrong and short-sighted – what really counts is the 'bang-for-the-buck' or something like ROCE. However, choose your moment and pick your battle. Try to cut products when growth is good, and cut costs when the EBIT is under pressure. A richer KPI set will help the VP of supply chain to better navigate the corporate agenda.

In summary, when comparing our KPI dashboard with the SCOR level 1 metrics, we were initially shocked. It compares companies on service and cost without accounting for the chosen strategy. This is outright dangerous. It will give every company the service target of the customer intimacy leader at the cost position of the operational excellence leader. The combination of the two is simply impossible. This is a grave error!

Conclusion

In Chapter 6 we expanded the value corner of our Supply Chain Triangle using the strategy model of Treacy and Wiersema and the model of Crawford and Mathews. In this chapter we have elaborated the cost and the capital employed corner of the triangle, using common financial KPIs. We have linked value, cost and capital employed to top-line, bottom-line and return metrics. We have explained how process metrics are in fact causal or diagnostic. They are able to predict where the result metrics, being value, cost, capital employed and top-line, bottom-line and return, will be going.

We have shown how different strategies are different routes to come to the same return, for instance ROCE. We have used the 'equalizer' of Crawford and Mathews to illustrate how different strategies put different priorities on process and value metrics. We have shown an example of how to build an iPad-like dashboard for a product leader and have built an example (but realistic) story around it.

Finally we have shown that the SCOR model is incomplete. It only includes service, cost and return metrics. It is impossible and even dangerous to compare the service and the cost level of companies if you can't account for the chosen strategies. Likewise it is impossible to define correct targets for capital employed if you don't know the width of the product portfolio and the strategic ambitions on that driver. We were surprised when we first discovered this, but we remain convinced – benchmarking using SCOR metrics only is dangerous.

In the next and final chapter, we want to summarize the findings of our book in a concept we will call the 'strategy-driven supply chain'. So far, the debate on supply chain has been stuck on whether you want to be lean or agile, with some authors arguing you can be both, by being 'leagile'.

We will argue that in general, complexity has grown, even for operational excellence players, and as a result supply chain had to become more agile by adopting best practices such as S&OP, design for supply chain, removing bad complexity and many more. However, it makes no sense to say lean and agile can be combined. It makes no sense trying to define a single type of supply chain. We believe some supply chains will always remain leaner, where others will always remain more agile. The type of supply chain you need depends on the chosen business strategy. The business strategy is key in defining the correct supply chain trade-off between value, cost and capital employed. That will be the essence of what we will call the strategy-driven supply chain.

CASE STUDY – Johnson Controls

The fast changing world of Johnson Controls, and the new decade of an engagement and ecosystem driven economy

Johnson Controls has been through a period of major transformation. In July 2015 it announced plans to divest itself of the division responsible for more than half of its turnover by spinning off its Automotive Experience car seat and interiors business.

A little more than a year later, in September 2016, it announced the completion of its merger with Tyco, creating a completely new industrial group with a $30 billion revenue and 117,000 employees, bringing best-in-class product, technology and service across controls, fire, security, HVAC and energy storage to serve the full spectrum of end markets including large institutions, government, commercial buildings, retail, industrial, small business and residential.

For Frank Vorrath, the VP global supply chain of Johnson Controls, this type of transformation is not the exception, but becoming the norm. When asked for his view on the role of supply chain, he starts: 'Traditional business models are being disrupted, by an exponentially increasing speed of change in markets. The answer is no longer functional organizations, where one company competes against another. Winning in the marketplace is about forming strong and sustainable ecosystems.'

He continues: 'It is obvious that it is the supply chain that connects the functions at the heart of all businesses with one another and with all customers. This creates the need for a Strategic Ecosystem Supply Chain Excellence System.' He observes that: 'Successful companies invest to build their own excellence system.' Building the one for Johnson Controls has been his major mission over the last few years.

Building a Strategic Ecosystem Supply Chain Excellence System

Figure 7.19 shows the Strategic Supply Chain Excellence System developed at Johnson Controls.

Frank Vorrath comments: 'Most global companies are still confused about the role and function of an integrated supply chain management. Companies don't use their full potential by making supply chains their main business value proposition in order to compete and win in a global marketplace.' He also observes: 'Supply Chain Excellence has been around for many years, but the approach to it has been very operational, tactical and functional. A vision and strategy for Supply Chain Excellence needs to be aligned with the overall business strategy of the ecosystem in order to create a highly competitive ecosystem.'

This is the reason that the system in Figure 7.19 starts by assessing customer needs and buying behaviour. According to Frank Vorrath: 'Companies have to rethink who they are in their core and what value they want to create for their customers to differentiate their product and service offerings. The entire ecosystem has to define their basis for competition linked to different customer buying behaviours and make them part of their overall ecosystem value proposition.'

As shown in Figure 7.19, customer needs and buying behaviour then translate into the three basic strategy options proposed by Treacy and Wiersema, which form the basis of the competition for the supply chain network. Different strategies lead to different trade-offs in the five performance attributes of SCOR we introduced earlier in Table 7.1.

Once the trade-offs in the performance attributes of SCOR are clear, we start designing our supply chain around it, shown in Figure 7.19 on the right as 'Supply Chain Design'. When designing the supply chain we need to look at people, processes, technology, organization and the network of assets, which includes the flow of information, cash and taxes in that network.

Another revolution: the 40/40/20 ecosystem and supply chain value creation rule

Frank Vorrath redefines the priorities with his 40/40/20 supply chain value creation rule. He explains: 'Historically, companies have invested in manufacturing or services by building a strong product and service portfolio to make their asset infrastructure a competitive advantage. But this alone will no longer lead to a sustainable business performance.'

According to Frank: 'More and more companies are realizing this, and are investing in people, processes, technology and effective performance measurement and management across their different value chain networks.' This requires a new way of thinking – the 40/40/20 ecosystem and supply chain value creation rule.' It is Frank Vorrath's belief that companies need to focus their investments:

- 40% on building people's mindset and behaviour, enabled by people skills;
- 40% on technology and an effective performance measurement and management;
- 20% on a more flexible network and asset infrastructure.

Figure 7.19 The Strategic Supply Chain Excellence System

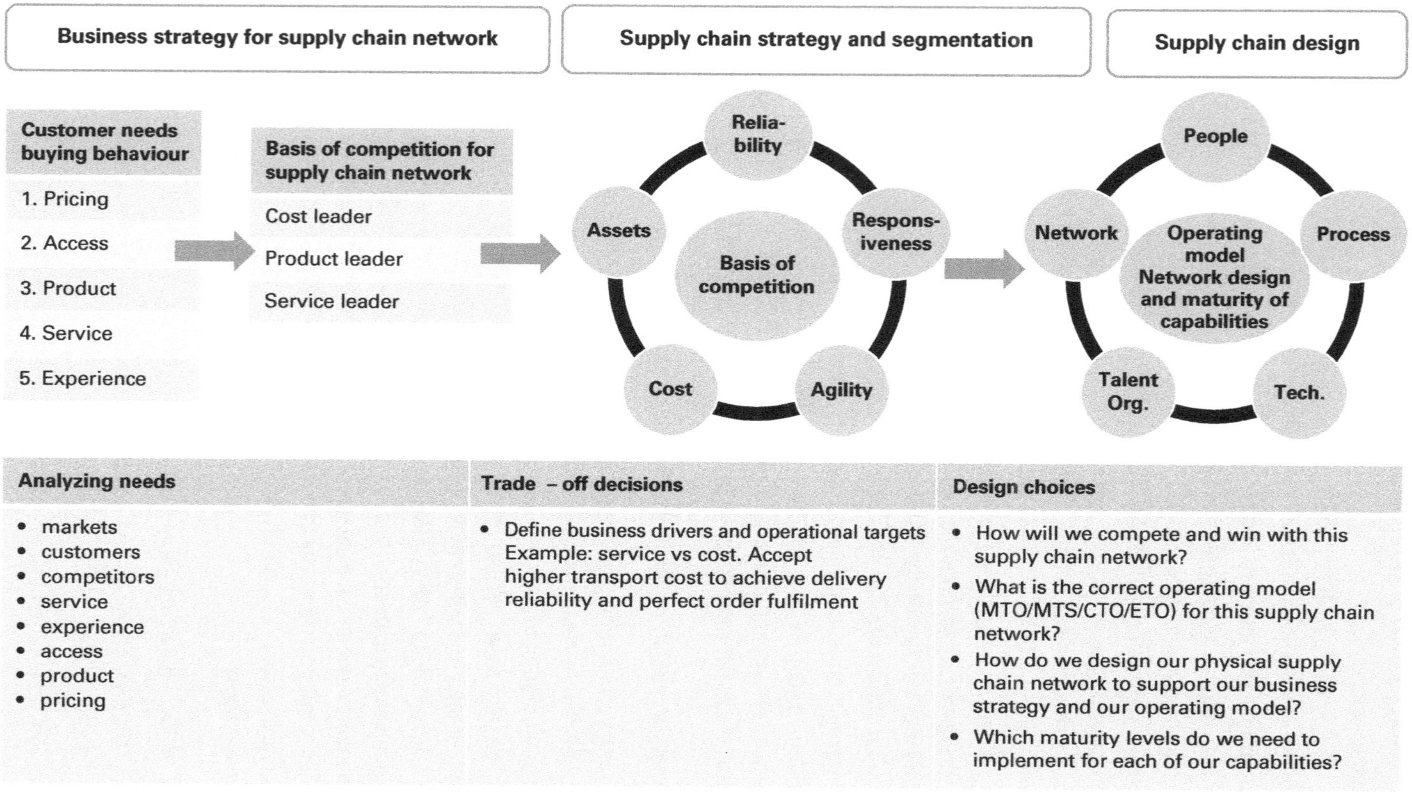

Business strategy for supply chain network	Supply chain strategy and segmentation	Supply chain design

Customer needs buying behaviour

1. Pricing
2. Access
3. Product
4. Service
5. Experience

Basis of competition for supply chain network

Cost leader

Product leader

Service leader

Basis of competition

- Relia-bility
- Respons-iveness
- Agility
- Cost
- Assets

Operating model
Network design and maturity of capabilities

- Process
- Tech.
- Talent Org.
- Network
- People

Analyzing needs

- markets
- customers
- competitors
- service
- experience
- access
- product
- pricing

Trade – off decisions

- Define business drivers and operational targets Example: service vs cost. Accept higher transport cost to achieve delivery reliability and perfect order fulfilment

Design choices

- How will we compete and win with this supply chain network?
- What is the correct operating model (MTO/MTS/CTO/ETO) for this supply chain network?
- How do we design our physical supply chain network to support our business strategy and our operating model?
- Which maturity levels do we need to implement for each of our capabilities?

He explains: 'The release of knowledge and skills into the ecosystem requires the right focus and investments in supply chain talent development and management. People are key to the transformation of companies like Johnson Controls. For this reason we are investing in a supply chain academy, in supply chain maturity frameworks and in supply chain capability assessments to identify training needs and link them to specific training offerings which drive the required skills enhancements.

'Secondly, a strong ecosystem will collaborate, share and integrate their supply chain technology platforms and will interact as an integrated ecosystem to meet the changing customer expectations at any point of time in different marketplaces. The entire ecosystem will make decisions in an aligned and collaborative way looking at the entire value stream network together.' If the key is in the network, having the right technology and metrics to manage the network is essential.

He continues: 'Thirdly, companies have to rethink who they are and what value they want to create for their customers to differentiate their product and service offerings. Questions about what is core and non-core will raise a new level of importance where the entire ecosystem becomes a shared platform for full-time sharing of capabilities, assets and resources related to processes, people, technologies, performance measurement and performance management.' Assets become less differentiating, and more become like utilities, where you pay per use.

Conclusion

Johnson Controls has gone through major transformation over the last two to three years. This has involved some soul-searching on what the core competences are, whether they are asset-driven or people-driven, and whether they are Johnson Controls-only or network competences.

As companies structure around networks, supply chain is the key discipline required for strategic coordination and delivering value to the customer. We agree with Frank Vorrath that leaders should acknowledge that, and invest in their supply chain competence, according to the 40/40/20 rule, over people, technology or assets.

References

APICS [accessed 20/07/2017] Quick reference guide: SCOR Model [Online] http://www.apics.org/docs/default-source/scc-non-research/apicsscc_scor_quick_reference_guide.pdf

Cecere, L M (2014) *Supply Chain Metrics That Matter*, John Wiley & Sons, New York

Crawford, F and Mathews, R (2007) *The Myth of Excellence: Why great companies never try to be the best at everything*, Crown Business, London

Pyzdek, T and Keller, P A (2014) *The Six Sigma Handbook: A complete guide for green belts, black belts and managers at all levels*, New York: McGraw-Hill Education, New York

Treacy, M and Wiersema, F (1995) *The Discipline of Market Leaders: Choose your customers, narrow your focus, dominate your market*, Basic Books, New York

Implementing the strategy-driven supply chain

08

In Chapters 1 and 2 we introduced our Supply Chain Triangle, and used the strategy model of Treacy and Wiersema (1995) to illustrate that strategy is about making choices, and that different strategies lead to different trade-offs in the Supply Chain Triangle – all with the same objective, however, of delivering 'bang-for-the-buck' or, in financial terms, return on capital employed (ROCE).

In Chapters 3, 4 and 5 we introduced benchmarking in two dimensions to illustrate the trade-offs, primarily between EBIT and capital employed. We used case studies to further illustrate how different strategies are indeed different 'routes' to generate ROCE, and how to account for the chosen strategy when setting targets for the underlying financial metrics like EBIT, inventory or fixed asset turns. It has helped in pointing out those different routes.

In Chapter 6 we broadened the findings of Treacy and Wiersema. Using the strategy model of Crawford and Mathews (2007) we illustrated that instead of just three strategic options, there are in fact more, – but that the essence of strategy remains making a choice, in this case about on which of the value drivers to dominate, on which to differentiate and on which to play at par or even below. The Crawford and Mathews model allowed us to give a more detailed and elaborate definition and treatment of the service corner of the Supply Chain Triangle, which we've renamed as a 'value' corner.

In Chapter 7 we continued through a more in-depth and financial definition of the cost and the capital employed corner of the Supply Chain Triangle, and arrived at a full KPI dashboard. Once more we showed how different strategies have the same objective of generating ROCE, but in different ways, with different targets and with a different priority, across the underlying metrics.

This chapter will conclude by showing the shift in strategy thinking from the 1990s to today, and how that shift requires a corresponding shift in supply chain thinking. Whereas the 1990s were dominated by service-based differentiation and the corresponding need for a responsive supply chain, we will argue that this vision is now too narrow. We will rediscover there are different options for differentiation, and as a result we keep seeing different supply chains from highly lean to highly responsive.

Secondly, we will try to summarize how we believe supply chains cannot be captured in two, three or even four archetypes. Following the model of Crawford and Mathews where multiple strategic options are open and valid, we believe each strategy will need its corresponding supply chain. If a supply chain is so closely linked to the strategy, it becomes an integral part of that strategy.

We will explain how Treacy and Wiersema (1995) and Kaplan and Norton (2004) talk about the 'operating model' as the engine to deliver a strategy, and how we believe the supply chain should be an integral part of that operating model. We'll argue that a supply chain is not a consequence of the strategy; that we cannot derive the supply chain strategy from the business strategy. We'll argue that the supply chain is simply an integral part of the strategy – the supply chain is 'strategy-driven'.

We'll conclude this chapter by giving a step-by-step overview of how to define and implement this 'strategy-driven supply chain'. This will bring together the value proposition work of Chapter 6 with an extended Treacy and Wiersema operating model (and Kaplan and Norton) around our Supply Chain Triangle. In the corresponding exercise, we have provided extra guidance on how executive teams can use the developed thinking to refine their own strategies and their own supply chains.

Strategy and supply chain in the 1990s

We believe the field of supply chain is ready for its next big step. To understand why, we need to reflect on its recent history. We will first review the dominant strategy thinking of the 1990s and see how supply chain ties into that. In the next section we will then reflect on how strategy thinking has changed over the last 30 years, and how we believe that should also change the thinking about supply chain.

Strategy in the 1990s and the promise of supply chain

One of the most influential and early books on the field of supply chain is probably *Logistics and Supply Chain Management* by Martin Christopher, initially published in 1992. In essence, the book makes the promise that supply chain management allows you to improve on both cost and service, delivering a much-needed breakthrough for companies in the 1990s.

We will analyse the dominant strategy thinking of that time and in the following section explain how that translated into the supply chain thinking of that time. We will then continue by discussing the shift in strategy thinking over the last 25 years, and the corresponding required shift in supply chain thinking.

Strategy thinking in the 1990s was still dominated by Michael Porter. In his classic Harvard Business Review paper 'What is strategy?' he argues that companies either go for a cost advantage or for a differentiation advantage. In *Logistics and Supply Chain Management*, Christopher talks about a cost advantage versus a value advantage. He also argues that the strongest companies have both a cost and a value advantage.

In principle, there are two types of value advantage: differentiating on product or differentiating on service. Christopher argues that: 'there is increasingly a convergence of technology within product categories, which means that it is often no longer possible to compete effectively on the basis of product differences'. In essence, he says that competition on the product dimension is void. We have adapted Christopher's original figure to reflect that thinking in Figure 8.1.

Figure 8.1 Strategy in the 1990s: product advantage erodes and cost leadership is reserved for the market leader (based on Christopher, 1998)

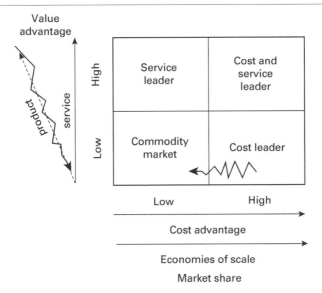

He continues that in mature markets, 'big is beautiful', meaning that size delivers a cost advantage, or even better, 'there will typically be only one competitor who will be the low-cost producer, the one with the greatest sales volume'. This limits the chances for companies to be a cost leader and have a cost advantage. Many companies are as such pushed into the 'commodity' quadrant of Figure 8.1. These are the companies which have neither a cost advantage nor a value advantage. These are clearly companies in peril.

In the situation of Figure 8.1, there is only one way out, which is upwards. It creates an imperative for companies to differentiate on service. Let's say that in the 1990s, service was 'the' way, and for most companies the 'only' way to seek competitive advantage, as shown in Figure 8.2.

It is in this competitive landscape and mindset that supply chain management promises to help deliver better service, and at a lower cost. As such, in the 1990s, supply chain management was seen as the holy grail, avoiding the need to choose between improving on either cost or service, but allowing companies to improve on both, as shown in Figure 8.3.

Supply chain thinking of the 1990s: the agile supply chain

So how do we deliver on the promise of Figure 8.3, improving on both cost and service? In his book, Christopher comes to the concept of the 'agile' or 'responsive' supply chain. He starts by describing the agile and the 'lean'

Figure 8.2 Strategy in the 1990s: the only way is up, differentiation on service is imperative (based on Christopher, 1998)

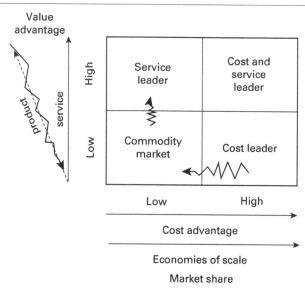

Figure 8.3 Strategy in the 1990s: the promise of supply chain, improving on both cost AND service (based on Christopher, 1998)

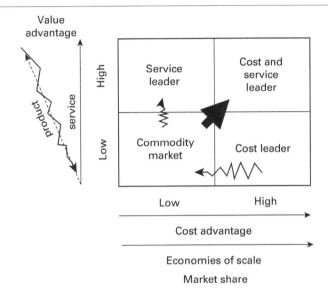

supply chain as two opposites. The agile supply chain is able to respond to big changes in volume and variety, in a short time frame. The lean supply chain is focused on providing a low-cost solution for big volumes with limited variety and variability.

Lean fans will argue that lean and agile are not opposite, that 'leanness' may be an element of agility. Christopher agrees, but at the same time argues that lean by itself will not enable an organization to meet the precise needs of the customer more rapidly. On the one hand, more leanness ensures that there is no 'dead weight' that needs to be moved when reacting to an unpredicted peak, which makes us more agile. On the other hand, lean is based on the levelling of demand, or 'heijunka', to create a stable and more constant flow through production. As such, we agree with Christopher that lean provides a better fit with a high-volume and low-variety/variability business.

Christopher continues to describe how organizations are facing ever-increasing levels of volatility in demand. He argues that for a variety of reasons product and technology life cycles are shortening, competitive pressures force more frequent product changes and consumers demand greater variety than ever before. It creates a kind of 'variety/variability' creep. It implies the world of high-volume and low-variety/variability is disappearing, making the lean supply chain obsolete! As such the agile or responsive supply chain (as they are interchangeably called) is proposed as the supply chain concept of the future.

One of the techniques of the agile or responsive supply chain is postponement. If we can create volume and economies of scale in an undifferentiated product, and then carry out differentiation at the last minute based on actual demand, that can create a low cost while still being agile. A commonly used example, also by Christopher, is the paint industry, where consumers can be offered customized colours through the use of paint mixing machines located at retail outlets. The retailers only need to stock a relatively small number of tints and the base paint to provide an almost infinite number of final colours. The paint manufacturer can utilize lean processes in producing base colours in volume, while providing an agile and timely response to the end users.

Other elements of the responsive supply chain, as described by Christopher, include synchronization of activities through sharing information, re-engineering of processes (also popular in the 1990s, as described by Michael Hammer (1990)), partnering with suppliers to reduce in-bound lead times, reducing complexity, managing end-to-end processes and utilization of appropriate performance metrics.

Christopher then develops each of these in separate chapters in the remainder of his book. It is probably one of the first textbooks with a comprehensive description of the broader supply chain management concept. They dominate supply chain thinking up till today. Today there is more talk about being 'outside-in' or being 'demand-driven' compared to the 1990s, but the base concepts remain the same. It is all about sharing information, partnering with customers and suppliers, managing end-to-end processes, the same basic recipe initially laid out by Christopher. His book and his thinking have shaped the supply chain thinking of a whole generation.

Though not an easy task, in the next sections we will try to describe how strategy thinking has evolved since the 1990s, and how we believe supply chain should move on from being agile to become 'strategy-driven'.

A shift in thinking: from agile to strategy-driven supply chains

Strategy in 2020: multiple options (and yes, you'll have to make choices)

Strategy thinking in the 1990s, as shown in Figure 8.2, is quite fatalistic. Product differentiation is not an option, and cost leadership is only for the market leader because size matters. That has created a kind of rat race to differentiate on service. Whereas in principle supply chain management can help to improve on both cost and service, in our experience the explosion and uncontrolled growth of services has led to an increase in costs for which the implementation of supply chain management has not necessarily been able to make up.

It also seems to split off the supply chain from the business strategy. Business strategy is about thinking which services to add, and then supply chain will have to make up for that by still lowering the cost. This, for us, expresses the typical strategy and supply chain thinking of the 1990s.

As a first step, we need to break down the 'fatalistic' strategy view of the 1990s. Yes, scale creates efficiencies, and size does matter, but we don't agree that only the market leader can gain a cost leadership position. Changes in technology can disrupt the marketplace and the position of cost leaders. Think about how Amazon has taken advantage of the internet to redefine shopping and threaten the position of cost leaders such as Walmart. Think about how hard discounters like Aldi and Lidl have disrupted food retail (in Europe), not driven by technology, but by smaller stores and private label assortments. Or how low-cost airlines like Ryanair and Southwest have disrupted the airline industry, by installing a culture, processes and management systems all relentlessly focused on reducing costs.

Yes, it has become more difficult to differentiate on product quality and specifications. In fact, playing on the product dimension is a high-risk game, as witnessed by the disruption of companies like Kodak or Nokia and to some extent even Sony.

But again, we don't agree that differentiating on product features is no longer possible. When Steve Jobs returned to Apple in 1996, the company was near dead. It made its way back to the top not through low cost or excellent service, but by making high-performance and eye-catching innovative products. How did Google become so dominant in the first place? Yes, a new technology created a new market, but out of all the search engines around in the early days, it simply had the best product. What has accounted for the success of a company like Johnson & Johnson over the last 20 to 30 years? Yes, its capability to innovate and make the best products for its chosen medical and consumer markets.

Figure 8.4 summarizes that evolution in strategy thinking.

Though it requires tough choices, even in so-called commodity markets companies have multiple ways to differentiate. We see proof in the market of at least the cost, the service, and the product dimension advocated by Treacy and Wiersema. Instead of talking about the 'commodity' zone, we prefer to talk about the 'bankruptcy' zone. Companies that don't

Figure 8.4   Strategy in 2020: there are multiple options, strategy is about making choices

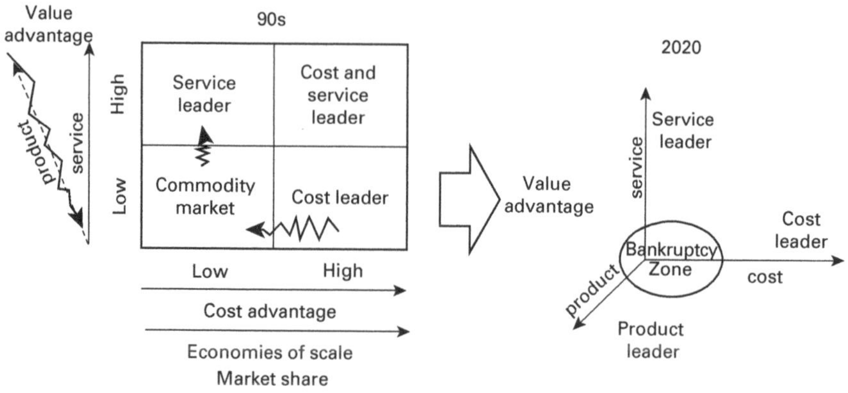

differentiate will have below-market results. Without differentiation they will end up being taken over by another company, or they will simply go bankrupt.

A second and more subtle effect of expanding into the three dimensions in Figure 8.4 is that it becomes clear companies have to make a choice. Yes, you'd like to be the company that dominates on cost, service *and* product, but excelling in three dimensions at the same time seems less likely than excelling in the two dimensions of Figure 8.3.

To further build this argument, remember the Crawford and Mathews (2007) model explained in Chapter 6. Crawford and Mathews talk about five dimensions, which we have expanded to seven dimensions to allow it to incorporate Treacy and Wiersema (1995). It becomes highly unlikely that you can excel in seven dimensions at the same time. That's exactly why Crawford and Mathews argue that you can dominate in one dimension, differentiate in a second, and will have to play at par on the others. If you don't make a choice, remember that your competitors will. They will outperform you on well-chosen dimensions, and leave you with an undifferentiated image in a highly competitive market.

So as a first argument, we believe strategy in 2020 has become more complex in that we believe there are multiple ways to differentiate and build a competitive edge. And second, unfortunately, this comes with the tough task of making choices. You can't have it all. It's no longer 'and', but 'or'. As the supply chain defines the cost and the capital employed, supply chain will be part of this strategic discussion, as opposed to strategy discussions in the 1990s.

Strategy in 2020: the expanding best practice frontier

The next questions to tackle are: 'What about the variety/volatility creep? Has that rendered the lean supply chain obsolete?' and 'What about the promise of supply chain to improve at both service and cost at the same time?' as shown in Figure 8.3.

Let's begin by answering that yes, we agree that variety and volatility is increasing, and yes, we agree that supply chain management can deliver improvements in service and cost at the same time, but no, we don't agree that this makes the 'low-cost' position void, as implied in Figure 8.1. Nor do we agree that supply chain management helps to avoid the strategic choice between service or cost. It simply redefines the boundaries, or what we will call the 'best practice frontier', and as such it pushes the choice between service or cost to a new level.

To understand the concept of the best practice frontier, we start by recapturing Figure 2.7 in Figure 8.5.

In Chapter 2 we argued that different strategies are different ways to deliver the same, or a comparable, ROCE. A product leader requires a higher capital employed and has a higher cost (R&D, marketing), but by selling unique products in high-end niches, they are able to command a significant premium from their customers which compensates for this.

The operational excellence leader has the lowest cost, and works at a minimal EBIT (as to guarantee the lowest price in the market), but compensates for that by working with less capital employed, or, stated differently, by making better use of their assets. The ROCE principle tells us that as an investor, it's OK that a product leader requires a higher capital employed, as long as they generate a higher EBIT. Or vice versa, it's OK that an opex player has a lower EBIT as long as they require less capital employed. As an investor I'm indifferent, as long as it leads to the same ROCE.

In a second step in Figure 8.5 we plot the three strategies as three dots in the three-dimensional space. The opex dot is based on the x, y and z values for the X, Y and Z axis, in this case cost, capital employed and service. The customer intimacy dot is based on the cost, capital employed and service levels of the customer intimacy strategy, and likewise for the product leader. Remember from Chapter 2 that we measure service by the gross margin. If we deliver more service, the customer will be willing to pay a higher premium. The gross margin measures the premium the customer is willing to pay, on top of the cost of goods sold.

Figure 8.5   Strategy in 2020: the three strategies of Treacy and Wiersema are different ways to reach the same ROCE

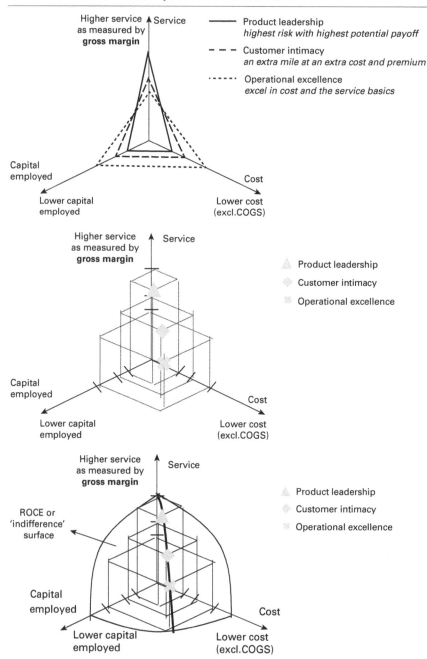

Thirdly, in Figure 8.5, we visualize that these three dots, the three strategies, are in fact just three strategic options on a surface of options all leading to the same ROCE. As an investor I'm indifferent that you need more capital employed as long as your EBIT is higher. In the graph you can reach a higher EBIT by attracting a higher premium (up on the vertical service axis), or by working at a lower cost (out on the cost axis). More capital employed means more complexity, so strategy-wise it's logical that you try to derive a higher premium from that extra complexity, so you move up and down along the surface, instead of left and right.

Figure 8.6 continues on that theme. We have retaken our three strategies as three dots on our surface of points leading to the same ROCE, and we have called it the 'best practice frontier'.

Let the best practice frontier be the maximum ROCE we can get to when we apply all best practices available. We assume that different strategies are equally likely to deliver the same ROCE; if that is not the case, it implies there would be better and worse strategies. That's an interesting question for extra research, and another book.

Secondly, Figure 8.6 explains what supply chain management has actually done for companies. Yes, Christopher is right that supply chain management has helped companies to improve on service, cost and capital employed, all at the same time. What this means is that it has actually pushed out and redefined the best practice frontier. It redefines the target at which companies need to aim, or it redefines the baseline, or the standard for competition, as you wish.

This also perfectly links to that second axiom of the 1990s that 'variety and volatility have increased'. Why is that? Is it because customers have asked for it? Or is it because the capabilities of companies have grown, as demonstrated by the shifting best practice frontier in Figure 8.6? It's almost the discussion of which was first, the chicken or the egg. It's probably fair to summarize that the adoption of new best practices, like more professional management of the supply chain, has shifted the best practice frontier, created new capabilities, and made customers more demanding, all at the same time.

The 'flaw' in the thinking of the 1990s is the false perception that, because of the increased variety and volatility, service is the only strategic option, and the responsive supply chain is the only possible answer. We now understand that is not the case. Yes, all supply chains have to become more responsive, but the supply chain of an operational excellence leader will always be leaner compared to that of a product leader.

Figure 8.6 Strategy in 2020: new best practices have created new capabilities and made customers more demanding

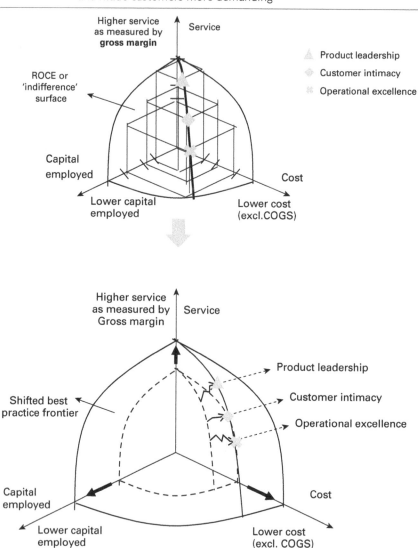

A shift in the best practice frontier, as shown at the bottom of Figure 8.6, can be triggered by new best practices such as 'supply chain management' in the 1990s. It can also be triggered by technological shifts. Think about what the internet and the emergence of pure online players like Amazon has done in retail. Online players don't have a network of physical shops. As a result they will have significantly lower fixed assets and as such a significantly lower capital employed. They will also carry less inventory, further lowering the capital employed. From a ROCE perspective this allows them to operate at a lower EBIT. If they have a comparable cost to the 'bricks' players, it would allow them to either cut prices or deliver more service, eg through a broader product portfolio, or even a combination of both.

It is clear that the online players have redefined the service expectation. We are getting used to a broader assortment, at cutting edge prices, and with a near-to-immediate delivery. The cost impact is less clear. It is to be expected that last-mile delivery has a higher cost compared to the cost of replenishing shops. However, 'bricks' players basically have to do both – keep their shops running, and organize an online channel. The cost and capital employed of a multi-channel approach is hard to compare to the cost and capital employed of an online-only model.

Moreover, some pure online players like Zalando are working at a loss. As investors expect these online players will disrupt and replace the 'bricks' players, they are happy to postpone profits and ensure a maximum focus on growth and market share.

You can feel that in retail the best practice frontier is currently being pushed out. That's not a smooth operation; it comes with a lot of turbulence. That implies it's not easy to define where it actually is or where it's going. But it is clear that in this shift some companies will be left behind and will face a difficult future.

Supply chain thinking in 2020: the strategy-driven supply chain

As shown in Figure 8.3, in the thinking of the 1990s, supply chain management was a way to escape the strategic choice between improving on cost or on service. While supply chain management has been delivering on that promise, for many years and for many companies, it is dangerous to assume that this will last forever. It has also created an attitude among sales personnel and CEOs that they can do whatever they want on the service side, without accounting for the impact on the cost or the capital employed, as supply chain improvement will always make up for that.

Where that unique ability to improve on two dimensions simultaneously has brought supply chain management higher up the executive agenda, supply chain has also put itself in a corner where it's continuously taking the punches of commercial decisions that have not necessarily been thought through for their impact on ROCE. As supply chain is nearly 30 years old, it is time for the young adult to finally grow up and claim its rightful position at the heart of the strategic debate.

Figure 8.7 tries to bring some nuance and objectivity to this discussion. It shows there is a difference for companies that are operating at the best practice frontier, the leaders, and those that are operating below the best practice frontier, the laggards.

If you are a laggard, the implementation of best practices like more professional management of the supply chain allows you to jump to that best practice frontier, and in that process improve on all three dimensions simultaneously.

Figure 8.7 Strategy in 2020: laggards can improve on several dimensions at the same time; leaders face strategic choices

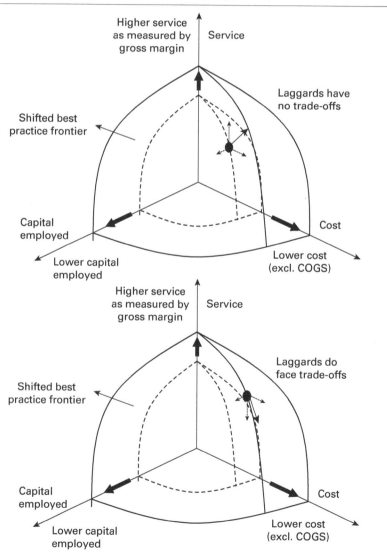

If you are a leader, you can try to shift the best practice frontier, eg by testing and applying new technologies like robotics or advanced analytics. If you can further push out the best practice frontier, this may allow you to continue improving on the three dimensions simultaneously. If you can't push the frontier, you may be faced with tough choices. Think of our case studies in Chapter 2 – a company like Barco which was moving from a product leadership into a customer intimacy position, giving in on gross margin, but lowering its cost and capital employed. Or a company like Casio, which from an operational excellence position providing cheap watches and components moved up to a product leader position, working at a higher cost and capital employed but earning a significantly higher gross margin from more advanced and more fashionable watches.

The general tendency for companies is still to turn to supply chain and demand that it 'reduce inventories by 30%'. Thirty years ago, when supply chain was still in its infancy, any type of supply chain project, whether it was a redesign of the distribution network or the introduction of an advanced planning system, probably had that potential. These days, we believe it's more realistic that supply chain will need to challenge the business and answer: 'OK – which non-performing SKUs are you going to cut?' Cutting SKUs is rightsizing the service to the customers. SKUs that don't deliver ROCE don't belong in the product portfolio. This is operating 'on' the best practice surface instead of 'below' the best practice surface.

While this may sound conceptual, remember there is a way to actually define the best practice surface, namely through the two-dimensional benchmarking we've developed in Chapters 3 and 4, as shown in Figure 4.1 and Figure 4.2. Given it is in two dimensions, we called it the best practice curve there, instead of the best practice surface.

What this means for supply chain is that instead of being outside of the strategy discussion, and being faced with 'just make the commercial strategy work', supply chain has become the centrepiece of the strategy discussion. As illustrated in Figure 8.8, different strategies correspond with different levels of cost and capital employed.

The strategy definition is only finished if we have evaluated the required cost and capital employed corresponding with a given service or commercial positioning. The supply chain strategy does not follow from the business strategy, it is an essential part of the business strategy. The commercial and the supply chain strategy are like the ying and the yang – they need to go together and together form the business strategy.

Another lesson learned from Figure 8.8 is that we don't believe in specific 'types' of supply chains. There have been many attempts to define and differentiate between the lean supply chain, the responsive supply chain and the

Figure 8.8 A strategy is only complete when supply chain has defined the appropriate cost and capital employed

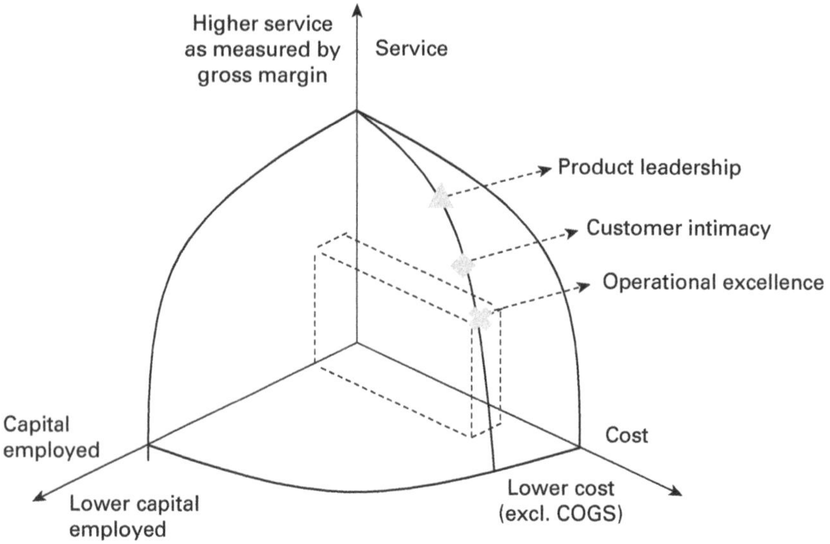

collaborative supply chain. Examples can be found in Gattorna (2003), and Christopher and Gattorna (2005).

We have already argued that where Treacy and Wiersema define three strategic positions, Crawford and Mathews have generalized that to any 5-4-3-3-3 profile among five possible value drivers, which gives 20 options. We agree with Crawford and Mathews there are different ways to be relevant for specific groups of customers. Each different strategy will have a different supply chain at its heart. In the next section we lay out how to define that supply chain, to be able to define the corresponding cost and capital employed.

Defining your strategy-driven supply chain

The overall process is relatively simple, but defines a significant change to current strategy practices. The first step is to define your value proposition. We will continue using the extended version of the model of Crawford and Mathews with its seven dimensions, as defined in Chapter 6. Different value propositions correspond with different price levels in the market (high end vs low end), and with different market sizes (niches vs mass market).

The next step is to define your operating model. We will extend the operating model of Treacy and Wiersema to include the supply chain and its assets. From your operating model and supply chain, you can derive the cost and capital employed, which in turn allows you to derive your ROCE. You may need to iterate step 1 and step 2 until you come to a realistic plan. Different value propositions will have different supply chains with different cost levels and different levels of capital employed.

In this approach the supply chain is not a consequence of the business strategy, it is a fundamental part of the business strategy. We also don't have something like a 'supply chain strategy'. The supply chain is driven by the business strategy and vice versa. Our supply chain becomes strategy-driven.

Defining your (competitive) value proposition

The first step is really about defining the targeted value proposition. It is defining the value corner of the Supply Chain Triangle as shown in Figure 7.1. It is about defining where you want to dominate, where to differentiate, and where you will play at par or even accept a performance below par. Figure 8.9 recaps the three options proposed by Treacy and Wiersema. Other options are possible such as dominating on experience and differentiating on product, for example in a trendy club in New York.

When we do this exercise with executive teams, we usually follow these steps. Firstly, we take the time to explore, explain and understand the value drivers of Crawford and Mathews. We start by giving a basic definition of the five original value drivers: what if you differentiate on price, what do we mean by access, what is the difference between service and experience, and so on. After the basic introduction, we ask the executive team to write down on Post-its what aspects of price and service they can think of relating to their specific competitive situation. By writing down examples, we make our thinking explicit.

Once they have written down examples defining the different dimensions, we can debrief one dimension at a time using Table 8.1, which is basically a summary of the descriptions in Crawford and Mathews (2007).

This may be a good time to split access into 'physical' and 'psychological', and product into 'breadth' and 'quality/depth'. We may start by asking who has Post-its on price, what did they write, and why. Things may pop up that are not related to the price dimension, but for instance to psychological access, as price visibility. Take the time to discuss.

When doing this exercise with the executive team there will be two important outcomes. Firstly, there will be a common understanding of what the different value drivers mean. Secondly, you will have mapped the drivers to your specific industry and competitive environment. The drivers are generic enough to be valid in any type of industry – only how you fill it in will be different. Doing this exercise easily takes two to three hours.

Figure 8.9   Defining your (competitive) value proposition based on the seven value drivers

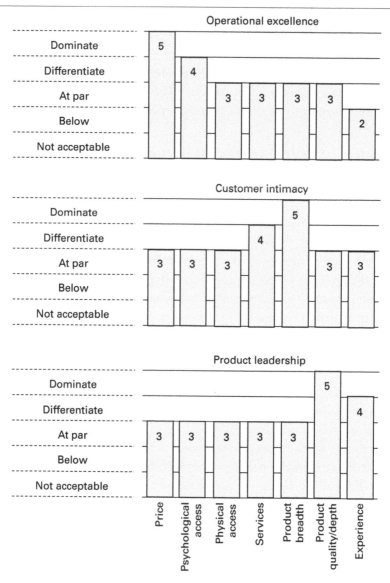

Once you have established a common understanding and a common language, take the discussion a step further by answering the following five questions:

1 Where are you today? Identify your 5-4-3-3-3-3-3 profile.

2 Where are your three to five key competitors? Identify their 5-4-3-3-3-3-3 profile.

Table 8.1 The seven value drivers of the extended Crawford and Mathews model

Price	Service	'Physical' access	'Psychological' access	Product breadth	Product quality/ depth	Experience
Honesty	Knowledgeable sales persons providing helpful advice	'Physical'... 'location'... 'real estate'... number of locations	'Psychological'... easily and successfully find what you're looking for	Breadth (range)	Quality (good-better-best)	Attractiveness of the store: décor, signage, layout,...
Consistency	Customization, tailoring. Eg service counter	Store layout	Opening hours		Depth	How employees dress to reflect/ complement the atmosphere
Low(est) price	Hassle-free return		Price visibility			Music, video enhance experience
	Availability					

3 What are the expected changes on the baseline? Which 5 will become a 4, or which 4 will become a 3?

4 Where do you want to be in two to three years' time?

5 What needs to be done to address the gap?

Starting with question 1, ask each of the members of the executive committee where they would give a 5, meaning we are currently dominating, where they would give a 4, meaning we are currently differentiating, and where they would give a 3 or a 2 meaning we are at par or lagging behind. Ask them to write their scores on Post-its, and gather the results on a sheet of paper. Focus on the 'as is'.

You will see different opinions and different perceptions around the table. Some of them may still be due to a difference in understanding of what the different value drivers mean. Given the scoring is relative to the market, there will be discussion on 'what is a 3' and 'what is a 4'. Quite likely there will also be examples and counter examples on where you are compared to the competition. All of this is good. It improves your understanding.

Try to come to a consensus scoring on where you are today, and then try to add a comparable scoring for where your three to five key competitors are. When saying competitors are better or worse in service, try to be specific. What are the services that they do/don't offer? Make groupings of Post-its to ensure you gradually further clarify what is being done in the market by which types of players.

Question 3 addresses any expected major changes in the market. If you are in retail, how will competition from pure online players redefine the boundaries? Will some of the 5s become 4s? Or will some of the 4s become a 3? Who will be affected by that – yourselves, or one of your competitors? What can happen as a result? When defining a value proposition, it is important to define it with an eye on the future.

Question 4 defines where you want to be. It is quite likely that your current proposition is different from what you want it to be. Part of that discussion will already pop up when answering question 1. Where are we, and where do we want to be? Some people may mistake the target for reality.

Question 5 addresses what needs to be done to sharpen our proposition. Again try to be specific. For each of the value drivers define: what are we going to do extra? What are we going to drop? Strategy is about making choices. It would be good to drop some actions on certain drivers if you want to improve on others. It creates more focus on the prioritized drivers. It will also help in communicating and implementing the strategy. If we only do 'more of that', it doesn't feel like we're making choices, though people have to make choices on a daily basis. If you can add 'and we'll do less of this', it will create a completely different message to the organization. Avoid the 'and-and' trap.

Your value proposition should come with a target price level. If your focus is on product quality, your price level will be different from one accompanying a focus on product breadth or on price. The price level is important for arriving at the ROCE at a later stage.

Exercise: Defining your value proposition

Gather your executive team and follow the approach outlined in the above section 'Defining your (competitive) value proposition'. A possible timeline is the following:

- 09:00 – 09:30: Clarify agenda and expectations
- 09:30 – 10:00: Introduction to the strategy model of Crawford and Mathews
- 10:00 – 12:00: Exercise and debriefing: 'Developing a common language and application to our industry'
- 14:00 – 17:00: Answering five strategic questions:
  - Where are you today? Identify your 5-4-3-3-3-3-3 profile
  - Where are your three to five key competitors? Identify their 5-4-3-3-3-3-3 profile
  - What are the expected changes on the baseline? Which 5 will become a 4, or which 4 will become a 3?
  - Where do you want to be in two to three years' time?
  - What needs to be done to address the gap?
- 17:00 – 18:00: Wrap-up and next steps

Providing an exact timing for this type of discussion is impossible. Take the time that is needed and be aware that any unanswered questions will pop up later in the strategy implementation and may create confusion. In this case fast is not necessarily good.

Some companies like to do this in a two-day offsite meeting. Be aware that some of this needs time to settle in, and some of it needs to be refined. We are more in favour of a series of workshops of half a day, or at maximum a full day. You need to be at your best and your sharpest.

Define your operating model and design your supply chain

Once you have defined your value proposition, the second step is to define the operating model through which you will actually deliver the value. If the value proposition is the end, the operating model is the means; it describes the 'inner workings'.

We will use Treacy and Wiersema to explain what an operating model is, and then show we have to extend it with the supply chain as a core element. After this, we will use that extended operating model (including the supply chain) to explain how different value propositions lead to different operating models, and to different ways of generating shareholder value, as measured by the ROCE.

Extending the Treacy and Wiersema operating model with supply chain

Treacy and Wiersema (1995) describe how companies that excel in the same value proposition have remarkably similar operating models. They argue that Arco and McDonald's are strikingly similar because both pursue operational excellence. Likewise, Sony and Johnson & Johnson look alike as both pursue product leadership. On the other hand, even within an industry, market leaders pursuing different value propositions, such as Walmart and Nordstrom, look completely different. In their study of 80 market leaders they found that homogeneity only exists among leaders in the same value discipline. You can send somebody from Sony to Johnson & Johnson, but if you send somebody from Nordstrom to Walmart they will think they are on a different planet.

For Treacy and Wiersema the operating model consists of operating processes, business structure, management systems and culture, all of which are synchronized to create a certain superior value. In the exact terminology of Treacy and Wiersema there is a difference between a 'value proposition', a 'value-driven operating model' and a 'value discipline'. In fact they argue that product leaders choose between one of three unique combinations of value proposition and operating model. They call those three unique combinations the three 'value disciplines' of operational excellence, customer intimacy and product leadership.

Table 8.2 summarizes the three operating models that match these three value disciplines. We won't discuss them in detail, but let's highlight some of the differences.

Table 8.2 The three value-driven operating models

Operating model	Operational excellence	Customer intimacy	Product leadership
Culture	• Disciplined teamwork • Process focused • Conformance, 'one size fits all' mindset	• Client and field driven • Variation: 'have it your way' mindset	• Concept, future driven • Experimentation, 'out of the box' mindset • Attack, go for it, win
Core processes	• Product delivery and basic service cycle • Built on standard, no frills fixed assets	• Client acquisition & development • Solution development • Flexible and responsive work procedures	• Invention, commercialization • Market exploitation • Disjointed work procedures
Management systems	• Command and control • Compensation fixed to cost and quality • Transaction profitability tracking	• Revenue and share of wallet driven • Rewards based in part on client feedback • Lifetime value of client	• Decisive, risk oriented • Reward individuals' innovation capacity • Product life cycle profitability
Information technology	• Integrated low-cost transaction systems • Mobile and remote technologies	• Customer databases linking internal and external information • Knowledge bases built around expertise	• Person-to-person communications • Technologies enabling cooperation and knowledge mgmt
Organization	• Centralized functions • High skills at the core of the organization	• Entrepreneurial client teams • High skills in the field	• Ad hoc, organic, and cellular • High skills abound in loose-knit structures

When looking at culture, it is obvious the product leader will be more focused on innovation and experimentation whereas the opex leader will be focused on control. That is also reflected in the organizational model. Control comes with hierarchy and centralization, whereas innovation will come with smaller multi-disciplinary teams able to make high-impact decisions.

What you get is what you measure, and what you measure is what you get. The management systems of an opex player will be focused on controlling cost and quality. The product leader will measure the innovation rate and the innovation capacity. The core processes of the operational excellence leader will be, no surprise, in manufacturing and delivery. For a product leader it will be innovation and product marketing. And finally, the IT systems will need to support these core processes and the management systems.

In general, the operating model of the customer intimacy leader is more oriented towards developing and delivering total solutions to the customer to maximize the 'share-of-wallet' and the life-time value of the chosen key customers.

Other authors come up with comparable, be it slightly different 'operating models'. Kaplan and Norton (2004) suggest 'strategy maps', that map how strategies create value. They talk about four core processes: operations management, customer management, innovation, and regulatory and social. They talk about human capital, information capital and organization capital, which in Treacy and Wiersema come back as the culture, information technology and organization. Treacy and Wiersema more explicitly mention the management systems. Kaplan and Norton more explicitly show the value proposition, which is supported by the operating model, and which is driving the shareholder value.

What struck us in these operating models, both from Treacy and Wiersema and Kaplan and Norton, is that it's difficult to map it to the cost and the capital employed of our Supply Chain Triangle, as initially laid out in Figure 7.1. The above models seem to be strong on the process side and on the intangibles like culture, but they miss the plant, property and equipment (to use a balance sheet term) and they don't say anything on the working capital either, both of which are key in assessing shareholder value, if we use the ROCE.

So a bit to our surprise, but at the same time not surprising at all, the existing strategy models seem to completely miss out the supply chain as a key component of their operating models. By supply chain, we in this context mean the fixed assets like plants and warehouse, and the working capital. We need that supply chain to assess the required capital employed. We also need it to be able to fully assess the cost. We need the cost and the capital employed to be able to assess the shareholder value.

Figure 8.10 shows an 'extended' version of the Treacy and Wiersema operating model.

Figure 8.10 The extended operating model of Treacy and Wiersema, including supply chain

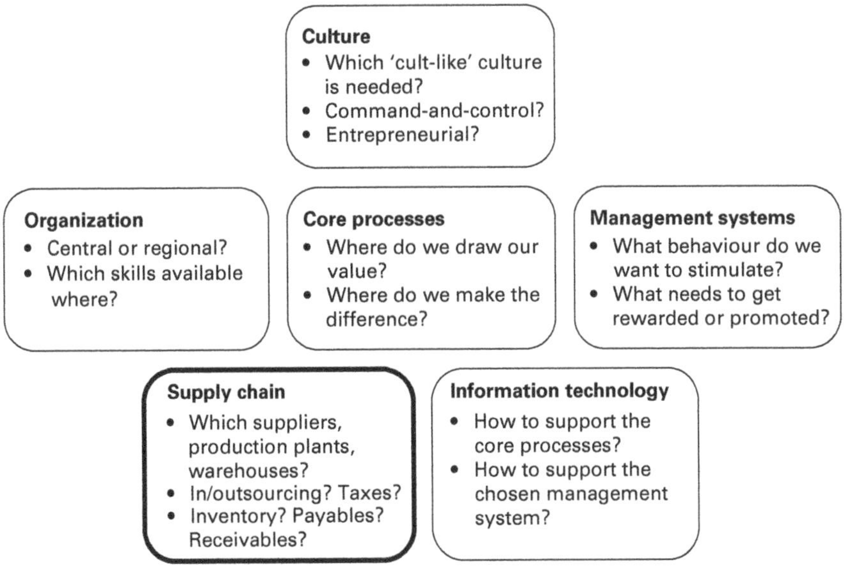

Culture
- Which 'cult-like' culture is needed?
- Command-and-control?
- Entrepreneurial?

Organization
- Central or regional?
- Which skills available where?

Core processes
- Where do we draw our value?
- Where do we make the difference?

Management systems
- What behaviour do we want to stimulate?
- What needs to get rewarded or promoted?

Supply chain
- Which suppliers, production plants, warehouses?
- In/outsourcing? Taxes?
- Inventory? Payables? Receivables?

Information technology
- How to support the core processes?
- How to support the chosen management system?

Likewise we could add a 'supply chain capital' layer to the strategy maps of Kaplan and Norton, next to the human capital, information capital and organization capital.

Mapping the value proposition to the extended operating model to define cost, capital employed and ROCE

Using the extended operating models, we can now continue our strategy exercise by mapping our value proposition to our operating model, to define the corresponding cost and capital employed, and finally derive the corresponding ROCE.

Figure 8.11 shows the extended operating model (of Treacy and Wiersema), as a kind of missing link in mapping the value proposition to the cost and capital employed.

Let's start by mapping the value proposition to the supply chain. In this mapping think about all questions you are likely to answer in a so-called 'network design' or supply chain design.

Which suppliers do we want? Where should they be located? Should we select on cost or on agility? What should our production footprint be? Is customization and local-for-local important? Or do we need specialized high-end equipment, and are the margins high enough to fly finished goods

Figure 8.11   From value proposition through operating model to cost and capital employed

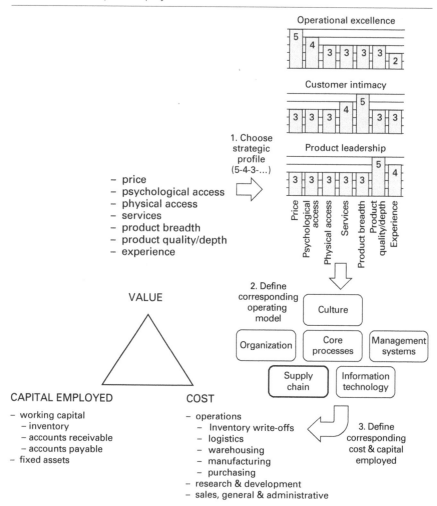

around the world? What will be insourced or outsourced? What is the impact on the capital employed versus cost?

How wide will our product portfolio be? What will the complexity of our products be? How deep is an average BOM? What is the average number of different raw materials or components going into a finished product? What is the impact on the inventory of raw materials, work-in-process and finished goods?

What does our distribution network look like? Can we ship from the plant? Do we need regional DCs? Do we need to go via distributors and finance part of their inventory in consignment? For which products? What is the impact on our finished goods inventories? What is the impact of tax optimization? Will we re-route flows to benefit from lower taxes in Ireland or Switzerland?

All of these questions should be answered in the light of the targeted value proposition. The answer to all of these questions is essential to define the cost and the capital employed levels. The answer will be different for different value propositions. So each supply chain will be truly strategy-driven.

As well as the supply chain, the IT systems, the resources required to power the core processes, the choice for a centralized versus a decentralized organization will also impact the cost level and possibly the capital employed. A decentralized organization may come at a higher cost, but it may be required to ensure being close to the customer and realizing your customer intimacy strategy.

Let's take the example of the Metro Group, which announced a new operating model for its Cash & Carry activities in mid-2015. In the financial report for 2016, the CEO Olaf Koch comments:

> The wholesale business is 100 per cent local, so it doesn't make sense to impose global solutions on a given location. Instead, any concept that's used must be oriented to the respective market situation. In other words: a food service concept in Spain may be fundamentally different to one in Italy. And you can only work on the concept if the relevant country unit has the necessary flexibility and freedom to act entrepreneurially. And that's exactly the task we gave the executives in the respective countries when we introduced our New Operating Model in mid-2015. This is an enormously important step in implementing our strategy on the ground.

So it is really the full operating model that is important when defining the cost and the capital employed, including but not limited to the supply chain. Different value propositions lead to different operating models (and supply chains), which may lead to different levels of cost and capital employed.

Once you have defined the levels of cost and capital employed, you should be able to define the expected shareholder value, as measured by the ROCE. You may need to iterate this process to come to the desired ROCE level. In our experience, companies are currently not thinking this through. We see many companies making strategic decisions on the product portfolio, assessing the impact on sales, sometimes on EBIT, but almost never on the capital employed, or on the ROCE. We see retail companies being concerned about the EBIT in the online channel, without accounting for the lower capital employed in that online channel. We are convinced that a more thorough analysis will lead to better strategies and more shareholder value.

Where Figure 8.11 above is helpful, as it builds on earlier figures like Figure 7.1, we actually prefer Figure 8.12 as a summary of this chapter, and of this book. It tells the same story, but it builds on the strategy maps of Kaplan and Norton.

The heart of Figure 8.12 (and of a strategy map) is the operating model. In Figure 8.12 we show the extended version, with the supply chain at the bottom. We have added the 'management processes' of Treacy and Wiersema as a core process (instead of 'regulatory and social' as per Kaplan and Norton). We know that the operating model is driven by the value

Figure 8.12 An integrated strategy and value generation model around the Supply Chain Triangle

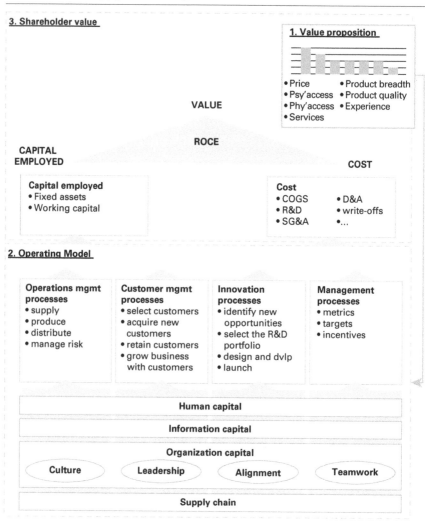

proposition. There can be no operating model without value proposition, and vice versa, hence the link between the value proposition at the top of the Supply Chain Triangle and the operating model.

The operating model, including the supply chain, defines the cost and the capital employed, as discussed above, completing the triangle and allowing to quantify the shareholder value based on the ROCE.

Exercise: Defining your operating model, cost, capital employed and ROCE

Continue your exercise with your executive team. Once you have defined your value proposition, try to assess the impact on the operating model as shown in Figure 8.11.

- What is the impact of the value gaps on your supply chain? Refer back to the list of questions outlined in the section 'Mapping the value proposition to the extended operating model'. How does this affect the cost and the capital employed?

- What's the impact on the organization model, the IT, the culture? And how do these affect the cost and the capital employed?

- What is the impact on your core processes? Operations? Customer management? Innovation? Management? Will we introduce more products? Or will we rationalize? Will we grow existing clients or explore new markets? Again, what is the impact on the cost and the capital employed?

If you're doing a strategy update, you can probably work with deltas on the existing cost and capital employed. Calculate the expected impact on the ROCE.

If you're doing a major strategy review, you may need to go deeper, and run a five-year budgeting exercise, trying to get to grips with how your new strategy will impact the future ROCE.

We understand these exercises are difficult. But at the same time they are also crucial. They are a commitment of the executive team to the shareholders, but equally to all stakeholders, including the employees. Better choices make for better work environments.

Implementing your strategy-driven supply chain

Finally, after having defined your strategy and the corresponding supply chain, it is crucial to carry out a good implementation. In *The Execution Premium* (2008), Kaplan and Norton argue that this is where many companies fail, that there is actually a 'premium' to be gained, for companies, by an effective strategy implementation. The book is an excellent read, with an excellent summary of the book as a first chapter.

Their model starts with the development of a strategy, part of which is what we have done in the previous section. Their text goes a bit broader in that it will talk about a mission-vision-values exercise, a full PESTEL analysis (Political, Economic, Societal, Technological, Environmental and Legal influences), a SWOT analysis and more. When doing a major strategy review, all of this is advisable. But don't forget to boil it down to a crystal-clear and differentiating value proposition, translate it into an operating model, and validate that it delivers the right shareholder value.

The second step is to plan the strategy. Kaplan and Norton work with so-called 'strategic themes', which can be seen as programmes consisting of multiple projects, across multiple processes and departments, with a common goal. An example could be to increase the % of revenues from new products to 25% in three years' time, which may have an impact on R&D, on marketing and sales, on operations, on the culture, and on the management and incentive systems.

All of these strategic themes should be summarized in a strategic plan, and should receive their own funding, called 'strategic expenses' or STRATEX, separate from the 'operational expenses' or OPEX. A separate budget is needed to ensure that strategic progress is not blocked by the operational managers.

Kaplan and Norton also stress the importance of defining measures – 'How will we measure success?' – and targets – 'Where do we want to be at what time?' – to ensure we don't just give it our best try, but that we are committed to results and pushing the strategy forward.

Next steps are a separate follow-up of the operations and the strategy implementation. Kaplan and Norton advise organizing separate meetings for the two, to avoid the strategic topics getting washed away by operational issues.

We refer the reader to *The Execution Premium* for a more detailed coverage of the individual topics. We wanted to close this chapter by at least pointing out the importance of further detailing the plan and ensuring the right type of follow-up. The framework of Kaplan and Norton is by far the best we have seen around for that purpose.

Conclusion

In this final chapter, we have started by summarizing the somewhat narrow strategy thinking of the 1990s and the impact on supply chain. By declaring that a product advantage was increasingly difficult and that cost leadership was the prerogative of the market leader, companies were pushed towards differentiation on service. In combination with an increase in variety and volatility, that creates a difficult context in which to operate.

In *Logistics and Supply Chain Management* (1999), Martin Christopher developed the concept of the responsive supply chain, which brought a much-needed breakthrough. The responsive supply chain comes with the promise that companies will be able to improve on service and on cost simultaneously. It is the start of the golden days of supply chain. As supply chain delivers on that promise, more and more companies adopt more professional management of the supply chain, and supply chain becomes gradually more important on the executive agenda.

For all the good that supply chain management brought to companies, its capability to improve on both service and cost found it disconnected from strategy. In fact, CEOs and VPs of marketing and sales had the luxury to define any type of value proposition. They would rely on supply chain to make it profitable, but only after the decision was made. These were the days when supply chain strategy was a translation of the business strategy.

We have made the argument that the strategy view of the 1990s was too pessimistic. We don't agree that cost leadership is only for the market leader. Nor do we agree that product leadership is void as a strategic option. On the contrary, we follow the thinking of Crawford and Mathews that there are multiple ways to be relevant for customers, but it requires tough choices and sharpening your value proposition.

We then analysed how existing strategy models miss supply chain as a core element of what is called the 'operating model'. The operating model is the engine through which we deliver the value proposition. As well as the culture, the organization, the IT systems and a set of core processes, the supply chain is an integral part of that engine. It is needed to arrive at an evaluation of the cost and the capital employed, which in turn are needed to arrive at an evaluation of the ROCE, which is our key measure for shareholder value.

Whereas in the 1990s we could define a strategy without making choices on service versus cost, we believe companies that have professionalized their supply chain are now confronted with those type of choices. That fact implies the supply chain can no longer be separated from the strategy discussion, but becomes an integral part of it. We argue that supply chains have become strategy-driven, and vice versa.

We concluded the chapter by providing a step-by-step explanation of how we believe companies can refine their strategies and their supply chains by starting with a value proposition, defining the corresponding operating model (of which the supply chain now is an integral part) to be able to assess the corresponding cost and capital employed, and ultimately evaluating the ROCE.

In our experience, not a lot of companies are iterating this full cycle today. We are however convinced that doing so will lead to better strategies, which will create more value for the shareholders and also for employees, who will get more satisfaction from working in better focused organizations. Let it be our hope that this book can contribute to that result.

CASE STUDY The strategy compass

Martijn Lofvers is the Founder and Chief Trendwatcher of Supply Chain Media. He is working on connecting supply chain professionals by gathering, generating and sharing supply chain knowledge, both within The Netherlands and internationally. He organizes workshops with his extended European network of Chief Supply Chain Officers on a broad set of supply chain topics. His Dutch *Supply Chain Magazine* and the international quarterly *Supply Chain Movement* are the de facto standard for supply chain interviews, management articles, vendor overviews (in subway maps) and news in Europe.

In recent years Martijn has performed research on differences in supply chain strategy and their drivers, which has resulted in what he has called the *Strategy Compass*.

Martijn starts from the model of Treacy and Wiersema to indicate that there are different ways to lead in a market. He describes six different supply chains around those three base strategies, as shown in Figure 8.13.

The first supply chain type is called *'long development, rapid deployment'*, and supports an R&D-dominant product leadership strategy, as opposed to *'fast, continuous renewal'*, which supports a marketing dominant product leadership strategy. Think about the difference between the medical devices business of Johnson & Johnson versus the fast fashion of Zara. Both are product leaders, but the first is more R&D-dominant, where the second is marketing-dominant.

Figure 8.13 Six supply chain types around the three Treacy and Wiersema strategies (©Martijn Lofvers, 2017)

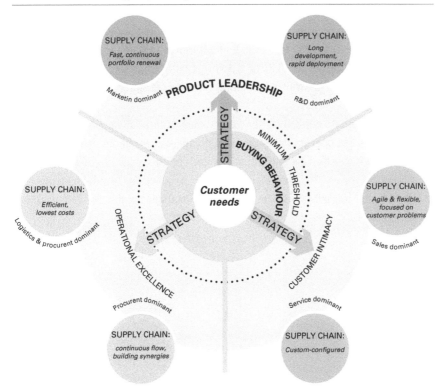

The customer intimacy strategy is either supported by an *'agile & flexible, focused on customer problems'* or a *'custom-configured'* supply chain. Thinking in the 5-4-3-3-3 logic of Crawford and Mathews, we could think of it in terms of putting 'product breadth' versus putting 'service' first. We tend to think of IBM as a player with a large catalogue, and being sales driven in trying to maximize the share of wallet in its bigger accounts, where something like the buildings business of Johnson Controls will more 'configure-to-order' and develop custom solutions to the heating and refrigeration problems in any complex building. We admit that differences are subtle and subject to discussion.

Operational excellence is either supported by a *'continuous flow, building synergies'* or an *'efficient, lowest costs'* supply chains, depending on whether the companies are production-dominant (manufacturing) or logistics and procurement-dominant (retail). In manufacturing the low-cost advantage needs to come from stabilizing the production and maximizing the turns on the manufacturing assets. In retail, the focus is much more on minimizing purchasing cost and maximizing the turns on the logistics assets. Private label manufacturers are typically following a low-cost strategy, as retailers want to differentiate on price using their private label products. As they're not branded, these companies, like McBride Plc, active in private label household and personal care, are typically less known than their branded counterparts like Henkel and P&G. Walmart and Ikea are probably well-known examples on the retail side.

Figure 8.14 builds on this and adds that different strategies and supply chain types go with a different set of KPIs, a different organizational structure, such as a different level of centralization, and a different set of core processes and systems.

Customer-intimate companies tend to be decentralized to ensure customer proximity, whereas operational excellence companies are centralized to ensure control over efficiency. This thinking aligns perfectly with the 'operating model' thinking of Treacy and Wiersema and of Kaplan and Norton, introduced earlier in this chapter. Figure 8.14 also adds numerous examples of the different supply chain types.

Figure 8.14   The strategy compass (©Martijn Lofvers, 2017)

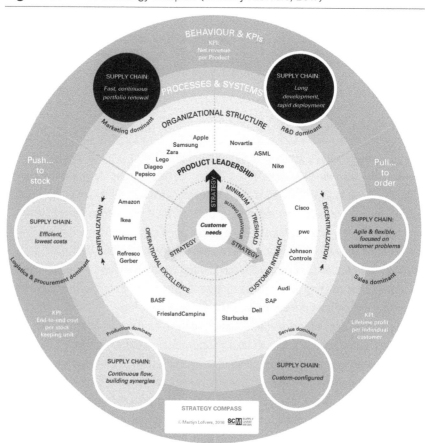

Table 8.3 Different product-market combinations may require different strategies and supply chains (©Martijn Lofvers, 2017)

Company	Category	Strategy	Supply Chain
Disney	Movie DVD	Operational excellence	Efficient, lowest costs
	Infinity	Product leadership	Long development, rapid deployment
Starbucks	Fresh coffee	Customer intimacy	Custom-configured
	Iced coffee	Operational excellence	Continuous flow, building synergies
Pepsico	Quaker	Product leadership	Fast, continuous renewal
	Lay's	Operational excellence	Efficient, lowest costs

When asked how he applies this thinking with executive teams, Martijn comments: 'Within the same company, different customer segments, or product segments, or product-market combinations, may follow different strategies and as such have different supply chains.' Table 8.3 shows some examples of discussions he had with executive teams. 'Where Pepsico follows a product leadership strategy for its Quaker oats, differentiating on product has become very difficult in potato chips, hence the operational excellence strategy for its Lay's chips.'

Martijn also links this to the product life cycle. 'A ground-breaking new product or product group typically requires a product leadership strategy, whereas a product near the end of its life cycle may have commoditized and require an operational excellence strategy.'

When segmenting and differentiating the strategy and the supply chain, we need to remember Treacy and Wiersema's warning that different strategies come with different operating models, as illustrated by Martijn in the outer circles in Figure 8.14. There is a limit to what we can do with one organization. If segmentation is required to be successful in different markets, we need to be aware that this comes with different supply chains and that different supply chains come with different KPIs, different organizations, and different processes and systems.

Martijn closes by saying: 'For years, supply chain management professionals have been searching for how their discipline adds strategic value. It's similar to the quest for the Holy Grail in the film *Indiana Jones and the Last Crusade*.' He is thrilled that we are finally there. 'Like the Holy Grail gives eternal life, the strategy compass will give the supply chain director a firm position on the board of directors. It makes supply chain management an integral part of the business, rather than a mere support function.' Let the supply chains indeed become strategy-driven!

References

Christopher, M (1999) *Logistics and Supply Chain Management: Strategies for reducing cost and improving service*, Financial Times/Pitman Publishing, London

Christopher, M and Gattorna, J (2005) Supply chain cost management and value-based pricing, *Industrial Marketing Management*, **34** (2), pp 115–21

Crawford, F and Mathews, R (2007) *The Myth of Excellence: Why great companies never try to be the best at everything*, Crown Business, London

Gattorna, J (ed) (2003) *Gower Handbook of Supply Chain Management*, Gower Publishing Ltd, Aldershot

Hammer, M (1990) Reengineering work: don't automate, obliterate, *Harvard Business Review*, **68** (4), pp 104–12

Kaplan, R S and Norton, D P (2008) *The Execution Premium: Linking strategy to operations for competitive advantage*, Harvard Business Press, Boston

Kaplan, R S and Norton, D P (2004) *Strategy Maps: Converting intangible assets into tangible outcomes*, Harvard Business Press, Boston

Metro Group [accessed 20/07/2017] Metro Group Condensed Report 2015/16 [Online] http://reports.metrogroup.de/2015-2016/condensed-report/

Porter, M (1996) What is strategy?, *Harvard Business Review*, **74** (6), pp 64–78

Treacy, M and Wiersema, F (1995) *The Discipline of Market Leaders: Choose your customers, narrow your focus, dominate your market*, Basic Books, New York

INDEX